"For far too many people the Bible remains a mystery, an impenetrable treasure hidden in a secret chest that us regular folk cannot access. Jeff L. loves you and the Scriptures enough to solve that problem by *Unlocking the Bible*. You are about to become wealthy beyond words in eternal riches for your soul. Let this exciting new book from Jeff L. take you there."

James MacDonald, pastor, Harvest Bible Chapel

"My friend Jeff has come up with another book that will help many of God's people enjoy Bible study and make progress in understanding and obeying the Scriptures. In these pages the new believer especially will find helpful information, and the more mature believer will find personal encouragement in Bible study."

Warren W. Wiersbe, author and former pastor
of Moody Church, Chicago

"Even after teaching through the Scriptures for over thirty-five years, I still love to read books about the Bible—its origin, reliability, and message, but *Unlocking the Bible* gives fresh perspective. In his book, Jeff Lasseigne shows us how to approach God's book, the Bible, with reverence and walk away with a confident understanding. Every generation needs to know these truths and Jeff has done us a great service to this one by helping us see the big picture of God's redemptive plan."

Skip Heitzig, pastor and author

"What a terrific book Pastor Jeff has written to help us learn the Bible, even making sense out of some of the more difficult passages. It's easy to understand, enjoyable, engaging, educational, and humorous. Once I began reading I did not want to put it down. It's written for anyone wanting to learn more about the Bible, from the Bible student to a seasoned Bible teacher. If you want to understand the Bible and you have a love for God's Word, you will love this book. I do!"

Tom Hughes, lead pastor of 412 Chur
.org, and author of *America*

"I have known and watched Jeff Lasseigne for many years. I have always appreciated Jeff in every aspect of his life and ministry. I'm not surprised that he has written *Unlocking the Bible*. Jeff loves our Lord and he loves His Word. I have watched him live out his calling and gifts for years at Harvest Christian Fellowship. He has pastored alongside Greg Laurie for many years and many have grown under the clear, effective, and anointed way in which he simply 'unlocks the Bible.' I assure you that you will be blessed by Jeff and his writing as much as his speaking. May the Lord bless you as you read."

Don McClure, Calvary Way Ministries,
Calvary Chapel Association

"I've known Pastor Jeff Lasseigne for decades. His thorough exposition of Scripture is remarkable. This book will prove to be an insightful tool for the new disciple as well as an intelligent resource for the seasoned saint."

Steve Wilburn, senior pastor, Core Church Los Angeles

UNLOCKING
the BIBLE

What It Is,

How We Got It, and

Why We Can Trust It

JEFF LASSEIGNE

BakerBooks

a division of Baker Publishing Group
Grand Rapids, Michigan

Published by Baker Books
a division of Baker Publishing Group
P.O. Box 6287, Grand Rapids, MI 49516-6287
www.bakerbooks.com

Printed in the United States of America

Part 2 of this book has been adapted from *Highway 66: A Unique Journey through the 66 Books of the Bible.* Copyright © 2004, 2014 by Jeff Lasseigne. Published by Harvest Ministries.

Library of Congress Cataloging-in-Publication Data
Names: Lasseigne, Jeff, 1955– author.
Title: Unlocking the Bible : what it is, how we got it, and why we can trust it / Jeff
    Lasseigne.
Description: Grand Rapids : Baker Books, 2016. | Includes bibliographical
    references.
Identifiers: LCCN 2016009695 | ISBN 9780801019173 (pbk.)
Subjects: LCSH: Bible—Introductions.
Classification: LCC BS475.3 .L373 2016 | DDC 220.6/1—dc23
LC record available at https://lccn.loc.gov/2016009695

In keeping with biblical principles of creation stewardship, Baker Publishing Group advocates the responsible use of our natural resources. As a member of the Green Press Initiative, our company uses recycled paper when possible. The text paper of this book is composed in part of post-consumer waste.

16 17 18 19 20 21 22   7 6 5 4 3 2 1

I dedicate this book
to the Harvest Christian Fellowship
Midweek Bible Study congregation,
whose love for God's Word inspires me
in my study, preparation, and teaching of the Bible.

Contents

Foreword

I'm pleased to recommend to you this practical and informative book from a truly gifted Bible teacher. Jeff Lasseigne has been my associate for nearly three decades at Harvest Christian Fellowship, where he has faithfully taught God's Word. God has gifted Jeff with a remarkable ability to examine, explain, and expound the Bible in his signature style: thorough, detailed, and easy to understand. Jeff's love for God's Word is evident in both his teaching and his life.

In a day and age where the culture has become, for the most part, biblically illiterate, it seems the average person no longer has even a basic understanding of what the Bible is about, much less its origins, its reliability, or its practical application. This book brings us back to the foundational importance of God's Word, and Jeff reasonably explains why we can trust it, how we can understand it, what it takes to study it, and even how to teach it.

If you are looking to deepen your understanding of the Bible, I wholeheartedly endorse *Unlocking the Bible*. May God bless you as you read it.

Greg Laurie, senior pastor, Harvest Christian Fellowship;
evangelist, Harvest Crusades and Harvest America

Acknowledgments

With a heart filled with gratitude, I would like to thank the following people for their encouragement, support, prayers, and contributions toward bringing this book to fruition: Pastor Greg Laurie, Brian Jackson, Andrew McGovern, Karen Zapico, Pastor Paul Eaton, Diane Jackson, and Pastor Brad Ormonde.

I would also like to express my appreciation to Chad Allen at Baker Books, along with the great staff there who have made this a pleasant process.

Introduction

A nine-year-old boy named Joey went to his Sunday school class, and the teacher spoke about how God delivered the Hebrew people from the clutches of Pharaoh and the Egyptian army. On the way home from church, Joey's mother asked him what he had learned that morning. Joey answered, "Our teacher told us how God sent Moses behind enemy lines on a rescue mission to lead Israel out of Egypt. When he got to the Red Sea, he had his engineers build a pontoon bridge, and all of the people walked across safely. Then he used his walkie-talkie to radio headquarters and call in an air strike when the Egyptians were closing in on them. They sent in bombers to blow up the bridge and destroy the enemy, and all of the Israelites were saved."

"Now Joey," his mom said, "is that really what the teacher told you this morning?"

Joey hesitated and said, "Well, not exactly, but if I told it the way the teacher did, you would never believe it!"

Believe it or not, the Bible is the most unique book ever written. The Bible is the world's all-time bestselling book, and nothing else even comes close. The Bible was the first book ever printed on the printing press, and portions have been translated into nearly two thousand different languages.

And yet, the irony is that it's also the most ignored book for so many. It is safe to say that the Bible is the most beloved, the most read, the most criticized, and the most neglected book in history. A recent Barna Group research poll reports that 88 percent of Americans own a Bible, and the average household has over four copies.[1]

That sounds promising, until we find that the same poll reveals that 59 percent of the people who claim to have no faith, or identify themselves as atheists, own a Bible. Clearly, many of those Bibles are simply collecting dust. That same Barna report reveals that just 13 percent of the people polled stated that they read the Bible every day. I'm one of those 13 percent, and I hope you are as well! The Bible is intended to be our daily bread, not an occasional cupcake.

The report also reveals that four out of ten people claim that they simply don't have enough time to read the Bible, but my answer has always been that we make time for what's important to us. Interestingly, more than 50 percent said that when they do make time to read Scripture, they don't know where to start reading. I'll address that question later on in this book.

An alarming finding from that report reveals that 47 percent of those surveyed believe that the Bible, the Koran, and the Book of Mormon all teach the same truth in a different way. Nothing could be further from the truth!

Finally, the percentage of people who are antagonistic toward the Scriptures has risen sharply in recent years, from 10 percent to 17 percent. Obviously, the more the light of God's truth shines on the darkness of the sinful lifestyles in our society, the more people raise their fist in defiance toward God and His Word.

In the first part of this book we'll look at how we got the Bible, how we can know it's trustworthy, the four hundred silent years between the Old Testament and New Testament, questions about the Apocrypha, how to study the Bible, how to teach the Bible, and more. At the same time, we'll tackle some of the more common questions that people have, such as: What is the Torah? Who decided which books should and shouldn't be in the Bible? When was the Bible divided up into chapters and verses? Why isn't the Bible in chronological order? Could more books ever be added? Why the different translations, and which are the best?

In part 2 we will look at individual books of the Bible and discover some of the unique details and perspectives of each one. My desire in putting this book together is that we might understand and appreciate that the Bible is not as difficult to read, study, and apply as some might think.

Billy Graham wrote,

> Millions of people today are searching for a reliable voice of authority. The Word of God then, is the only real authority we have. It is in the Holy Scriptures that we find the answers to life's ultimate questions: Where did I come from? Why am I here? Where am I going? What is the purpose of my existence? One of the greatest needs in the church today is to come back to the Scriptures as a basis of authority.[2]

Dr. Graham continues,

> One of the greatest tragedies today is that, although the Bible is an available, open book, it is a closed book to millions—either because they leave it unread or because they read it without applying it to themselves. No greater tragedy can befall a man or a nation than that of paying lip service to a Bible left unread, or to a way of life not followed.[3]

My hope and prayer for you as you read through this book is that you will fall more in love with Jesus as you receive and understand His Word.

PART 1

THE BIG PICTURE

1

How We Got the Bible

Many years ago, I was trying to share the gospel with a co-worker, and when I made reference to the Bible, he said, "The Bible is nothing more than a collection of fables written by a bunch of old Jewish men." So I smiled and said, "What if you're wrong, and the Bible actually is God's Word? What will you say when you stand before the Lord?" He winked at me and said, "I'll think of something."

Good luck with that!

Let's begin with some basic facts about the Bible.

What Is the Bible?

Dr. David Jeremiah writes, "The Bible is the Word of God in the words of man," and I like that definition.[1] John MacArthur says, "The Bible is a collection of 66 documents inspired by God."[2] Greg Laurie likes to call the Bible "the user's manual for life." In the simplest of terms, the Bible is the Word of God. It is God's written revelation of Himself and of His will for mankind.

Our English word *Bible* means "book." It comes from the Latin word *biblia* and the Greek word *biblios*. Interestingly, the word *Bible* is not found in the Bible, but that's not a major mystery. All of the New Testament was written by the end of the first century, and then it wasn't until the second century that the church began calling it "the Bible," so that particular title is not found in Scripture. The Bible is far beyond any book and is nothing less than God's voice from heaven. It's not the book of the month or the book of the year; it's the book of eternity!

There are over a dozen names and titles in the Old and New Testaments that are used for the Bible. For example, in Psalm 19:7 it's called "the Law of the LORD," and David writes, "The law of the LORD is perfect, refreshing the soul" (NIV). In Romans 1:1–2 Paul calls it "the Holy Scriptures," and he writes of "the gospel of God which He promised before through His prophets in the Holy Scriptures." The word *Scripture* means "sacred writings." Other religions have their sacred writings: the Muslims have the Koran, Mormonism has the Book of Mormon, and the atheists have the complete works of Dr. Seuss!

In Ephesians 6:17 Paul gives the Bible two more names: "the sword of the Spirit" and "the word of God." In John's Gospel Jesus called it "truth" in His prayer to the Father, when He said, "Sanctify them by Your truth. Your word is truth" (17:17). Those are just a few of the many names and titles for the Bible.

From the divine perspective the Bible is one book with one Author and one message. From the human perspective it's also recognized as a collection of sixty-six books with different authors and subjects. It's not unlike the human body in some ways. We have one body, but that body is made up of many different parts, all working together. So the one book of the Bible is divided up into sixty-six different books, and those sixty-six books are divided up into two testaments—the thirty-nine books of the Old Testament and the twenty-seven books of the New Testament.

The word *testament* means "covenant" or "agreement." The Old Testament is God's covenant with Israel, and that covenant included any non-Jew who believed by faith. Paul calls that first covenant "the Old Testament" in 2 Corinthians 3:14. The New Testament is God's covenant with mankind about salvation in Jesus Christ (see Matt. 26:28). The Old Testament prepared people for the coming of the Savior while the New Testament tells us that the Savior has come—and is coming back again!

The Old Testament covenant can be summarized by the word *law* while the New Testament covenant is summarized by the word *grace*. In John 1:17 we read, "For the law was given through Moses, but grace and truth came through Jesus Christ." The Old Testament is associated with Moses and Mount Sinai. The New Testament is associated with Jesus and Calvary. The Old Testament begins in Genesis 1:1 with God; the New Testament begins in Matthew 1:1 with Jesus Christ. The Old Testament ends in Malachi 4 with "a curse," while the New Testament ends in Revelation 22 with "grace."

Why Is the Bible So Important?

1. *It's God's communication to us.*

When God created Adam and Eve, He spoke with them personally; face-to-face, if you will. But when they sinned, they broke off their fellowship and communication with God. So while God has occasionally spoken to individuals such as Moses and Abraham, He primarily communicates to us through His written Word. The good news is that one day, when Christ returns, our communication will once again be face-to-face.

2. *It reveals God's nature to us.*

Without the Bible, we wouldn't know who God is or about any of His characteristics and attributes. But in the pages of Scripture we learn that God is eternal; He has a triune nature of Father, Son, and Spirit; He is holy; He is omnipresent, omnipotent, and omniscient; and so forth. We wouldn't know those things apart from God's revelation to us through His Word.

3. It answers our greatest questions.

Through the Scriptures, we find the answers to such questions as: "Where did I come from?" (God created us in His own image.) "Why am I here?" (To know God and bring Him glory.) "What happens after death?" (We go to either heaven or hell.) There's the often-told story about comedian and actor W. C. Fields, who was a staunch atheist and a heavy drinker. Toward the later part of his life he was caught thumbing through a Bible, and when he was asked what he was doing, he famously replied, "Looking for loopholes."

4. It addresses our greatest needs.

In Scripture, we learn that everyone is a sinner in need of a Savior, and that Savior is Jesus Christ. We also discover that forgiveness and salvation only come through faith in Christ—through His sacrifice and resurrection. At the same time, the Bible shows us how we are to live in this world as we prepare ourselves for the next.

Where Did the Bible Come From?

Short answer: it came from God!

More than two thousand times in the Old Testament alone, the Bible declares that God is speaking. Time and time again, we find phrases like, "The LORD said," or "God declared," or "The Word of the LORD came." In the New Testament there are more than three dozen instances where people speak of the "Word of God" in referring to the Old Testament (see Luke 4:4) and specific statements that Scripture is literally "God-breathed" (2 Tim. 3:16 NIV) and that God spoke through holy people (see 2 Pet. 1:21). What the Bible says, God says!

The Bible came from God, and that transmission process included using "holy men of God" (2 Pet. 1:21). The actual writing and recording of the Old Testament took place over a thousand-year period, starting with Moses—either writing Job or Genesis—and then ending chronologically with the book of Nehemiah, written by Nehemiah and Ezra.

After that thousand-year period of the Old Testament being written, there were four hundred years when God did not speak or provide any revelations. That period is commonly referred to as "the four hundred years of silence," and I will address that topic later in the book. Then finally, the New Testament was written in about a fifty-year period, between AD 45–95, being completed by the end of the first century. So when we take the thousand years of the Old Testament, followed by the four hundred years of silence, and add in the hundred years of the first century, we have about fifteen hundred years during which the Bible was written and recorded by God's chosen vessels.

In addition to being completed over a period of fifteen hundred years, the Bible was written by at least forty different writers whom we know of. As I already mentioned, the first writer and recorder was Moses. On the other end of the spectrum, the very last writer was the apostle John, near the end of the first century. Other Bible writers included prophets such as Samuel, Jeremiah, and Malachi. Some of those writers were shepherds such as Hosea and Amos.

Joining them we have a soldier (Joshua), a scribe (Ezra), a prime minister (Daniel), a tax collector (Matthew), and a doctor (Luke). Other New Testament writers were fishermen such as Peter and John. So the Bible was written over a period of fifteen hundred years, by at least forty different writers who came from a wide variety of backgrounds and occupations. These facts are important to note, because while there was a wide variety in the circumstances, years, and people, the message and theme of Scripture are consistent.

The various books of the Bible were written on three different continents: Africa (Moses in the Sinai desert), Asia (Ezekiel in Babylon), and Europe (Paul in Rome). The Bible was also written in three different languages: the Old Testament in Hebrew, with a few parts in Aramaic, and then the New Testament in Greek. The writers were also in very different and oftentimes difficult circumstances. For example, Moses was in the wilderness, Ezekiel was a captive in Babylon, Paul was a prisoner in Rome, and John was banished to an island.

Parts of the Bible were written to individuals. Other parts were written to specific groups or to God's people in general. But in spite of all that variety, the Bible is the history of God's dealings with humankind. It has two dominant themes: humanity's sin and God's salvation. This fact reveals its divine nature.

Another detail helps us to appreciate the divine nature of Scripture: the people in the Bible are presented to us with flaws and all. Someone trying to write a book that proposed to be the Word of God would paint all of its people in the most favorable light. But the Bible gives us the heroes of the faith with all their flaws and failures on display.

For example, faithful Noah got drunk. The great Abraham lied about his wife, Sarah. Humble Moses got angry and missed out on the Promised Land. Wise Solomon started out well and ended terribly. Brave Peter denied the Lord three times. Missionaries Paul and Barnabas exchanged heated words over Mark. And the list goes on. The Bible is about a real Savior—and real sinners!

How Was the Bible Put Together?

You may have heard of "the canon of Scripture." The word *canon* is not referring to an outdated military weapon that fires cannon balls! The English word *canon* comes from the Greek word *kanon*. In Greek culture, a *kanon* was a measuring rod, ruler, or staff. Today's counterpart would be a ruler or a tape measure.

So the term *canon of Scripture* refers to the books that are in the Bible, which have measured up to the standards of being divinely inspired by God. In other words, when the Old Testament and New Testament were put together, there was a standard used to determine which books did, and did not, belong in the Bible. What was that standard and measurement?

Let me first say that in the early centuries of the church, Christians were sometimes put to death for having copies of the Scriptures because of the great persecution that existed in those times. So while our question today is, "Which books belong in the Bible?" back then the question was, "Which books are worth dying for?" Let me also point out that God—not people—decided which books ended up in the Bible. With the guidance of the Holy Spirit, people simply recognized which books were divinely inspired. In fact, as soon as God's Word was received and recorded, it was already inspired of God whether people recognized it or not.

Let's begin with the Old Testament books. We know that God directed certain individuals to write down their revelations and experiences. For example, in Exodus 17, after Joshua and the armies of Israel defeated the Amalekites, we read, "Then the LORD said to Moses, 'Write this for a memorial in the book and recount it in the hearing of Joshua'" (Exod. 17:14). Later, in Exodus 24:4, we're clearly told, "And Moses wrote all the words of the LORD."

Those earlier writings were kept alongside the ark of the covenant. We read about this in Scriptures such as Deuteronomy 31, which reads:

> So it was, when Moses had completed writing the words of this law in a book, when they were finished, that Moses commanded the Levites, who bore the ark of the covenant of the LORD, saying:

"Take this Book of the Law, and put it beside the ark of the covenant of the LORD your God." (Deut. 31:24–26)

Then after the temple was built, the sacred writings were kept inside it. That special attention and reverence given to those writings testifies to how God's people recognized it to be the Word of God.

When the time of captivity came, and the Jews were carried off to Babylon, it is believed that they took those writings with them. Later on, they were probably collected by Daniel. In Daniel 9:2, we read, "In the first year of [the king's] reign I, Daniel, understood by the books the number of the years specified by the word of the LORD through Jeremiah the prophet, that He would accomplish seventy years in the desolations of Jerusalem." Daniel was saying he knew that the captivity would last seventy years because of Jeremiah's written prophecy. So Daniel refers to "the books," which would be the writings of Moses, Samuel, and Jeremiah—and all of it was Scripture.

After the Babylonian captivity ended and the Jews returned to their homeland, it is believed that Ezra the priest and other leaders of Judah continued to collect the writings and safeguard them in the newly built second temple. In Nehemiah 8, the people gathered together in front of the temple and Ezra read to them from "the Book of the law of Moses" (see Neh. 8:1–8). So about four hundred years before the birth of Christ, all the Old Testament books had been written and collected.

Many scholars believe that Ezra led the council of leaders who identified Holy Scripture from other religious writings. Most of the Old Testament books were written by a recognized prophet of God such as Moses, Samuel, David, Isaiah, and Zechariah. The remaining Old Testament books were written by godly leaders such as Joshua, Nehemiah, and Ezra. All of the Old Testament books gave clear evidence of being inspired of God. And ultimately, just as God inspired those who wrote the words, God inspired His people to know which books belonged in the canon of Old Testament Scripture.

The same is true for the New Testament canon of Scripture. God determined the canon and then the church discovered the canon. The canon of Scripture was not created by the church; rather, the church recognized it. But there are a few different details about the New Testament canon process. All of the books for consideration in the New Testament had to be written by an apostle or by a known associate of the apostles. At least twenty-three of the twenty-seven New Testament books were written by apostles, making the authorship qualification easier.

Only Mark, Luke, Acts, and Hebrews were questioned in the area of authorship. John Mark, who wrote the second Gospel, was the spiritual son and disciple of Peter, so he had Peter's stamp of approval and apostleship on his book. Luke wrote the third Gospel, as well as Acts. Luke sought out the eyewitness accounts of the other apostles in composing his Gospel account (see Luke 1:2–3). Luke was also a very close associate of Paul on his missionary journeys, so he knew many details firsthand. The writer of Hebrews is unknown, but it was accepted by the early church fathers because of its inspired content and its close connection to the Old Testament book of Leviticus.

Besides authorship by an apostle, the early church leaders also gave careful consideration to the canon of Scripture based upon spiritual content, doctrinal soundness, and most importantly, recognition of divine inspiration. It also helped that all of the New Testament was written during the lifetimes of many of the apostles and witnesses of Christ. Within twenty-five years of Jesus's death, the New Testament was already being written, and it was completed before the end of that first century—all within a fifty-year period. In fact, if you set aside the five books written by John (his Gospel, his three epistles, and Revelation), the rest of the New Testament was completed in just twenty-five years—by AD 70.

It's worth noting that early on, before any so-called official recognition, Peter was already calling the epistles of Paul holy

Scripture. In 2 Peter 3:16, Peter speaks of evil people twisting the words of Paul in his epistles, just as they do with "the rest of the Scriptures." Peter was bearing witness that Paul's letters were inspired Scripture, which brings us to a very important discussion on the subject of inspiration.

Second Timothy 3:16 tells us that all Scripture, including both the Old Testament and the New Testament, is given to us "by inspiration of God," which literally means that it's "breathed out from God." The Scriptures do not breathe out God; God breathes out the Scriptures. All of the various prophets and apostles who received and recorded the divine words of God were led and guided by the Holy Spirit. This is called "divine inspiration."

The men themselves weren't inspired; only God's Word is inspired—or divine and perfect. Later in this book we'll talk about Bible translations, but let me say here that the translations are not inspired. What I mean is that only the original writings were perfectly inspired by God, while the copies and translations that we now have, though holy, are not inspired in the true sense of "divine inspiration." It doesn't make them any less reliable, and we'll talk more about that in a later chapter.

Second Peter 1:20–21 is another passage on this subject of divine inspiration: "Knowing this first, that no prophecy of Scripture is of any private interpretation, for prophecy never came by the will of man, but holy men of God spoke as they were moved by the Holy Spirit." Once again, these verses explain that no Scripture is of human origin but rather godly men were used as human instruments as God spoke to them, and through them, to communicate His holy words.

Over 3,800 times in the Bible, the writers call what they were writing "the Word of God." Peter also explains that "no Scripture is of any private interpretation" (v. 20), which means that these godly men weren't figuring out divine truth by their own human wisdom or efforts. God was supernaturally revealing it to them.

It reminds us of when Peter confessed that Jesus was "the Christ, the Son of the living God" in Caesarea Philippi, as recorded in Matthew 16:16. Jesus explained to Peter afterward, "Flesh and blood has not revealed this to you, but My Father who is in heaven" (v. 17).

So the New Testament was all written by the end of the first century, and not many years later, in about AD 140, the formation of the New Testament canon began. During the next fifty years, most of the New Testament books were officially recognized as inspired and as part of the canon of Scripture, with a few exceptions.

A few New Testament books and letters took a little longer, due to different concerns. As I already mentioned, we still don't know who was the human author of Hebrews. In the famous words of early church father Origen, "Only God knows certainly," but to that we would add that we absolutely know that God wrote Hebrews.[3]

Another epistle that was questioned was the letter of James. That's because James placed a strong emphasis on works and actions demonstrating genuine faith, and on the surface almost seemed to contradict the New Testament emphasis of salvation by faith alone. One of the criteria for canon consideration was agreement with the rest of Scripture. Eventually, it was understood that James was describing the fruit of our salvation (good works) while Paul was describing the root of our salvation (faith alone). The fact that James was the half-brother of Jesus, and had been the leader of the early church in Jerusalem, also helped in the process of getting his epistle included in the canon.

All twenty-seven of our New Testament books were officially recognized and canonized by the year 397. And so, in basic terms, that's how we got our Bible!

Can Any More Books Be Added to the Bible?

The answer is no! After the final New Testament book (Revelation) was written, we find a clear warning at the end: "If anyone adds to these things, God will add to him the plagues that are written in this book; and if anyone takes away from the words of the book of this prophecy, God shall take away his part from the Book of Life" (Rev. 22:18–19).

That particular warning is specifically in regard to the prophecy of Revelation, but there are similar warnings in Scripture against tampering with God's Word. In Deuteronomy 4:2, we read, "You shall not add to the word which I command you, nor take from it." Again, in Deuteronomy 12:32, it says, "Whatever I command you, be careful to observe it; you shall not add to it nor take away from it."

Then in Proverbs 30:5–6 we find, "Every word of God is flawless. . . . Do not add to his words, or he will rebuke you and prove you a liar" (NIV). Also, in Galatians 1:8, Paul said, "If we, or an angel from heaven, preach any other gospel to you than what we have preached to you, let him be accursed." So this is a consistent warning throughout Scripture.

Conclusion

Studying these issues concerning the Bible is vital, because the Bible itself is so vital to us as believers. Without inspired Scripture, we would have little knowledge of God or communication from God—only what we hear and see in creation.

The Bible is God's written Word to you, and in it He tells you that He loves you!

2

Why We Can Trust the Bible

A lady was sunbathing at the beach when a little boy in swimming trunks, carrying a towel, walked up and said to her, "Excuse me, ma'am, but do you believe in God?" She was surprised by his question, but smiled and replied, "Why yes, I certainly do." Then he asked her, "Do you go to church every Sunday?" Still taken aback, she answered, "Absolutely." Then he asked her, "Do you read your Bible and pray every day?" Again she said, "Yes," and now her curiosity was really aroused. Finally the little boy sighed and said, "OK, then, will you hold my money for me while I go swimming?"

In this chapter we're going to consider the question of trust and, in particular, why we can trust the Bible. A Barna Group survey tells us that only half of those who identify themselves as Christians firmly believe that the Bible is completely accurate in its teachings and principles.[1] That's an alarming statistic, and it reveals that many professing believers have trust issues when it comes to God's Word. That's a problem, because the basis of our Christian faith comes from what the Bible reveals about God, creation, sin, salvation, and eternity.

More to the point, if the Bible is not completely reliable, then how can we trust it at all? Who's to say which parts of the Bible are true and which ones are not? It all becomes very subjective. Vance Havner summed it up quite well when he said:

> I am certain that the Bible is the Word of God. Either it is or it isn't, and either all of it is the Word of God or we never can be sure of any of it. It is either absolute or obsolete. If we have to start changing this verse, apologizing for this, and making allowances for that, we might as well give up and walk away.[2]

The inerrancy of Scripture is one of the essentials of the Christian faith and is nonnegotiable. The word *inerrancy* means "freedom from error and untruths." As I mentioned previously, inerrancy does not apply to the various translations of the Bible; it applies to the original inspired words of God. While the translations are not perfect, they *are* very reliable and we'll talk more about that in later chapters. But right now, we're talking about trusting the truths, teachings, and principles of God's Word.

The issue of trusting the Bible is oftentimes not a question of its reliability but rather of satanic attack, rejection of its teachings, unbelief, and sinful lifestyles. In the very beginning Satan attacked Eve with a barrage of doubts and denials about what God had actually said (see Gen. 3:1–7). When Jesus stood before Pilate, Pilate sarcastically asked Him, "What is truth?" and wasn't even interested in the answer (see John 18:38). Today, in our post-Christian culture, anything goes. John Blanchard was correct in saying that "men do not reject the Bible because they find faults in it, but because it finds fault in them."[3]

So while many people claim to be Christians and to believe in God, it's often on their own unbiblical terms. They reject doctrines such as hell and judgment, or reject what the Bible says about homosexuality or abortion. They pray to a "higher power," believing that the major religions all teach the same thing and that God has many names, like Buddha and Allah. But if the Bible truly is the Word of God, then we must believe it, obey it, study it, defend it, and trust it. To reject the truth of Scripture is to reject God Himself.

I'd like to give you ten reasons why you can trust the Bible.

1. Self-Claims

The Bible itself claims to be perfect and inspired:

- "All Scripture is given by inspiration of God." (2 Tim. 3:16)
- "The law of the LORD is perfect, converting the soul; the testimony of the LORD is sure, making wise the simple." (Ps. 19:7)
- "The words of the LORD are pure words, like silver tried in a furnace . . . purified seven times." (Ps. 12:6)

John Wesley said, "If there be any mistakes in the Bible, there may as well be a thousand. If there be one falsehood in that book, it did not come from the God of truth."[4] As we read in Proverbs 30:5, "Every word of God is pure."

Now, the fact that the Bible itself claims to be inerrant is enough for most of us as believers. However, those who disagree would argue that we're trying to prove the Bible by quoting the Bible, and that's a fair objection. So while I begin, without apology, with the fact that the Bible itself claims to be inerrant, we also have independent means of demonstrating that the Bible is reliable and trustworthy.

2. Manuscripts

We do not possess any of the original manuscripts for the Old Testament or New Testament, but we do have lots of copies. The reason we don't have originals is pretty straightforward: the Bible was written on materials that weren't made to last—scrolls made of parchment and papyrus. After two thousand years, they have deteriorated. However, many copies were made of the originals. The fact that they're copies, though, raises red flags for people, so let's talk about that.

There are more than 24,000 manuscript copies and pieces of manuscript supporting the New Testament. And while we don't possess any of the original manuscripts, some of the earliest New Testament copies were made as little as twenty-five years after the original. The New Testament was written well over 1,900 years ago, and yet we have over 24,000 pieces of manuscript to support it, which is substantial. *In fact, the New Testament has far more manuscript evidence than any other ancient work.*

By comparison, the thirty-seven plays of William Shakespeare have no surviving original copies and there are missing sections in every one of his works. But Shakespeare's writings are only about four hundred years old, and were all written after the invention of the printing press, which gives their survival rate a huge boost in comparison to the biblical manuscripts, which were handwritten and hand-copied. Nevertheless, no one seriously questions the works of Shakespeare, and their authorship is accepted with much less manuscript evidence.

Going back to the Bible, the New Testament book that has the least amount of manuscript evidence is Revelation, but even then we have more than three hundred Greek manuscripts of the text, which is a lot. Someone well said, "The same God who amazingly provided the Bible has amazingly preserved it."[5] Or as Spurgeon put it, "God writes with a pen that never blots, speaks with a tongue that never slips, and acts with a hand that never fails."[6]

Now, as far as the Old Testament is concerned, we have much less manuscript evidence that has survived. Once again, the reasons are fairly obvious and logical: the amount of time that has passed since Old Testament times is greater than that since New Testament times, so fewer manuscripts have survived. Another factor is that the Jewish people had such a high regard for Scripture that when manuscript copies became worn out, they took careful steps to dispose of them in a prescribed manner, which involved burying them. The Jews disposed of older manuscripts to protect readers from misreading God's Word because of worn out spots in the text.

One of the most exciting discoveries of the last century, without a doubt, was that of the Dead Sea Scrolls. In the summer of 1947, a young Bedouin shepherd named Ahmed was looking for one of his goats that had strayed from the flock. Eventually, Ahmed stumbled onto a cave located in the wall of a large cliff. Thinking that his goat might have wandered into that cave, he picked up a rock and threw it inside, hoping to scare it out. But instead of hearing the sounds of a frightened goat, he heard the sound of pottery shattering.

So Ahmed ran home to his father and told him that there were ghosts living inside the local caves. His father assured him that there were no ghosts, but perhaps lost treasure of gold and silver coins were stored in some pottery. So the next day, Ahmed and his father went back to the cave, and going inside, they discovered eight large clay jars. From out of that broken jar, they found three leather parchments. Disappointed that it wasn't treasure, the father sold the leather scrolls to a local trader, who intended to sell them to a shoe cobbler who was going to use the leather to make shoes.

Fortunately someone intervened, and eventually the scrolls got into the hands of some Israeli scholars. As Ahmed's father surveyed the strange writing on the parchments inside that cave, little did he realize the significance of the monumental discovery his son had made. Just five hundred yards away from that cave was a body of water that would end up giving Ahmed's discovery its official name: the Dead Sea Scrolls.

The climate and conditions of that area are optimal for the preservation of such scrolls, and after this discovery, archaeologists combed through a total of 270 different caves by the Dead Sea. Eleven of them turned up clay jars with scrolls. When all was said and done, five hundred Old Testament scrolls and fragments of scrolls were discovered. Research revealed that a Jewish religious sect called the Essenes had hidden them there during the time of Christ, in the early first century.

There were fragments representing every single book of the Old Testament except Esther, and a complete scroll of Isaiah. And most importantly, those scrolls were a thousand years older than any other Old Testament manuscript copies that we had up until that time! And yet, when compared with the previous manuscripts, there were no contradictions or deletions—only minor differences in the punctuation of the language. So again, the same God who supernaturally provided the Bible supernaturally preserved it.

Now let me also add a quick word about the Old Testament copies themselves. The scribes who copied the Old Testament Scriptures followed very strict guidelines in doing their work. For example, they first counted every word of the section they were copying, then made note of the middle word and then the middle letter. So let's say that they were copying an Old Testament section that contained five hundred Hebrew words. They would write that exact number down. Then they would count and identify the middle word, and let's say that word was *Jerusalem*. They would write that down. Then they would identify the middle letter—in this case, it would be the letter *s*, which they would also write down. Then after they were finished writing their copy, they would go back and count each word in the new copy. If the total matched five hundred words, then so far, so good. Next they counted to the middle word, and then to the middle letter. If the middle word wasn't *Jerusalem*, or the middle letter wasn't *s*, they would destroy their copy and start over.

If they made any mistakes as they were copying a manuscript, they would immediately stop, destroy it, and start over. They recognized the holiness of God's Word and did everything humanly possible to keep it accurate. But in spite of their best efforts, mistakes were made. Some examples of mistakes included adding one too many zeros to a number. Another type of error might have been the misspelling of someone's name or a city. But even those errors were minimal and did not affect the context or intent of God's message.

3. Fulfilled Prophecy

I've heard some believers say, "I'm not really into prophecy." But 27 percent of the Bible is prophecy! Prophecy is history written in advance. Prophecy in Scripture has a twofold purpose: to foretell the future and to explain the positive and negative results of those future events.

The Bible contains hundreds of prophecies about the future of the world, nations, cities, and humankind. In the Old Testament alone are over three hundred prophecies just about Jesus Christ. For example:

- Where Jesus would be born (Bethlehem), in Micah 5:2.
- Which tribe He would descend from (Judah), in Genesis 49:10.
- How He would be born (virgin birth), in Isaiah 7:14.
- How He would be betrayed for thirty pieces of silver, in Zechariah 11:12–13.
- How He would suffer for our sins, in Isaiah 53.
- That He would be crucified (even before crucifixion existed!), in Psalm 22:16.
- How the Roman soldiers would gamble for His garment, in Psalm 22:18.
- One of His seven statements from the cross ("My God! My God! Why have You forsaken Me?"), in Psalm 22:1.

- How He would rise from the dead, in Psalm 16:10.
- How He would ascend into heaven, in Psalm 68:18.

All three hundred of those Old Testament prophecies were fulfilled perfectly and precisely. Only God can predict the future with 100 percent accuracy, and He always does! Of the thousand prophetic passages in Scripture, half of them have been fulfilled to the last detail.[7] Fulfilled prophecy is one of the strongest reasons why we can trust the Bible! I appreciate the statement that says, "If you want to know what happened yesterday, read the morning paper; if you want to know what happened today, listen to the evening news; if you want to know what will happen tomorrow, read the Bible!"[8]

4. The Resurrection

I mention the resurrection of Christ not only because the Old Testament foretold it but also because it's the main and most important event of the New Testament. The same Jesus who rose from the dead, demonstrating that He is God, also proclaimed, "Heaven and earth will pass away, but My words will by no means pass away," giving divine weight and authority to the Scriptures (Matt. 24:35).

As Paul wrote in 1 Corinthians 15:6, there were over five hundred eyewitnesses to the fact of the resurrection. Those same witnesses, including the apostles, were then willing to die for the message of the gospel and the truth about Jesus. The resurrection of Jesus is a well-attested historical fact.

5. Archaeology

The great mystery writer Agatha Christie was married to an archaeologist, and she used to say, "An archaeologist is the best husband a woman can have. The older she gets, the more interested he is in her." It's worth noting that a Jewish archaeologist named Nelson

Glueck, the most prominent archaeologist in his day, wasn't a Christian or even an orthodox Jew. In fact, he once admitted that his faith wasn't built on a literal interpretation of the Bible. In other words, he had no motive for trying to prove the Bible to be true. And yet he went on record as saying, "It may be stated categorically that no archaeological discovery has ever contradicted a biblical reference."[9]

Another famous archaeologist, William M. Ramsay, set out to disprove the geography of the New Testament, being extremely skeptical of the geographic information in the book of Acts. However, his extensive travels and findings convinced him that the New Testament was completely accurate, leading him to write helpful books such as *St. Paul the Traveler and Roman Citizen*, which I have in my library.

So let me give you two quick archaeological discoveries that speak of the reliability of Scripture, in addition to the Dead Sea Scrolls. The first is called the Tel Dan Stele (not to be confused with the 1970s rock group Steely Dan). This inscribed stone was discovered during excavations in the northern Israel area of Tel Dan in the early 1990s. Before this discovery, many secular archaeologists claimed that King David in the Bible was a mythical figure like King Arthur rather than a historical king, and that outside of the Bible there wasn't any evidence for the reign of King David.

Then came the discovery of the Tel Dan Stele. On that stone are inscribed the words "House of David," with reference to his kingdom. The stone was unearthed among the ruins of a city dating back to the ninth century BC. The stone has been universally verified as authentic, dating back to David's dynasty, and now gives us solid proof of David and his kingdom outside of the Bible. It was a huge discovery, to say the least. I've seen the Tel Dan Stele in the Israel Museum.

A similar challenge and discovery had to do with Pontius Pilate, the Roman governor who questioned and then condemned Jesus, handing Him over to the soldiers to be crucified. Like David, there was no solid evidence outside of the Bible for the existence of a Roman governor named Pilate in the early first century, so Bible critics rejected him as a mythical figure—that is, until 1961, when a team of Italian archaeologists discovered a limestone tablet in the area of the theater at Caesarea.

On that tablet was an inscription that read "Pontius Pilate—Prefect of Judea." This stone was dated to the first century and was universally verified as being authentic—giving us solid proof about a Roman prefect, or governor, named Pontius Pilate.

Let me just say that archaeological discoveries like these don't prove the Bible, because the Bible itself is absolute and archaeology is not. Psalm 119:89 says, "Forever, O LORD, Your word is settled in heaven." But for those sincerely seeking to understand the Bible, archaeology does confirm Bible history.

6. Israel

From the days of the Pharaoh in Egypt to the days of Adolf Hitler in Nazi Germany—for the past four thousand years—the chosen people of God have been persecuted and killed. Time and time again, their very existence has been threatened but they have miraculously survived. God has protected them because He has a promised future for Israel.

After AD 70, when the Romans invaded Jerusalem, destroying the temple and parts of the city, the Jewish people were without a homeland. Then, against all odds, almost 1,900 years later, on May 14, 1948, Israel once again became a nation, though many Middle Eastern nations have attempted to destroy Israel since that time and continue to pose a serious threat to Israel.

At the end of Romans 11, Paul explains that Israel will survive. Zechariah states that the eyes of the Jews will be opened to the Messiah, the One "whom they pierced" (Zech. 12:10), in the tribulation. In Ezekiel 48 and Isaiah 66, we also learn that God will restore Israel in the millennial kingdom, and each tribe will receive a section in the Promised Land. Christ Himself will rule and reign, with His throne situated in Jerusalem and Zion. The past, present, and future survival of Israel is great evidence that the Bible is God's Word.

7. The Indestructible Book

Not only has Israel been under attack since its inception but so has the Bible. From the enemy nations of the Old Testament to the Roman emperors of the New Testament to modern-day atheists, people have tried to discredit and destroy the Bible. But while all of those people die, the Bible lives on!

The well-known French philosopher Voltaire famously declared that within twenty-five years, the Bible would be forgotten and Christianity would become obsolete. But forty years after Voltaire's death in 1778, his home was turned into a printing shop for Bibles and other Christian literature! Listen to words of Bernard Ramm:

> A thousand times over, the death knell of the Bible has been sounded, the funeral procession formed, the inscription cut on the tombstone, and the committal read. But somehow the corpse never stays put. No other book has been so chopped, knifed, sifted, scrutinized, and vilified. But the Bible is still loved, read, and studied by millions. This Book will never die![10]

8. Unity

In the last chapter we talked about how the Bible came to be, including how its sixty-six books were written over a period of about fifteen hundred years by at least forty different writers—in a wide variety of circumstances and occupations, on three different continents, and in three different languages. And yet, remarkably, the message of the Bible is in complete unity.

From beginning to end, there's one unfolding story of God's plan of salvation for mankind—in the Person of Christ. Jesus Himself said to the unsaved religious leaders, "You search the Scriptures, for in them you think you have eternal life; and these are they which testify of Me" (John 5:39). Despite all of the diversity of its components there is remarkable unity in the Bible.

9. The Message

The remarkable message of God's Word is the message of grace. What religious book would declare that we are totally depraved and lost sinners separated from God, headed for eternal judgment—and then declare that forgiveness, salvation, and deliverance of judgment is found in the Person of Christ, by faith? All other religions and religious writings tell humankind what they must do to achieve salvation, through human works and achievements. The Bible's message of grace stands alone, shining like a beacon from heaven.

10. Changed Lives

How many people have had their lives radically and eternally changed by the biblical message of the gospel? Everyone who is a Christian! The authority and power of God's inspired and supernatural Word is best seen in the transformation of countless lives. Drug addicts, derelicts, deadbeats, and decent people who thought they were OK have been converted and transformed by God's Word.

Throughout history, men and women of God have been willing to die for the precious truths of Scripture. Various forms of torture have been used in the attempt to force people to renounce their faith in God and His Word. They were burned, boiled, and beheaded—but still preferred torture and death to renouncing their faith. All of the great apostles, except for John, died excruciating deaths for the truth. They went from hiding in fear to fearlessly proclaiming God's Word. Their lives and deaths testify to the fact that the Bible truly is the Word of God.

One of my favorite conversion stories is that of the brilliant writer and Christian apologist C. S. Lewis. While teaching at Oxford, England, in 1925, Lewis was an atheist. His mother had died of cancer when he was only nine, causing him to reject any notion of God's goodness. By age fourteen, Lewis had rejected any kind of faith, and the wounds he received as a soldier during World War I only strengthened his resolve against God.

According to his autobiography, *Surprised by Joy*, Lewis described himself as being "the most dejected and reluctant convert in all England."[11] In 1931, Lewis had dinner with J. R. R. Tolkien, author of the famous Lord of the Rings trilogy and a fellow professor at Oxford. As they were discussing the subject of myths, Tolkien proposed to Lewis that the so-called myth of Christianity was actually true. Tolkien explained to Lewis that Jesus Christ truly did live, walk the earth, die, and rise from the dead.

For the next several days, under heavy conviction, Lewis began to search the Scriptures, almost looking for ways to discredit the truth beginning to take hold in his heart. In his own words, Lewis wrote that he was "kicking, struggling, resentful, and darting his eyes in every direction looking for a chance of escape."[12] Finally, while riding to the zoo with his brother, talking about Christianity, C. S. Lewis was converted.

He later wrote, "When we set out I did not believe that Jesus Christ is the Son of God, and when we reached the zoo I did."[13] Lewis would go on to write over a hundred great books, including *The Problem of Pain*, *Mere Christianity*, and *Surprised by Joy*. Lewis also gave us great works of fiction based on scriptural truths, like *The Screwtape Letters* and the Chronicles of Narnia series. The Bible is able to change lives. It truly is the inspired Word of God, which we can trust and cherish!

On an interesting side note, Lewis died on November 22, 1963. If that date sounds familiar, it's because it's the day President John F. Kennedy was assassinated in Dallas, Texas. With the eyes of the world squarely focused on that tragic event, Lewis quietly slipped into eternity, virtually unnoticed.

3

Understanding the Old Testament

A little boy was sitting on his living room couch, thumbing through the large, old family Bible. He was fascinated as he looked through the Old Testament. Suddenly, something fell out of the Bible, and when he reached down to pick it up, he saw it was an old leaf that had been pressed between the pages. Very excitedly, the little boy called out, "Mommy, look what I found!" The mother smiled and said, "What have you got there, honey?" With astonishment the little boy replied, "I'm not sure, but I think it might be Adam's underwear!"

We turn now to the subject of understanding the Old Testament. Often at the beginning of a new year, people will make a commitment to read through the Bible from Genesis to Revelation. Reading the Bible in a year is a wonderful goal and I've done it many times as a Christian. But despite good intentions, it's easy to get bogged down in the Old Testament with its unfamiliar names, unpronounceable places, and uninspiring genealogies. Perhaps you can identify with the words of author Max Anders, who described the experience by saying, "I stubbed my toe on Leviticus, sprained my ankle on Job, hit my head on Ecclesiastes, and fell headlong into the mud on Habakkuk."[1]

In my opinion, reading through the Old Testament is kind of like driving across the United States, which I've also done many times. If you jump on the freeway and just start driving from one coast to another, you can follow the signs and basically make your way in the right direction. But without any kind of map, you start to lose perspective of how the different states connect together, where you're at, and how you're getting there. Ultimately, it becomes a long, meandering journey.

So whenever I went on one of those trips, I always took a large atlas with me that included a detailed road map of each state as well as a map of the entire United States. That way, I could pause to get a good overall sense and understanding of where I was going and where I had been. In the same way, if we don't have a basic sense and understanding of the Old Testament, then as we simply try to read it book by book it will begin to feel like a series of disconnected stories and events. So in this chapter, I'd like for us to take a step back and seek to get an overall sense of the Old Testament.

Going back to the very basics, the Bible is divided up into two main sections: the Old Testament and the New Testament. As I previously mentioned, the word *testament* simply means "covenant" or "agreement." The Bible, then, is one book made up of two testaments, consisting of sixty-six individual books: thirty-nine in the Old Testament and twenty-seven in the New Testament. The primary dividing line between the Old Testament and New Testament is Christ. The Old Testament takes us from creation to the silent years just before the time of Christ, and then the New Testament takes us from the birth of Christ to the future heavens and earth.

Since the Bible is a single book, the Old and New Testaments complement each other. In the Old Testament paradise is lost in Adam; in the New Testament paradise is restored in Christ. The Old Testament deals with God and the nation of Israel while the New Testament deals with God and the church. The Old Testament lays the foundation for the coming of the Messiah; the New Testament presents us with the Messiah's arrival. In the words of Augustine, "The old covenant is revealed in the new, and the new covenant is veiled in the old."[2]

It's been pointed out that a better title for the Old Testament might be "the First Testament," because the word *old* implies that the first thirty-nine books are obsolete and irrelevant. But as Paul points out in 2 Timothy 3:16, all Scripture is profitable. We need both the Old Testament and the New Testament in order to understand our past, our present, and our future.

Categories of the Old Testament

You've heard of the basic food groups. Well, the Word of God is our spiritual food, and one of the most helpful ways for understanding the Old Testament is knowing how its thirty-nine books break up into four basic groups.

1. The Law (five books)	Genesis–Deuteronomy
2. History (twelve books)	Joshua–Esther
3. Poetry/Wisdom (five books)	Job–Song of Solomon
4. Prophecy (seventeen books)	Isaiah–Malachi

Sometimes "prophecy" is divided into separate groups of "major prophets" and "minor prophets," creating five groups, but I prefer four. The Old Testament was originally divided up into two sections: the law and the prophets. In Luke 16:16, Jesus said to the Pharisees, "The law and the prophets were until John," referring to John the Baptist. So Jesus was saying the Old Testament was divided up between the law and the prophets, while the time period went up to the days of John the Baptist. But then later in Luke's Gospel, in the final chapter, Jesus expanded the Old Testament. While speaking to the two discouraged disciples He met on the road to Emmaus, Jesus said to them, "All things must be fulfilled which were written in the Law of Moses and the Prophets and the Psalms" (24:44).

Today it's very helpful to remember this fourfold division while reading through the Old Testament, because then we know what type of information we can expect to find in the various books. If you're reading Isaiah, you'll expect to find prophecy. If you're reading Joshua, you'll know it's history.

Let's look at these four divisions of the Old Testament a little more closely.

The Law—Genesis through Deuteronomy

The first five books of the Bible are referred to as the Torah by Jewish people. *Torah* is the Hebrew word for "law," though it's also translated as "teaching" or "instruction." The first five books are also referred to as the Pentateuch, which is Greek for "five scrolls" or "five books" (*penta/teuchos*). These are also commonly called the Five Books of Moses, because he is recognized as their writer. There are numerous Old Testament and New Testament verses that identify Moses as the writer (including Exod. 17:14; Deut. 1:1; Luke 24:27; and John 5:46).

Genesis is the foundational book of the Bible, the book of beginnings. The Greek word *genesis* means "origin." The Hebrew title of the book, *Bereshith*, translates, "In the beginning," which are the first three words of the Bible. So Genesis is the book of beginnings, telling us about the beginnings of the universe, earth, humankind, sin, salvation, marriage, family, faith, worship, government, nations, language, and so forth. What Genesis doesn't tell us about is the beginning of God—because God is eternal, with no beginning or end.

The way I like to remember Genesis is by simply dividing its fifty chapters into two sections:

1.	Chapters 1–11	Four main events: creation, fall, flood, nations
2.	Chapters 12–50	Four main people: Abraham, Isaac, Jacob, Joseph

In the first section we have the four main events, starting with creation. In Genesis 1:1, we read that "In the beginning God created the heavens and the earth." This is the beginning, not of God but of recorded history—the beginning of time and space. Genesis 1 gives us the outline of God's creation, while Genesis 2 gives us added details. It's been well said that if you can believe Genesis 1:1, you'll have no trouble believing the rest of the Bible.

Make no mistake—rejecting Genesis and its foundational truths is an absolute game changer for life and eternity. Rejecting Genesis leads people to embrace evolution, alternate lifestyles, same-sex marriage, abortion, euthanasia, lawlessness, and on the list goes—including rejection of God. If you reject the truths of Genesis, you're left with believing the lies of Satan, like when he said to Eve, "Did God really say . . . ?" (Gen. 3:1 NIV).

Eve believed the lie, so in Genesis 3 we have the second main event: the fall. Adam and Eve were created by God without sin. But they were also created with a free will. Using their free will, they chose to disobey God's words and to believe the lies of the devil. In the six-day creation account, we don't read about God creating the angels. In Job 38, however, we do read that the angels were there rejoicing when God laid the foundations of the world. So it would appear that God had already created the angels beforehand.

All angels were created as holy and, as we learn from Isaiah 14 and Ezekiel 28, Lucifer was one of those holy angels next to the throne of God. But in his free will, he was filled with pride and rebelled against God. A third of the angels joined Lucifer in his rebellion and they were all expelled from heaven. Here's an important life lesson for all of us: whatever we don't turn into praise will turn into pride.

Soon afterward Lucifer, now known as Satan, attacked God's first created human beings by lying to and deceiving Eve. As a result, the fall of humankind took place and sin entered the human race. With it came physical death. Romans 5:12 clearly says, "When Adam sinned, sin entered the world. Adam's sin brought death, so death spread to everyone, for everyone sinned" (NLT). But the good news comes just a few verses later, in verse 18, when Paul writes, "Yes, Adam's one sin brings condemnation for everyone, but Christ's one act of righteousness brings a right relationship with God and new life for everyone" (NLT).

Genesis 3 is one of the "three important third chapters" in the Bible. The other two are John 3 and Romans 3 in the New Testament. Combining those three chapters in Scripture gives us the "Three Rs" in Bible history: ruin (Gen. 3), redemption (John 3), and regeneration (Rom. 3).

Throughout history, it's often been assumed that the forbidden fruit that Eve ate and then gave to Adam was an apple. But the fruit on that tree is never identified in Scripture. It might have been an apple or it may have been a fig, since Adam and Eve used fig leaves to cover the shame of their nakedness afterward. As someone pointed out, "The problem in the Garden wasn't with the apple on the tree, it was with the pair on the ground."

Speaking of apples, all of us are familiar with Apple, Inc., because so many of us use their products—phones, tablets, and computers. But what many of us may not know is that Apple was cofounded in 1976 by three men. First there was Steve Jobs, the best-known of the three, who eventually became the CEO of Apple. Jobs passed away in his midfifties. The second member of the cofounding team was Steve Wozniak. He wasn't as recognizable as Jobs until he appeared on *Dancing with the Stars*. (He's good with computers, but lousy at dancing!) Wozniak developed the Apple I and Apple II computers in the late 1970s, contributing significantly to the computer revolution.

That brings us to the third cofounding member, someone most of us have never heard of: Ronald Wayne. Wayne sketched the first logo, created the first manual, and wrote the original partnership agreement. In the terms of their founders' agreement, Ronald Wayne was made a 10 percent shareholder in Apple. Today, that 10 percent share would be worth more than forty-seven billion dollars! But less than two weeks after that agreement was signed, Ronald Wayne sold his 10 percent share of Apple for a measly eight hundred dollars! That story reminds me of Adam and Eve—selling out their share of paradise for a few bites of fruit.

When we are apart from God, our bad decisions in life usually lead to worse decisions. But the good news—scratch that—the great news is that God can forgive our bad decisions. And one good decision can change the course of our lives, like the decision to follow Christ!

As I already alluded to, after Adam and Eve had sinned, they attempted to cover the shame of their nakedness with fig leaves. But then we read in Genesis 3:21 that God gave them animal skins with which to cover themselves. That means an animal was slain in order to provide those clothes, which became a foretaste of animal sacrifices for the atonement of sin. And that was the foreshadowing of Jesus, the Lamb of God, coming to lay down His life to permanently atone for the sins of all who would believe.

Adam and Eve's sin spread to all humanity. That rampant sin and rebellion permeating the human race escalated rapidly, reaching a breaking point in Genesis 6. God determined that the wickedness of humankind was so widespread that He would judge the world, bringing us to our third main event: the flood. But in His great mercy and grace, God also gave humanity the opportunity to be saved. God instructed His faithful servant Noah to build an ark. As far as we know, it was the first boat ever built in the history of the world. Plus, it had never rained on the earth at this point (see Gen. 2:5). There are many amazing aspects to Noah's story—first and foremost is the longsuffering of God in pronouncing that humanity would be given 120 years to respond to His warning of global judgment. How merciful and longsuffering God is. And yet only eight people (Noah and his family) experienced that amazing grace.

Another amazing aspect to this story is the faithfulness of Noah! Who builds a boat where there's no water? And who faithfully preaches the Word of God for 120 years with no converts? Noah did these things and more. In the 1989 movie *Field of Dreams*, there's a definite "Noah and the ark" element in the story. Kevin Costner plays the part of a farmer and baseball lover who hears a voice one day while walking through his cornfields in Iowa. The voice simply says, "If you build it, they will come." Later on, he sees a vision of a baseball field in the middle of his cornfield. Against all common sense, and with ridicule from everyone, he decides to mow down a large portion of his cornfield and build a baseball diamond. During the process, Costner's character looks like a complete fool. Noah would have looked like a complete fool building a boat in the middle of nowhere, warning about a flood when it had never rained before.

But then again, Moses looked pretty foolish when he went before the king of Egypt and announced that God wanted His people set free. The Israelite army looked pretty foolish marching around the city of Jericho for several days. David looked really foolish running toward the giant Goliath with nothing except a sling and a stone. The wise men looked pretty foolish following a star and searching for an infant king. Peter looked foolish stepping out of the boat and expecting to walk on water. Jesus looked foolish hanging naked on a cross. I bet a lot of people thought you were absolutely foolish when you gave your heart and life to Christ.

So Noah built it and indeed they came—not the people, but the animals! The people that God had created in His own image rejected Him, while the animals were smart enough to make their way to the ark. They joined Noah and his immediate family on the ark, just before the rains began to fall. Once the flood waters started to rise, I promise you that no one was laughing at Noah or thinking him a fool any longer—but then it was too late.

This brings us to the fourth main aspect in the first part of Genesis: the nations. The story of the tower of Babel is recorded in Genesis 11. After the flood, God instructed humankind to spread out and repopulate the earth (see Gen. 9:1). But in pride and rebellion, they did the exact opposite and tried to establish one city, with a tower symbolizing their power and human achievement. The people were in rebellion to God's authority. The Jewish historian Josephus wrote that the people built the tower because they refused to submit to God.

God dealt with them by confusing their words, creating several new languages. The Hebrew word *babel* means "to confuse." This "confusion" caused the various groups of people to separate and congregate with people who spoke the same language. In the process, these various groups began to spread out, bringing about the different nations of the world.

Now we reach the second section of Genesis (chs. 12–50), which is best remembered by four main people: Abraham, Isaac, Jacob, and Joseph.

In James 2:23, Abraham is called "the friend of God," something that isn't said about any other person in Scripture. Abraham in particular is foundational, because we read in Galatians 3:7 that all believers in every generation are called "children of Abraham." He's not only the father of the Jewish people; he's also the father of the faith. This brings us to a common question about the Old Testament: How were people saved in Old Testament times?

The answer is the same way people are saved today—by faith. First of all, no one was ever saved in the Old Testament by trying to keep the law. As Paul wrote in Romans 5:20, "God's law was given so that all people could see how sinful they were" (NLT). The purpose of the law was to show people their sin and then point them to God for salvation. Read what Galatians 3:11 says: "No one is justified by the law in the sight of God . . . for 'the just shall live by faith.'" Those words, "the just shall live by faith," are written three times in the New Testament. However, in all three instances the writers are quoting an Old Testament verse, Habakkuk 2:4. The message of being saved by faith comes from the Old Testament, and Abraham is the foundational example of this truth.

In Genesis 15, before Abraham was circumcised and before the law was given, we read that God gave him a promise: he would become the father of many nations and descendants. And in Genesis 15:6 we read that Abraham "believed in the LORD, and He accounted it to him for righteousness." Abraham was saved just like we are saved: by grace through faith. To emphasize this truth, we read in Romans 2:28–29 that a true Jew, and true child of God, is not a person of Jewish descent or circumcision but one who believes by faith like Abraham did. In the same way, we read that David was also saved by faith in the Old Testament, and in Romans 4:7 Paul quotes David's statement, "Blessed is the one whose transgressions are forgiven" (Ps. 32:1 NIV).

There's so much more that I'd love to say about Abraham, but to keep things concise let's move to his son Isaac. God promised Abraham and his wife, Sarah, a child of their own in their old age, and God gave them Isaac. So through Isaac, God's covenant promise of many descendants and nations was fulfilled (see Gen. 22). Isaac was married to Rebekah and they had twin sons, Esau and Jacob. Jacob became a spiritual son of faith while Esau remained an unsaved and unspiritual man who willingly traded away his spiritual birthright.

A big part of understanding the Old Testament is by remembering the covenant that God made with Abraham, referred to as the Abrahamic Covenant. Basically, back in Genesis 12, God promised Abraham, "I will make you a great nation . . . and you shall be a blessing. I will bless those who bless you, and I will curse him who curses you; and in you all the families of the earth shall be blessed" (vv. 2–3).

So catch this, please: God repeated that covenant promise to Abraham's son Isaac, and again to his grandson Jacob (see Gen. 26:1–5; 28:13–15). But God never repeated it again to anyone else. That's why, in the Old Testament, we often read the words of God spoken to others, such as Moses, whereby God says, "I am the God of your father—the God of Abraham, the God of Isaac, and the God of Jacob" (Exod. 3:6). God's promises of blessings to all future generations came through Abraham, Isaac, and Jacob.

That brings us to Abraham's great-grandson Joseph, and we might wonder: Why is so much of Genesis devoted to the life of Joseph? The answer is because Joseph is the person in whom we see the Jewish people move from being a family to becoming a nation. As we read up to, and through, the life of Joseph, it's all about his family—his father and his many brothers. Through Joseph's difficult circumstances of betrayal and false accusations, as well as through his faith, by the end of Genesis the whole family ends up in Egypt. And then as we turn the page into Exodus, Israel is now a nation of many people.

In Exodus, it's not long before we find the Israelites, Jacob's descendants, suffering under the bondage of a new Pharaoh in Egypt. After a period of four hundred years, as the Israelites cried out to God for deliverance, the wheels were set in motion. Actually, the wheels had been set in motion some eighty years earlier, with the birth of Moses. When Pharaoh tried to have all the Hebrew baby boys drowned in the Nile River, God intervened and baby Moses ended up being adopted by Pharaoh's daughter. Then years later, it was Pharaoh's own army that drowned, not Moses or the Hebrew people!

The fact that Moses was adopted by Pharaoh's daughter and raised in the Egyptian palace wasn't just a matter of God protecting Moses but also God preparing Moses. Moses received the finest education available anywhere in the world at that time. And since he would end up writing and recording the first five books of the Bible, his education was part of God's plan and purpose.

Moses would also end up leading two million Hebrews through the desert, so mathematics certainly came in handy! Then there was his training in astronomy, which would help him during the endless miles of desert travel with no compass but the stars. As far as learning architecture, Moses would have been trained in the courts of Pharaoh to build the pyramids, but he had a higher calling from the courts in heaven to build the tabernacle. Moses was trained in music, which later would become useful in worship. And Moses was trained in warfare, which would prepare him to lead his people against the enemies of God.

After his first forty years, as a prince of Egypt, Moses came to understand that the Hebrew slaves were actually his relatives. At one point, when Moses stumbled upon an Egyptian taskmaster beating one of the Hebrew slaves, he took matters into his own hands and killed that Egyptian. But the very next day, Moses learned that what he had done was not a secret. Pharaoh soon heard about it, so Moses fled into the wilderness. In time he met and married a Midianite woman and began to raise a family. For the next forty years Moses was a shepherd in the wilderness.

Moses had been well educated in all the ways of Egypt, but he still needed those forty years to learn the ways of God. And most importantly, he learned to wait on the Lord for His perfect timing. When Moses tried to take matters into his own hands in helping the Hebrew people, he failed miserably. But here's some more good news: in God's kingdom, failure is never final! Our God always gives us second, third, and fourth chances (and more!) to succeed in Him. Moses became the patron saint of second chances. In the words of Mark Batterson, "Failure is the fertilizer that grows character."[3]

After forty years of shepherding sheep and goats in the middle of nowhere, at age eighty, when Moses thought his life was basically over, God was now ready to call him into service. God doesn't call the qualified; He qualifies the called. Exodus records so many marvelous miracles, starting with God speaking to Moses through a burning bush at Mount Sinai.

After God called Moses He sent him to appear before Pharaoh, demanding that Pharaoh set God's people free from bondage and slavery. When Pharaoh hardened his heart and refused, God sent ten different plagues by the hand of Moses, devastating Egypt. The tenth and final plague introduced the Passover to God's people—God's judgment passing over them after they applied lamb's blood to the doorposts of their homes. This foreshadowed the Lamb of God, Jesus Christ, removing our judgment at the moment when we apply His shed blood to the doorposts of our hearts by faith.

As Moses led the people out of Egypt, Pharaoh hardened his heart again and pursued the Hebrews with his soldiers and chariots. But then came the next great miracle: God parted the waters of the Red Sea, allowing the Israelites to pass through safely on dry ground. Afterward, God brought the waters back down upon the pursuing army, drowning them all. From there Moses and the people went on to Mount Sinai, where God gave them His law.

In the book of Leviticus God spoke to the people about His requirements for holy living. God gave them instructions for the sacrificial system, as well as the priesthood and the various feasts. He taught them about purity and morality. The emphasis of Leviticus is that of holiness, as God told the people, "Be holy, because I am holy" (Lev. 11:44 NIV).

In the book of Numbers the people were still assembled at Mount Sinai, preparing for their eleven-day journey to the Promised Land, Canaan, or modern-day Israel. But as they got closer to Canaan, the faith of the people began to crumble, to the point of unbelief and rebellion. So God disciplined that adult generation, causing them to wander in the wilderness for forty years. These events are used in the New Testament to warn us as believers today about the serious consequences of sin and unbelief (see 1 Cor. 10; Heb. 3–4; 1 Pet. 2; and Jude).

The law then concludes with the book of Deuteronomy. Moses is 120 years old and at the end of his life. The adult generation of Israelites has died in their wilderness wanderings, and the next generation is ready to follow Joshua into Canaan. Deuteronomy takes place over a period of about thirty days, as Moses gives the people several speeches about the blessings of obedience and the consequences of disobedience (see Deut. 1:3; 34:8; Josh. 1:2). Then Moses climbs a mountain at the border overlooking the Promised Land, dies, and is buried by God.

According to Deuteronomy 34, Moses died just outside the Promised Land and was not allowed to enter it because he had misrepresented God at an earlier time. God had instructed Moses to speak to a rock to give the people water, and instead Moses lost his temper and struck the rock. So God disciplined Moses by not letting him cross over into the Promised Land. However, Moses did eventually make it in! In the Gospels, Moses is there in the Promised Land, standing on the Mount of Transfiguration, talking with Jesus and Elijah.

At the end of Deuteronomy Moses died outside Canaan while Joshua was chosen by God to lead Israel forward. Moses, as the lawgiver, represented the law, while Joshua, whose name is the Hebrew equivalent of the name Jesus, represented grace. The law (Moses) couldn't bring God's people into their inheritance, but grace (Joshua) could and did. The law, or anything other than God's grace, can't and won't bring us into our eternal inheritance.

On that subject, believers sometimes ask the question of whether or not we still obey the Old Testament law. It may surprise you to know that the answer is both no and yes. The answer is no, because the Old Testament law was given to Israel and not to the New Testament church. Many of those laws had to do with Jewish dietary regulations, animal sacrifices, and ceremonies. Most importantly, when Jesus died on the cross, He cancelled out our debt to the law (see Col. 2:14). Romans 10:4 declares that "Christ is the end of the law for righteousness to everyone who believes."

But in conjunction with that, we still obey the principles of the law. Jesus said, "Do not think that I came to destroy the Law or the Prophets. I did not come to destroy but to fulfill" (Matt. 5:17). Just like prophecy is fulfilled, Jesus was saying that He fulfilled the Old Testament law. When Jesus was asked what the greatest commandment in the law was, He said, "'You shall love the LORD your God with all your heart, with all your soul, and with all your mind.' This is the first and great commandment. And the second is like it: 'You shall love your neighbor as yourself.' On these two commandments hang all the Law and the Prophets" (Matt. 22:37–40).

So most of the Old Testament laws applied specifically to the Jewish people, and those other moral principles that still apply to us are kept by loving God and loving others (see Deut. 6:5 and Lev. 19:18). Take the ten commandments, for example—as we love God, we won't worship idols or take His name in vain. And as we love others, we won't commit adultery, lie, steal, or commit murder. So in that way, the Old Testament laws help us to understand how we can love God and love people.

History—Joshua through Esther

In the book of Joshua we come to the beginning of the second Old Testament group, the history of God's people. Joshua picks up right where Deuteronomy left off. The book of Joshua is about

God's people arriving in the land God promised to them: Canaan, or modern-day Israel. Joshua is summarized by Israel crossing the Jordan River into Canaan, overtaking Jericho, conquering Canaan, and then occupying the land God gave to them.

Joshua is the first book of the Bible named after its main character. And in Joshua we find the first recorded conversion of a Gentile: a woman named Rahab. Like the end of Deuteronomy, where Moses gave the people God's words of warning and blessing, Joshua ends his book in the same way. Joshua's now famous words at the end of his life, which still apply to us today, were, "Choose for yourselves this day whom you will serve. . . . But as for me and my house, we will serve the LORD" (24:15).

As we come to the next book, Judges, it doesn't take long for God's people to choose apostasy over allegiance to God. The days of the judges have been called "the Dark Ages in Israel's history." The fourteen different judges were men and women whom God raised up to deliver His people from oppression. Sadly, their continuous cycles of oppression were the direct result of their disobedience and unfaithfulness. Over and over again, the people turned away from the Lord to worship false gods. Then God would discipline them by allowing them to become oppressed by various enemies. Next they would repent and cry out to God for help. In response, God would raise up a judge to deliver them. Then, after some temporary peace, they repeated the cycle over again—a total of seven times in this book. As the popular saying goes, "Insanity is doing the same thing over and over again and expecting different results." A phrase that is repeated several times in Judges is, "In those days there was no king in Israel; everyone did what was right in his own eyes" (17:6; 21:25).

But in the midst of Israel's dark apostasy, the story of Ruth appears—a beautiful lily in a stagnant pond. In stark contrast to the people in Judges, Ruth emerges as a woman of purity, humility, and loyalty. It's the only instance where a book of the Bible is devoted to the life of one woman. And it's one of just two books in the Bible named after a woman; the other is Esther.

Ruth marries Boaz and becomes the great-grandmother of David—and more than a thousand years later, Jesus is born through that line of David and Ruth. Boaz was the direct descendant of Rahab the harlot, who was saved in Jericho by faith! And like Rahab, Ruth is another Old Testament Gentile convert to the faith. Both Rahab and Ruth have their names included in the genealogy of Jesus in Matthew 1.

The book of Ruth is followed by 1 and 2 Samuel. First Samuel is divided by its three main characters: Samuel, the prophet; Saul, the first king of Israel; and then David, the shepherd boy who succeeded Saul as king. Samuel was a great spiritual leader over Israel, in contrast to the high priest at that time, Eli. Eli was weak and wishy-washy, with two sons who assisted him at the tabernacle but were very wicked boys. Sadly, Eli failed to discipline them.

So, as in the days of Judges, God allowed an enemy nation in Canaan to oppress Israel: the Philistines. In the last days of Eli, God's people were so disobedient that Eli's grandson was named Ichabod, which means "the glory has departed." I read about a young preacher who was a candidate to pastor a church in the Fort Worth area of Texas. In his Sunday sermon as a candidate, his message was on Eli, Israel's sin, and God's glory departing. At the key moment of his "Ichabod" sermon, he got excited and said, "If we don't follow God, and we refuse to obey Him, He will say to us, 'Michelob!'" A little embarrassing. I don't know if he became the pastor or not!

Later, as Samuel grew old, the Israelites clamored to have a king like the other nations had. The people were not content with God as their King; they wanted a human monarch like the other nations. This greatly displeased Samuel, but God allowed it. In fact, God gave the people exactly the kind of king they clamored for in the person of Saul, and at that point Israel went from being a theocracy (ruled by God) to a monarchy (governed by kings).

Being far more secular than spiritual, it didn't take long for Saul's reign to fall apart. Two verses give us the summary of Saul's life. In 1 Samuel 14:35, we read that "Saul built an altar to the LORD." Saul got off to a good start, trying to honor God in his leadership. But in the very next chapter, we read that "he set up a monument for himself" (15:12). Whenever we stop building altars to the Lord and start building monuments to ourselves, we're in big trouble spiritually.

God chose a man after His own heart to succeed Saul as king—a shepherd boy named David. David really comes to the forefront when he runs an errand for his father and ends up at the Valley of Elah, where the Philistine giant Goliath is taunting Israel's army. Goliath is blaspheming God and provoking Israel, so David steps up and volunteers to fight the giant. David defeats Goliath with only a sling and a stone—and it's worth noting that the Old Testament penalty for blasphemy was stoning! Saul eventually dies, and David becomes Israel's new king. So:

- Judges is the book of no king (self).
- 1 Samuel is the book of man's king (Saul).
- 2 Samuel is the book of God's king (David).

In 2 Samuel David dies and his son Solomon ascends the throne. This might be a good time to pause and address another often-asked question related to the Old Testament: Where did Old Testament believers go when they died? In the New Testament, when a believer dies his or her soul immediately goes to be with the Lord in heaven (see Phil. 1:23 and 2 Cor. 5:6–9). In the meantime the deceased body remains behind, awaiting the return of Jesus, when it will be raised up and transformed into a new, eternal body, united again with the soul.

In the Old Testament, before the resurrection of Christ, believers went into Sheol (also called Hades in the New Testament). Both the wicked and the righteous went there in the Old Testament (see

Ps. 9:17 and 16:10). We find the same dynamic in Luke 16, before Christ's death and resurrection. A believer named Lazarus and an unsaved rich man both die and go to Hades. It is divided, with two sides: Abraham's bosom for believers and the place of torment for the unsaved. Today, though, believers go directly to heaven by Christ's provision on the cross, while the unsaved remain in Hades, awaiting their final judgment.

The story of David's son Solomon is the sad account of someone starting great but ending terribly. Solomon began his rule dedicated and devoted to the Lord. God blessed him with unprecedented wisdom and wealth. God also allowed Solomon the privilege of fulfilling his father's vision: building a permanent house of worship for the Lord—a temple instead of a tabernacle. Everything went swimmingly for Solomon until he started doing things God told him not to do. That included making alliances with foreign nations and having many foreign wives, and then his ultimate collapse—worshiping the false gods of those foreign wives. Gifted Presbyterian minister Clarence Macartney rightly described Solomon as being "the wisest fool in the Bible."[4] Solomon's divided heart led to a divided kingdom.

Now this brings us to a key point and an important piece of the puzzle if we're going to better understand the Old Testament: the divided kingdom. Not understanding this creates a lot of confusion when reading through the Old Testament. As a result of Solomon's spiritual compromises, a civil war erupted after his death, causing the kingdom of Israel to become divided.

The northern kingdom, ten tribes, became Israel.

The southern kingdom, two tribes, became Judah.

After the kingdom is divided, we start reading references to Israel alongside references to Judah. Both kingdoms had their own separate kings during the next few hundred years. For example, the first king in the northern kingdom of Israel was Jeroboam, while the first king in the southern kingdom of Judah was Rehoboam. And from there it all starts sounding like a children's song: "The Jeroboam's connected to the . . . Rehoboam!" Most of those Jewish kings were bad, failing to honor and obey God and worshiping idols. A handful of them were good and stayed faithful to God.

In the next books, 1 and 2 Kings, we read about the ups and downs of the two kingdoms and their various kings. In God's efforts to bring His people to a place of repentance and obedience, He raised up prophets such as Elijah and Elisha to confront the kings and call the people back to faithfulness. Just as Moses represented the law in the Old Testament, Elijah represents the prophets. As I mentioned before, Jesus referred to the entire Old Testament as "the law and the prophets" in Luke 16:16.

Moses and Elijah represent the law and the prophets and that's why we see them standing with Jesus on the Mount of Transfiguration in Matthew 17 and Luke 9. The three of them were discussing Jesus's impending death and departure. Witnessing all of that were Peter, James, and John. And it was Peter, uncertain of what was going on—or what to say—who suggested that they build tabernacles for Jesus, Moses, and Elijah. Apparently, Peter wanted to camp out and make that unique experience last longer.

But God's voice sounded from heaven and said, "This is My beloved Son, in whom I am well pleased. Hear Him!" (Matt. 17:5). God was reminding Peter and the others that Moses and Elijah, representing the law and the prophets, all pointed to Jesus. They were not on equal ground, since Jesus is the fulfillment of all the Scriptures. To emphasize this point, after Peter and the boys hit the ground, Moses and Elijah were gone when they got back up, while only Jesus was still standing there.

Personally, I'm convinced that the two witnesses who will appear in Jerusalem during the tribulation period referenced in Revelation 11 will be Moses and Elijah. For one thing, the miracles that they will perform, such as bringing forth plagues and calling down fire from heaven, point us to the Old Testament ministries of Moses and Elijah. And by standing together with Jesus at the transfiguration, they were previewing the second coming. But at the same time, they represent the law and prophets of the Old Testament that prepared the way for Messiah, so it's fitting that they would appear again to a Christ-rejecting world in the last days.

Both 1 and 2 Chronicles give us more information and history on the various kings of the divided kingdom. By the way, the Hebrew Bible has the same Old Testament Scriptures as our English Bible does, with one difference. The Hebrew Bible is divided up into twenty-four books rather than thirty-nine. They are the same writings, but the Jews don't divide the books of Samuel or Kings. And they combine the books of Ezra and Nehemiah, and so forth. I just wanted to mention that little fact as part of our look into the Old Testament.

Moving on to Ezra, Nehemiah, and Esther, we have more books of history, but it's history that takes place on the other side of the Babylonian captivity. I'll come back later and make some brief comments about those last three books in the category of history, but for now, let's talk about the third Old Testament group of books.

Poetry/Wisdom—Job through Song of Solomon

Let me begin this section by pointing out that while the five books of poetry/wisdom appear together in the middle of the Old Testament, they were actually written at different times during the history of the Old Testament. Job's story most likely took place in the Genesis era and was written by Moses shortly thereafter. The Psalms, at least half of which were written by David, were compiled in the period of 2 Samuel. The other three books (Proverbs, Ecclesiastes, and Song of Solomon) were all written by Solomon in the time period of 1 Kings.

So this brings us to another question: Why isn't the Bible in chronological order? It's probably not hard to figure out the answer at this point; the books of the Bible are grouped together by their subjects. And as we've been discussing, those Old Testament categories are the law, history, poetry/wisdom, and prophecy. Now, within those individual groups, the books are usually ordered chronologically. For example, in the category of prophecy, the prophecies of Isaiah occurred before those of Jeremiah so Isaiah's book appears before Jeremiah's book.

The category we are currently looking at is commonly referred to as poetry or poetry/wisdom. The wisdom heading is easy to understand, but perhaps not the poetry heading. Essentially, the psalms of David and the proverbs of Solomon are written in poetical form. There's no meter or rhyme per se, but a rhythm of thoughts and parallels. There's also a poetical aspect to Job. In the words of the famous poet Tennyson, Job is "the greatest poem, whether of ancient or modern literature."[5]

Job describes for us the wisdom of learning to trust God in times of suffering and trials. Psalms teaches us the wisdom of worshiping and praising God. In Job we're taught to know ourselves; in the psalms we're taught to know God! Proverbs, then, teaches us the wisdom of seeking wisdom! As someone pointed out, "He that would be wise, let him read the Proverbs; he that would be holy, let him read the Psalms."[6] The psalms are the believer's devotions, while the proverbs are the believer's walk.

Solomon wrote three thousand proverbs and more than one thousand songs (see 1 Kings 4:31–32). No wonder he was so wealthy—with all those royalties! Solomon also wrote Ecclesiastes, which describes his journey in seeking the meaning of life. In the end, Solomon came back full circle to God, learning that our greatest needs and desires are found in Him. Solomon also wrote Song of Solomon, the only book in the Bible devoted to the subject of marital love.

It's been pointed out that Solomon wrote three different books at three different stages in his life. He wrote Song of Solomon as a young man in love. He wrote Proverbs as a middle-aged man in wisdom. And he wrote Ecclesiastes as an older man, having learned life's lessons the hard way.

Prophecy—Isaiah through Malachi

The common title of "prophet" is used over three hundred times in Scripture. A prophet was someone who was called or appointed to proclaim the message of God to others. Simply put, prophets spoke on behalf of God. Their message was most often a warning or challenge to God's people. The prophets were also people whom God used to foretell the future. There are at least a thousand prophecies in the Bible, half of which have already been fulfilled. The prophecies of the Old Testament prophets often had both a near-future and distant-future fulfillment. These final seventeen books of the Old Testament were essentially written in those five hundred years leading up to the four hundred silent years before Christ's birth.

The seventeen books of prophecy are divided into two categories: the major prophets being the first five books and the minor prophets making up the other twelve books. The difference between the major and minor prophets is basically size. The twelve minor prophets are not minor in message or meaning but smaller in volume. For example, the combined books of all twelve minor prophets is roughly equal in length to the single book of Isaiah. Isaiah contains sixty-six chapters, and the minor prophets combined have sixty-seven chapters. There are sixteen different authors of the seventeen prophetical books, with Jeremiah writing two of them, Jeremiah and Lamentations.

Now, as we come down the homestretch of this overview of the Old Testament, let's return to the history category. (It sounds like I'm playing Jeopardy—"I'll take history for $800.") I saved Ezra, Nehemiah, and Esther for last because their historical information takes us to the other side of the seventy-year Babylonian captivity and the end of the Old Testament. Earlier, I mentioned the divided kingdom. There is one more major detail to add to each kingdom.

> The ten tribes of the northern kingdom, Israel, underwent the *Assyrian captivity.*
>
> The two tribes of the southern kingdom, Judah, underwent the *Babylonian captivity.*

When the northern tribes went astray, forsaking God and worshiping idols—after years of repeated and unheeded warnings to repent—God allowed the northern kingdom to be invaded and oppressed by the Assyrians. Some of the Jews were taken as captives back to Assyria. One of the noteworthy things the Assyrians did, historically, was to force some of those northern Jews to intermarry with them, forming a mixed race. Those mixed Jews resettled in an area known as Samaria, in northern Israel, and so became known as Samaritans.

For the next hundred years or so after that, God sent prophets to the southern kingdom to warn them that the same type of invasion, oppression, and captivity would fall on them if they failed to repent and return to the Lord. Remarkably, the southern kingdom of Judah also failed to repent, so God used King Nebuchadnezzar and the Babylonians to invade Judah and take it captive to Babylon. The prophets Daniel and Ezekiel were among those captives. During that Babylonian invasion, the temple in Jerusalem that Solomon built was looted and destroyed.

Writer Max Anders tells a story of a man jumping off the top of the Empire State building to end his life. After falling a little ways, the man cries out to God and says, "Oh, Lord, I'm sorry for this stupid mistake; please forgive me!" God's voice calls to him on the way down and says, "Of course I forgive you, and I love you—and that will never change. And by the way, I'll see you in just a moment!"[7] The point of that story is that while God is always willing and wanting to forgive us, that doesn't take away the consequences of our sins. And for the kingdom of Judah, God would forgive them and restore them, but not until after the discipline of their captivity. Jeremiah prophesied that the captivity would last for seventy years and, of course, it did.

Then the Jews were allowed to return home to Canaan to reestablish their lives. The story of their return after the exile is told in Ezra and Nehemiah. The time period covered by these two books is about one hundred years. Both books begin in Persia and end up in Jerusalem. And both books are named for their central characters. In the book of Ezra the first six chapters describe the rebuilding of the temple while the final four chapters describe the rebuilding of the people. In the book of Nehemiah we see the temple work being finished and the continuation of the spiritual work of God's people.

The second temple was much smaller in size and lesser in grandeur than Solomon's temple, but that was the price of sin. Years later, King Herod expanded and enlarged that second temple, and that work continued for forty-six years (John 2:20). Then, as Jesus predicted, that second temple was also destroyed, this time by the Romans in AD 70. According to Revelation 11, a third temple will be erected in the tribulation period that the Antichrist will desecrate at a later point.

The book of Esther is a story that takes place in the time period of Ezra—after the exile, and thirty years before Nehemiah. Like the stories of Joseph and Ruth, the theme of God's providence is front and center in Esther. And like the early chapters of Exodus, Esther is also the story of Satan using a wicked man in an attempt to destroy and eradicate the Jewish people—something that would be attempted again in our recent history by Adolf Hitler.

Conclusion

Without some basic understanding, sense, and perspective, trying to read through the Old Testament can feel like reading a series of disconnected stories and events. But now, I hope, having seen how the Old Testament is divided up and how it's all connected, your reading of the Old Testament will be enhanced and much more understandable.

4

The Sounds of Silence

In his book *For What It's Worth* Paul Harvey compiled a collection of humorous and true stories, many of which he shared during his years on national radio. In one of those stories a large group of people were attending a convention to hear a complex presentation on economics. During the dinner portion of the program, a young lady was seated next to a Chinese gentleman.

The young lady noticed that he didn't say a word all evening but only smiled and nodded his head. So she assumed he was staying silent because his English wasn't very good. Trying to be helpful, she turned to him at the dinner table and asked, "Would you likee some soupee?" The Chinese gentleman took the soup, still smiling and nodding politely.

After the dinner was finished, the time had arrived for the keynote speaker. Suddenly the Chinese gentleman rose up from his seat, walked to the podium, and proceeded to give a brilliant dissertation on economics, all in impeccable English. After rousing applause from the audience, the man returned to his seat, smiled at the very embarrassed young lady, and then couldn't resist asking her, "Did you likee my speechee?"

It's easy to mistake silence for being something that it isn't. If someone close to us is acting quiet, we often assume that something is wrong. As I've gotten older, I find myself craving silence more and more! Our society has become so noisy, and I don't like it. Between the leaf blowers, car stereos, and loud motorcycles, I often want to escape to a deserted island.

The subject of silence is also addressed in the Bible in many different ways. When Job's three friends were giving him so-called words of wisdom, which were actually hurtful to Job in his suffering, he said to them, "Oh, that you would be silent, and it would be your wisdom!" (Job 13:5). Job's friends would have been a lot more comforting had they kept their mouths shut!

In contrast, when Esther was reluctant to appear before the king on behalf of her Jewish people, who were in grave danger, Mordecai said to her, "If you remain completely silent at this time, relief and deliverance will arise for the Jews from another place" (Est. 4:14). In that instance, remaining silent would not have been good. Ecclesiastes 3:7 reminds us that there's a time to speak and a time to keep silent. And in Revelation 8:1, when Jesus opens up the seventh seal to unleash further judgment on the earth, "there was silence in heaven for about half an hour."

But the longest period of silence in the Bible was actually about four hundred years! It's not listed in any of the chapters or verses; it took place between the Old Testament and New Testament. It's called "the four hundred years of silence," or "the silence era," because after Nehemiah, which is the last book of the Old Testament chronologically, God is silent for four hundred years, until the birth of Christ.

No words, prophecies, revelations, or visions come forth from the Lord during those years. God's people had been cured of their idolatry after the Babylonian captivity. However, they persisted in other areas of disobedience. So for all intents and purposes, God gave them the silent treatment! This four-hundred-year gap is also often called the intertestamental period, which means "between the testaments." And those four centuries were quite busy with change. God's voice might have been silent but His hand was still moving. Those changes gave shape to the circumstances and conditions that we find as the New Testament begins.

When we finish reading the Old Testament and then turn the page to the New Testament, the landscape is dramatically different! Rome is now the world power instead of the Medo-Persians. The king had been Artaxerxes, but now it's Herod the Great. And there are now religious parties called Pharisees and Sadducees. How did all those major changes come about?

Let us consider what was happening historically, politically, religiously, and spiritually in this time leading up to the New Testament.

Historically

C. S. Lewis is attributed with saying that "History is a story written by the finger of God."[1]

Many historical changes that took place during those four hundred years were predicted by Daniel. In Daniel 2, King Nebuchadnezzar had a dream that Daniel interpreted for him. In his dream Nebuchadnezzar saw a giant statue with a head of gold, chest and arms of silver, belly and thighs of bronze, and legs of iron (see vv. 32–33). This dream was a prophetic insight into the future kingdoms that would follow Nebuchadnezzar. Then in chapter 7, Daniel himself receives a vision from the Lord along the same lines—a prophecy from God about future world powers.

> In the first year of Belshazzar king of Babylon, Daniel had a dream and visions of his head while on his bed. Then he wrote down the dream, telling the main facts.

Daniel spoke, saying, "I saw in my vision by night, and behold, the four winds of heaven were stirring up the Great Sea. And four great beasts came up from the sea, each different from the other. The first was like a lion, and had eagle's wings. I watched till its wings were plucked off; and it was lifted up from the earth and made to stand on two feet like a man, and a man's heart was given to it.

"And suddenly another beast, a second, like a bear. It was raised up on one side, and had three ribs in its mouth between its teeth. And they said thus to it: 'Arise, devour much flesh!'

"After this I looked, and there was another, like a leopard, which had on its back four wings of a bird. The beast also had four heads, and dominion was given to it.

"After this I saw in the night visions, and behold, a fourth beast, dreadful and terrible, exceedingly strong. It had huge iron teeth; it was devouring, breaking in pieces, and trampling the residue with its feet. It was different from all the beasts that were before it, and it had ten horns." (Dan. 7:1–7)

When I was a kid growing up in Southern California, one of the trips our family would take every few years was to the San Diego Zoo. (It's always nice to visit the relatives!) As we read this description here in Daniel, you might feel as though you're riding on a bus through the zoo. Daniel describes a vision in which he sees some amazing animals—or Dr. Seuss characters!

In verse 1, we learn that Daniel's vision takes place when Belshazzar was ruling over the land. He was Babylon's final king before they were conquered and replaced as the world power. On the night in which Belshazzar was holding a drinking party with a thousand guests, right outside the city walls the Medo-Persian armies were laying siege (see Dan. 5). That night the Medo-Persians penetrated the city, killed Belshazzar, and conquered the Babylonian empire.

But before that happened Daniel received this vision from the Lord, which foretold future world powers. In rapid succession, Daniel was given a vision of four bizarre-looking creatures: a lion with eagle's wings, a bear with three ribs in its mouth, a leopard with bird wings, and some unidentified animal with iron teeth and ten horns. I never saw animals like that at the San Diego Zoo! Today, animals still symbolize various nations, such as the eagle for the United States and the lion for Great Britain.

The first animal, the lion with the wings of an eagle, represented the Babylonian empire that was in power when Daniel received this vision. In Babylon there were huge statues of winged lions guarding the gates of the royal palace. Its wings being plucked off in verse 4 speaks of how Nebuchadnezzar was humbled by God for a period of seven years.

Then, in verse 5, Daniel describes the second beast. The bear, raised up on one side with three ribs in its teeth and eating much flesh, is a picture of the Medo-Persian empire, which conquered the Babylonians. The bear is much slower than the lion but more powerful—and like a bear, the Medo-Persians were a slow-moving but powerful force. The three ribs in its teeth represent their initial conquests over Lydia, Babylon, and Egypt. The one raised side speaks of the fact that Persia was the more dominant part of the Medo-Persian alliance. The eating of much flesh portrays the fact that this empire slaughtered many people.

After the Persians took power, their king was Cyrus the Great. He was a wise and fair-minded ruler who acted favorably toward the Jewish people. At the end of their seventy-year captivity, the Jews were encouraged by Cyrus to return to their homeland in Israel, to resettle and rebuild their temple in Jerusalem, which the Babylonians had destroyed.

Nearly fifty thousand Jews decided to return to Israel from Babylon, while the others remained in Babylon or settled elsewhere. The temple was eventually rebuilt, though it was much smaller than the magnificent temple Solomon had built. Cyrus also made Shushan the capital city of his Persian empire, which gives us the background for the Old Testament stories of Esther and Nehemiah. After Cyrus a man named Ahasuerus, also known as Xerxes, eventually became the new Persian king. The story of Esther takes place at that time.

Afterward the son of Xerxes, named Artaxerxes, became the new Persian king. Nehemiah was the cupbearer to Artaxerxes when the Lord stirred his heart to help in Jerusalem, where construction in the city had stalled and remained unfinished. So Nehemiah requested and received permission from Artaxerxes to travel from Shushan to Israel to help with the completion of the city walls and gates.

Nehemiah and Ezra encouraged the people to finish the work and to follow the Lord. Unfortunately, the people reverted to many of the former sins that had led to their captivity. The rebukes and reforms that were begun with Nehemiah carried on until the close of the Old Testament period. The final words that conclude the Old Testament in Malachi 4 are God's, saying, "Behold, I will send you Elijah the prophet" (v. 5). Four hundred years later, the New Testament opens with the coming of John the Baptist, in the spirit of Elijah.

Daniel 7:6 describes the third beast of Daniel's vision, a leopard with four bird wings. The leopard symbolized Greece and its greatest military leader, Alexander the Great. This now takes us into those years between the Old Testament and New Testament. The power of Greece had been on a steady rise under the leadership of Philip. Philip was a Macedonian, and the city of Philippi is named for him. Philip helped Greece begin to rise to power but was murdered in 336 BC.

The mantle of leadership fell to his son Alexander at the age of twenty. (Interestingly, Alexander was educated by Aristotle.) The wings on the leopard represent the fact that Greece was remarkably quick in conquering the world. Rushing forward like a speeding leopard with wings, Alexander conquered the world in just a few years. He was undefeated in battle and considered one of the most successful military commanders of all time.

When Alexander invaded Israel, he treated the Jews well and spared Jerusalem. He even helped the Jews to settle in places like Alexandria in Egypt. But as brilliant a military leader as Alexander was, his reign was cut short by his own self-destructive lifestyle. John Walvoord said, "Alexander conquered more of the world than any previous ruler, but was not able to conquer himself."[2] He died just before turning thirty-three from a malaria-induced fever that was worsened by his heavy drinking and depraved lifestyle. In his short life, Alexander had conquered more land than any of his predecessors.

Something else connected to Alexander, and his conquering of the world, is what became known as Hellenism, or the Hellenistic period. This refers to the widespread influence of Greek culture on the world as the Greek language and Greek way of life spread, including the establishment of Greek colonies in various locations. I mention this because of its influence that carried over into the New Testament. For example, in Acts 6 is a dispute taking place in the early church between Hebrew and Hellenist believers. The Hebrews were the native Jews of Israel while the Hellenists were the Jews born outside Israel and influenced by Greek culture. The Hellenists felt that the Hebrew widows were receiving preferential treatment in the daily food distribution. Later on, when the Romans displaced Greece as the world power, the Hellenistic period basically ended, though its influence definitely continued.

In Daniel 7:6, the four heads of the leopard signify how Alexander's kingdom would be divided among his four generals after he died. One of those generals was succeeded by a man named Antiochus Epiphanes, also known as "Antiochus the Madman." He started ruling in 175 BC from his headquarters in Syria. He attempted to conquer the world but was stopped by the Romans, who would eventually become the next world empire. So Antiochus channeled his rage in a different direction.

Like other demonic leaders before him, Antiochus hated God and he hated God's people, the Jews. So he turned his demonic fury upon them, because Antiochus was an antichrist. He chose to follow the Greek god Zeus and he forced his subjects to worship him. He made life as miserable as he could for the Jewish people, and he forbade them from practicing circumcision, observing the Sabbath, and worshiping God—all upon the penalty of death. He also sold thousands of Jewish families into slavery. He ordered all copies of Scripture destroyed and executed anyone caught with some. At one point, he had one hundred thousand Jews slaughtered.

The demonic rule of Antiochus lasted over six years, and the Jews suffered terribly. In his ultimate act of desecration, Antiochus erected an altar to the Greek god Zeus in the Jewish temple and then sacrificed a pig on the altar, spilling swine blood in the temple. But God intervened by the hand of a Jewish priest named Mattathias, who lived about seventeen miles from Jerusalem.

One day a representative from Antiochus came to his little village of Modin and told the people, "You are hereby ordered by King Antiochus Epiphanes to bow down before the altar of Zeus, our Greek god." Mattathias was outraged and decided to take action. When he saw a fellow Jew bowing down to worship Zeus, he killed that man, killed the king's agent, and then demolished the altar. Afterward, Mattathias took his five sons and fled to the rocky hillsides nearby.

From there, others joined in their revolt against Antiochus and his Syrian forces. At that point, it was Mattathias's third son, Judas Maccabees, who began to lead the guerilla warfare against the Syrians. He was both brave and brilliant in his military leadership, and he earned the name Judas the Hammer, winning battle after battle against impossible odds. This became known as the Maccabean Revolt.

In December of 164 BC, Judas and his militia recaptured most of Jerusalem. He commanded the Jewish priests who had remained loyal to God to cleanse the temple and erect a new altar. On December 25 the temple was rededicated back to God. Antiochus escaped from Judas, but he couldn't escape from God. He was stricken with and then died from complications of ulcers and worms. (In the immortal words of Groucho Marx, "I've had a wonderful time, but this wasn't it.")

There is a popular Jewish tradition that says that only one undefiled jar of oil could be found for lighting the candles in the temple at the rededication. Normally, a jar of oil would last for one day. However, this tradition states that the oil miraculously lasted for eight days. Today, during the Christmas season, our Jewish friends celebrate what is known as the Hanukkah, which means "dedication," in commemoration of when the temple was rededicated under Judas Maccabees. It's also called the Festival of Lights. It all refers back to the Jewish tradition about the single jar of oil lasting for eight days. And it all took place about 160 years before Christ—during that time between the Old Testament and New Testament.

After the Maccabean revolt and overthrow of Antiochus, the brother of Judas Maccabees, Simon, was made the Jewish leader over what became known as the Hasmonean dynasty. This is when Israel finally returned to self-rule—for about a hundred years—led by priest-kings and judges. This dynasty was very strong but basically ended when the Romans emerged as the dominant world power and took control of Israel.

That brings us back to Daniel's fourth beast—an unidentified animal with huge iron teeth and ten horns. This is describing the Roman empire. The Roman empire lasted for some five hundred years, longer than the first three empires combined.

Rome was known for its excessive cruelty. It was the Romans who crucified Jesus and Peter, beheaded James and Paul, destroyed Jerusalem and the temple, banished John to the island of Patmos, and killed thousands of Christians. The presence and power of

Rome had been growing for many years, and they eventually conquered the Greeks.

In 63 BC the Romans conquered Israel under Pompey, and Israel began to experience Roman rule. Antipater was appointed ruler over Judea until he was succeeded by his son Herod the Great. When Herod took control the Hasmonean dynasty ended, but in a purely political move Herod married a Hasmonean princess to strengthen his throne.

Herod was a brutal and cruel ruler who killed countless numbers of his family, including that princess wife. At one point, Herod had forty-three members of the Sanhedrin put to death because they had dared to summon him to trial. Herod had his own mother and some of his sons executed, prompting the saying in that day, "It's safer to be one of Herod's swine than to be one of his sons." We also remember the slaughter of the children in Bethlehem that Herod ordered in his attempt to kill the Christ child.

But while Herod was absolutely deranged, he wasn't stupid. He was a master builder, and to appease the Jews he greatly expanded the Jewish temple that had been rebuilt after their captivity. Herod started ruling in 37 BC, which began the Herodian dynasty that included successive Roman rulers from Herod's family. His reign lasted until 4 BC, the year that Jesus was born.

We also see in Luke 2:1 that, as the New Testament period began, Caesar Augustus was the Roman emperor. Herod was the king, and Pontius Pilate became the governor about the time Jesus began His ministry. Pilate was directly involved in Jesus's trial and crucifixion. He would be succeeded by other governors such as Felix and Festus, whom we read about in Acts 23–24.

Caesar Augustus would be succeeded by emperors such as Tiberius, Claudius, and Nero, to name a few. The significant fact about Augustus, for us as believers, is that he gave the decree that "all the world should be registered" in Luke 2:1, referring to a census of the Roman Empire. Obviously, it was the hand of God that caused this, because it required Joseph and Mary to travel to Bethlehem to be registered in their tribal home town (see Luke 2:4). God set the world in motion in preparation for the birth and arrival of Jesus in Bethlehem, where Micah 5:2 prophesied He would be born.

All of that helps to give us a brief overview and understanding, historically, of what took place before, during, and after that four-hundred-year period between the Old Testament and New Testament.

Politically

Earlier, we talked about the Maccabean revolt against Antiochus, the demonic Syrian ruler. Those Maccabean patriots in Israel became the template for a group of Jewish patriots known as Zealots.

The Zealots were born out of the revolt against Roman rule in the years just before Christ's birth. One of Jesus's disciples was a Zealot; his name was Simon (see Luke 6:15). The Zealots thought it was treason to pay taxes to the Romans, and interestingly, Jesus called both a Zealot (Simon) and a tax collector (Matthew) to be His disciples! It was the Zealots who started the great Jewish revolt in AD 66, leading to the Romans destroying the temple in AD 70.

Religiously

Let's talk about a subject that creates confusion for some people: the Apocrypha. *Apocrypha* means "hidden," and it refers to fifteen books that were written in the four hundred years before the New Testament period began. The Apocrypha is roughly the same in size as the New Testament. Some of the books contain good historical details, but none of them are inspired Scripture.

The Roman Catholic Church believes that these writings are scriptural and therefore includes them in their Old Testament. This decision was made in the mid-1500s, primarily in response to the

Protestant Reformation. Here are a few quick reasons why these books aren't universally accepted as biblical or inspired:

1. There is no claim within the Apocrypha of being inspired of God. The Bible—Old Testament and New Testament—repeatedly states that it is the Word of the Lord, but there are no such claims in the Apocrypha.

2. The Apocrypha has unbiblical teachings, such as praying for the dead, praying to saints in heaven, purgatory, worshiping angels, and giving money to the church to help atone for sins.

3. There are errors and contradictions within the Apocrypha, something that is never true of inspired Scripture.

4. The Jews and the early church rejected the apocryphal writings as inspired Scripture. Even Jewish historian Josephus rejected them overall.

5. Their authorship is uncertain. In both the Old Testament and New Testament canon of Scripture, the criteria of consideration included authorship by a prophet, apostle, or recognized spiritual leader.

Now let's talk briefly about synagogues. When we open the Bible to the New Testament, we find synagogues, which aren't mentioned in the Old Testament. Synagogues began to arise in the days of the Babylonian captivity. The temple had been destroyed, so the Jewish captives needed a place to gather for fellowship and prayer. This started in homes, and eventually small meeting places were constructed in the community. After some of the Jews returned to Jerusalem and a smaller temple was rebuilt, the synagogues still continued, led by elders. The main reason for this was that many Jews were still living outside of Jerusalem, in places such as Persia, Egypt, Greece, and Rome.

Synagogue is a Greek word meaning "congregation." Synagogues continued to rise up during the intertestamental period and were in every large Jewish community. In time, the synagogue became the local place of Scripture reading and prayer while the temple became the place of worship and sacrifice. The rabbis determined that the heads of ten Jewish families were required in order to organize a local synagogue.

When Paul and his missionary companions traveled to Greece, they went to Philippi in Acts 16. We read there that Paul and his friends went out by the river, where some Jewish women were holding a prayer meeting on the Sabbath day. This indicates that within that small Jewish community there weren't ten Jewish men who were the heads of households, which was required to establish a synagogue.

The significant thing for us as Christians, regarding the synagogues, is that they became the template for the early church and its places of worship. Just like synagogues, the early church also began by meeting in homes. Eventually, small buildings were erected as places of worship, fellowship, and Bible study. We still refer to the church family as the congregation, a translation of the Greek word *synagogue*.

Now let's talk about the religious leaders who come to the forefront in the New Testament, starting with the Pharisees. From the writings of Josephus, we learn that the Pharisees arose during that Hasmonean dynasty mentioned earlier, when Israel was ruling itself between 140 and 37 BC, right after the Maccabean revolt. Pharisees were both religious and political. The word *Pharisees* means "separated ones," and some believe it referred to separation from common people. However, it's more likely to have meant separation from Greek influence, which was both worldly and widespread.

Pharisees were spiritually conservative and legalistic, though Josephus wrote that they interpreted the law of God more accurately. They believed in angels, a bodily resurrection, and life after death. As time went on the Pharisees became self-righteous, and by the time Jesus squared off with them in the Gospels, He called them hypocrites, blind guides, and fools (see Matt. 23). Some Pharisees who converted to Christianity included Nicodemus, Joseph of Arimathea, and of course Saul, who became the apostle Paul. There were about six thousand Pharisees during the time of Jesus.

Sadducees were the other primary religious and political party that arose at the same time as the Pharisees. From the very beginning the two groups were at odds with each other. That's because the Sadducees were liberal and in favor of Greek influence. They were more interested in politics than religion. They did not believe in angels or the resurrection, and they only believed that the first five books of the Old Testament were binding.

Sadducees primarily came from wealthy and prominent families, so they were closed off from the common people. When the second temple was destroyed by the Romans in AD 70, the Sadducees essentially disappeared. There is no record in or outside of Scripture of any Sadducee ever receiving Christ. As the saying goes, that's why they were so "sad, you see"!

Scribes were responsible for copying the Scriptures, and they go back into the Old Testament period. They became quite numerous in the Maccabean period, and in the New Testament they're also referred to as lawyers, in the religious sense, because they interpreted the law of Moses (see Luke 10:25). Scribes lined up religiously with the Pharisees, and Jesus coupled the two groups together in His strong rebukes of their hypocrisy and self-righteousness (see Matt. 23).

Essenes were another religious group I should mention quickly, though they are not mentioned by name in the New Testament. They were a monastic community that isolated themselves from society, living out in the desert around the Dead Sea in an area called Qumran. Not much is known about their early history except that they were possibly an offshoot of the Pharisees. Some scholars believe that John the Baptist was part of the Essene community.

They were the ones who placed copies of the Old Testament in clay jars and hid them in caves by the Dead Sea. The Essene community disappeared from the landscape in the later part of the first century. Some nineteen hundred years later, in 1947, the Dead Sea Scrolls were discovered there in the Qumran caves, and the Essenes' rigid way of life became well known.

Finally, there was the Sanhedrin. Before the Pharisees and Sadducees, the Jews established the Sanhedrin as the recognized leadership in Israel in about the third century BC. They were like a religious supreme court made up of chief priests, scribes, and elders. After the Pharisees and Sadducees were formed, they made up the majority of the Sanhedrin. The Sanhedrin consisted of seventy members and was presided over by the high priest, who could cast the seventy-first and deciding vote if the council was deadlocked on a decision.

The Sanhedrin was limited in power by the Romans, though they were often ignored and left to carry on. The Romans denied the power of capital punishment to the Sanhedrin, which is why the false charges against Jesus had to be brought to Pontius Pilate, the Roman prefect (see John 18:31). The Sanhedrin was also involved in hearings against Peter, John, Stephen, and Paul (see Acts 4–7; 22–24). After the destruction of Jerusalem and the temple in AD 70, the Sanhedrin was abolished.

Spiritually

The first major translation of Scripture from one language into another was the Septuagint. *Septuagint* is Latin for "seventy," referring to the seventy Hebrew scholars who did the translation work. This was the translation of the Old Testament from Hebrew into Greek, and was the result of that heavy Greek influence, Hellenism, we talked about earlier. Most likely, the Septuagint was created for Hellenistic Jews who wanted their Greek-speaking children to have a copy of the Old Testament they could read.

The final thing we want to understand, heading into the New Testament, is the messianic hope of the Jewish people. The Messiah and Savior was prophesied and promised many times over in the Old Testament as the One who would come to save the Jews. But here's the key point: some were expecting a spiritual savior—which Jesus was—while many were looking for a political savior to deliver them from the oppression of Rome—which wasn't why Jesus came.

During those four hundred years before the New Testament, that messianic hope was building stronger and stronger. So when Jesus arrived claiming to be the Messiah, it captured the attention of the Jewish world. And all of that takes us to page 1 of the New Testament! Galatians 4:4–5 tells us that "When the fullness of the time had come, God sent forth His Son, born of a woman, born under the law, to redeem those who were under the law, that we might receive the adoption as sons."

Conclusion

There might be times when we don't feel as though God is speaking to us—times when He's silent. So why might that be? Here are seven quick takeaway thoughts for application.

1. *Disobedience*—Israel was in ongoing disobedience, reaching the point where God didn't speak to them for four hundred years.
2. *Patience*—God has spoken, but we're still waiting on the Lord for His timing.
3. *Trust*—Sometimes God wants to strengthen how we trust Him and walk by faith.
4. *Devotions*—Every time we read and study God's Word, He's speaking. But if we're not in the Word, then we're not listening!
5. *Sovereignty*—God has lots of things going on behind the scenes, but we may not see them.
6. *Waiting*—God is waiting on us to talk to Him—in prayer!

7. *Faith*—If you're in the Word, God is speaking to you, whether you "feel" it or not. We walk by faith, not by feelings, and there will be seasons in every believer's life when we don't "feel" like He's there. But remember God's promise: "I will never leave you nor forsake you" (Heb. 13:5).

5

Understanding
the New Testament

I ran across a true story about four high school seniors in Sullivan, Missouri. They had intentionally skipped morning class and arrived late, telling their teacher that they all rode in the same car, which had a flat tire and that's why they were late. The teacher knew better, but smiled sympathetically and informed them that they had missed a test that morning. Then she told them she had a simple makeup test they could take. She asked each of the four boys to sit at a desk in different corners of the classroom and gave them all the same test with one simple question: Which tire on the car was flat?[1]

When it comes to the Gospels, a common question is, "Why four Gospels; why not just one comprehensive Gospel that covers the entire life and ministry of Jesus?" For starters, it helps to remember what John said at the very end of his Gospel: "There are also many other things that Jesus did, which if they were written one by one, I suppose that even the world itself could not contain the books that would be written" (21:25). John was emphasizing that as the Son of God, Jesus is infinite—and therefore, the things that could be written about Him are endless. But before we look further into the four Gospels, let's talk about how we can better understand the New Testament as a whole.

The primary dividing line between the Old Testament and New Testament is Christ. The New Testament completes the panoramic story begun in the Old Testament about God's plan of salvation for the world through Christ. In Matthew 26, Jesus shared the Passover supper with His disciples in the upper room, and as He instituted the cup of communion, He said to them, "This is My blood of the new covenant, which is shed for many for the remission of sins" (v. 28). In that verse, we usually focus on the cup of communion and the shed blood of Jesus on the cross. But we can also see how Jesus explained that His shed blood and sacrifice was establishing a new covenant (or new testament), replacing the old covenant of animal sacrifices.

> But now He has obtained a more excellent ministry, inasmuch as He is also Mediator of a better covenant, which was established on better promises.
>
> For if that first covenant had been faultless, then no place would have been sought for a second. Because finding fault with them, He says: "Behold, the days are coming, says the LORD, when I will make a new covenant with the house of Israel and with the house of Judah—not according to the covenant that I made with their fathers in the day when I took them by the hand to lead them out of the land of Egypt; because they did not continue in My covenant, and I disregarded them, says the LORD. For this is the covenant that I will make with the house of Israel after those days, says the LORD: I will put My laws in their mind and write them on their hearts; and I will be their God, and they shall be My people. None of them shall teach his neighbor, and none his brother, saying, 'Know the LORD,' for all shall know Me, from the least of them to the greatest of them. For I will be merciful to their unrighteousness, and their sins and their lawless deeds I will remember no more."

In that He says, "A new covenant," He has made the first obsolete. Now what is becoming obsolete and growing old is ready to vanish away. (Heb. 8:6–13)

The Old Testament was incomplete and imperfect. It was always meant to be temporary, pointing toward the future coming of Christ and a better covenant. The blood of the Old Testament animal sacrifices could never remove sin permanently. It could only cover sin temporarily. But Christ's blood provides permanent cleansing and forgiveness—that's the message of the New Testament.

The contrast between the Old Testament and New Testament has been well stated by Saint Augustine: "The new is in the old concealed; while the old is in the new revealed."[2]

As with the Old Testament, we can better understand the New Testament by knowing how its twenty-seven books break into four basic groups. In the Old Testament those groups are law, history, poetry/wisdom, and prophecy. In the New Testament the groups are:

1. Gospels (four books)	Matthew–John
2. History (one book)	Acts
3. Epistles (twenty-one books)	Romans–Jude
4. Prophecy (one book)	Revelation

The Gospels tell us how, when, and why Christ came; Acts gives us the history of how the message of Christ spread; the epistles tell us how to live that message personally as believers; and Revelation gives us the future outcome of God's message.

You'll recall that the Old Testament category of prophecy is sometimes divided up into two subcategories, the major prophets and the minor prophets. And within the New Testament, the epistles are also sometimes subdivided into the separate categories of Pauline and non-Pauline epistles—that is to say, those letters written by Paul and those written by others. We'll discuss that more later.

The New Testament is less than one-third the length of the Old Testament and was all written in Greek, whereas most of the Old Testament was written in Hebrew, with a few sections in Aramaic. The twenty-seven books of the New Testament were all written within a short period of time, about fifty years, from AD 45–95. Like the Old Testament, the New Testament is more topical in layout than it is chronological.

Out of the eight known New Testament writers (we don't know for certain who wrote Hebrews), Luke is the only Gentile author. Paul is the predominant writer, with thirteen epistles (fourteen if he also wrote Hebrews, which is possible). John wrote five books, and while Luke wrote just two, the volume of his writings makes up about 28 percent of the New Testament and his Gospel is the longest book in the New Testament.

Gospels

Sometimes this first category is called "biography," but I prefer the heading "Gospels." The word *gospel* literally means "good tidings" or "good news." The good news is summed up well by Paul: "that Christ died for our sins according to the Scriptures, and that He was buried, and that He rose again the third day, according to the Scriptures" (1 Cor. 15:3–4). The New Testament gospel message is God's promise of salvation through Jesus Christ for all who believe. That's not just good news; that's absolutely great news!

The four Gospels combined make up about 46 percent, or nearly half, of the New Testament. The four Gospels appear first in the New Testament not because they were the first books written but because they're the foundation upon which the rest of the New Testament is built. Between all four Gospels, we have approximately fifty days of Jesus's ministry recorded (out of three and a half total years of ministry).

Let's address the question of why there are four Gospels. I offer you three reasons for consideration.

1. More complete picture.

Let's say that you and three of your friends went to see a movie together. Afterward, you all went to grab a bite to eat and to discuss the movie you just saw. In that conversation, all of you would remember the same major plot points while all of you would also add minor details that stuck out to you personally. Between the four of you, you'd have a more complete recollection of what the movie was about.

In the same way, while the Gospels all contain many of the same major events, each Gospel adds unique details not found in the other three Gospels. As a result, we have a more complete picture and presentation of Christ's life, ministry, death, and resurrection. For example, all four Gospels record the death and resurrection of Jesus but only Matthew tells us about the visit of the Magi after Jesus was born. Or consider that all four Gospels record the feeding of the five thousand but only Mark tells us that Jesus was a carpenter. All four Gospels tell us about the triumphal entry of Jesus into Jerusalem on Palm Sunday but only Luke describes the salvation of the dying thief on the cross. And while all four Gospels tell us that Judas betrayed Jesus, only John tells us about Jesus raising Lazarus from the dead. The four different Gospels are not contradictory but rather complementary, giving us a more complete picture of Christ's life and ministry.

2. More complete perspective.

All four Gospel writers tell us about the life, ministry, death, and resurrection of Jesus, but each writer focuses on a different aspect.

Matthew was writing to Jewish readers, presenting Jesus as the king and messiah of the Jews. Matthew wanted to show his fellow Jews that Jesus was the prophesied Messiah in the Old Testament, so he uses more quotes from the Old Testament than the other Gospel writers.

Mark was writing to Roman readers, presenting Jesus as a humble servant. He portrayed Jesus as a man of action who performed many miracles, and so Mark's Gospel records more miracles than the other three.

Luke was writing to an audience of Greek readers, presenting Jesus as the perfect man. With the gentle touch of a family doctor, Luke focuses on the compassion of Jesus toward Gentiles, Samaritans, women, children, and lost sinners.

John was writing to a very wide audience, and his unique emphasis was on the deity of Jesus as the Son of God. Over 90 percent of John's Gospel presents unique details not found in the other three Gospels.

All of this, then, gives us a more complete perspective. Here's another way of seeing the different perspectives:

- Matthew presents Jesus as the Promised Savior.
- Mark presents Jesus as the Powerful Savior.
- Luke presents Jesus as the Perfect Savior.
- John presents Jesus as the Personal Savior.

3. More complete testimony.

One writer in the last century pointed out that in a court of law, if four different witnesses gave the same exact testimony about a detailed event, the judge would instantly suspect that those four witnesses had conspired to tell the same false story (like those high school students with the flat tire). But if four witnesses told the same basic story from four different perspectives, it would then be very credible. And so it is with the four Gospels.

An important fact about the first three Gospels (Matthew, Mark, and Luke) is that they are known as "the synoptic Gospels." The Greek word *synoptikos* means "to see together" or "to share a common viewpoint." So these first three Gospels contain a lot of the same biographical information about Jesus, from each writer's unique perspective. These synoptic Gospels were all written within about ten years of each other.

Then, toward the end of the first century, the last living apostle of Christ, John, was inspired by God to write a fourth Gospel in about AD 85. That's more than fifty years after Christ ascended to heaven and at least twenty-five years after the other Gospels were written. By then heresy was springing up in the early church, so John's Gospel is more theological and presents Jesus as the Son of God. It was also written specifically to help unsaved people believe. In John 20:31, we read, "these are written that you may believe that Jesus is the Christ, the Son of God, and that believing you may have life in His name."

Synoptic Gospels	John's Gospel
Jesus's humanity	Jesus's deity
Begins with Jesus on earth	Begins with Jesus in eternity
Biographical, historical	Theological
Parables	Allegories (no parables)
Galilean ministry	Judean ministry

Now, speaking of Galilee and Judea, something else that is extremely helpful in understanding the Gospels as we read through them is their geography (in other words, a basic knowledge of the main cities, regions, and bodies of water). Many believers read about events in Nazareth, the Sea of Galilee, or the region of

Samaria but don't understand them geographically. The geography of the Gospels is pretty simple and yet very helpful.

Let's begin with the four main bodies of water.

1. *Mediterranean Sea* (west coast of Israel). Just as the Pacific Ocean runs all along the west coast of California, the Mediterranean Sea (often called "the Great Sea") runs along the entire west coast of Israel. Caesarea, on the coast, is where Peter led Cornelius to Christ and where Paul sailed from as a prisoner headed to Rome.

2. *Jordan River* (runs from north to south). The Jordan River starts from the melted snows of Mount Hermon, near Dan, in northern Israel. It flows directly down into the north end of the Sea of Galilee, then continues out the south end of the Sea of Galilee and meanders south until it dead-ends in the Dead Sea. The Jordan River, just north of the Dead Sea, is where Jesus was baptized by John as He began His public ministry.

3. *Sea of Galilee* (northern Israel). The Sea of Galilee is actually a large freshwater lake. This is the area where Jesus called some fishermen (Peter, James, John, and Andrew) to be His disciples and become fishers of men. It's where Jesus began His ministry, fed the five thousand, taught sermons and parables, and healed the sick.

4. *Dead Sea* (southern Israel). I once heard elderly comedian George Burns say, "When I was a kid, the Dead Sea was only sick." Like the Sea of Galilee, the Dead Sea is actually a large lake. But unlike Galilee, it's a saltwater lake. In fact, its salt content is five to six times that of our ocean waters! The Dead Sea is the lowest point on the surface of the earth, at about 1,300 feet below sea level. From the north end of the Sea of Galilee to the south end of the Dead Sea is 130 miles.

Now let's talk about the three main regions in Israel.

1. *Galilee* (northern Israel). This is the area of Caesarea Philippi (where Peter confessed that Jesus was the Son of God), the Sea of Galilee, Capernaum, Cana, and Nazareth.

2. *Samaria* (upper Israel). This is where the Samaritans lived, where Jesus met the woman at the well, where He healed the ten lepers, and the area that He traveled through while going back and forth between Galilee and Jerusalem.

3. *Judea* (southern Israel). This is where Bethlehem and Jerusalem are (just five miles apart). It's also where Bethany is (the home of Martha, Mary, and Lazarus, and where Jesus spent lots of His time), just two miles from Jerusalem. It's also the area of the Dead Sea, the Judean wilderness, and Jericho (about seventeen miles from Jerusalem).

Finally, let's talk about four key cities in the Gospels.

1. *Bethlehem*—where Jesus was born (five miles from Jerusalem).

2. *Nazareth*—where Jesus's family went to live (north).

3. *Capernaum*—where Jesus began His ministry and spent lots of time.

4. *Jerusalem*—where the temple was, and where Jesus was crucified and rose from the dead.

Since parables and miracles were a big part of Christ's ministry, let me say a word about that. Parables were short, simple stories used to communicate spiritual truths. About a third of Christ's teaching in the Gospels was in the form of almost forty different parables. Also in His ministry, Jesus performed at least three dozen recorded miracles. The purpose of His miracles was to demonstrate that He had divine power and therefore that His words and messages had divine authority.

Now let's tackle a couple of the common questions associated with the Gospels. Let's begin with questions about the genealogies.

Why are there genealogies in two Gospels, but not in the other two? And why are they so different?

The genealogy of Jesus is recorded in Matthew's Gospel and in Luke's, but not in Mark's Gospel or John's. The reason for that isn't too hard to understand when we remember the different Gospel perspectives we talked about earlier.

Matthew was presenting Jesus as Messiah and King, while Luke was presenting Jesus as Savior to humanity—so the genealogies were helpful for their purposes. But Mark's Gospel was written to a Roman audience, presenting Jesus as the humble servant—and the Romans were not interested in the genealogy of a servant. John's Gospel was written to present Christ as God, so rather than writing an earthly genealogy, John wrote of Jesus being in eternity past with the Father, and as God come in the flesh.

Why do Matthew and Luke's genealogies seem so different? Once again, both writers had different goals. Matthew, presenting Jesus as King and Messiah of Israel, started his genealogy with Abraham, the father of the Jews. Luke presented Jesus as the savior of humanity, so his genealogy goes all the way back to Adam.

Another difference is that Matthew's genealogy takes us through His earthly father, Joseph, while Matthew's genealogy takes us through His mother, Mary. Finally, Matthew starts in the past and works forward to show that Christ is King and Messiah, in fulfillment of the Old Testament. Luke's genealogy starts with Christ's arrival as Messiah and then works backward to the throne of David and on back to Adam, God's first creation.

Another common question that I hear is, "Why isn't there more information about the early years of Jesus?" All four Gospels focus on the mission and purpose for why Christ came: to lay down His life as a ransom for many. In fact, more than 40 percent of the Gospels specifically focuses on the passion week of Christ—the week in which He died and then rose again. That's the meat of the Gospel message. So with that in mind, we don't have a lot of information about the first thirty years of Christ's life, other than some of the events surrounding His birth and then the one specific incident at the temple when Jesus was twelve. That's the incident recorded in Luke 2, when the family of Jesus went to the temple in Jerusalem for Passover and afterward Jesus stayed behind.

At the end of Luke 2, Luke gives us a couple of verses that are intended to summarize those hidden early years of Jesus: "Then [Jesus] went down with [Joseph and Mary] and came to Nazareth, and was subject to them, but His mother kept all these things in her heart. And Jesus increased in wisdom and stature, and in favor with God and men" (2:51–52). Jesus never ceased being divine, but in His humanity He was subject to His parents, went to the synagogue, worked with Joseph, and stayed relatively secluded until He was thirty, when He began His public ministry. Tradition states that Joseph died in Jesus's later teen years, so, being the eldest son, Jesus would have helped to care for the family by working.

But most importantly, Jesus lived a perfect life. When we come to faith in Christ, here's what takes place: our sins are imputed to Him on the cross, while His perfect life and righteousness are imputed to us. Second Corinthians 5:21 says, "For [God] made Him who knew no sin to be sin for us, that we might become the righteousness of God in Him."

History

In recent years, some flight attendants and pilots on commercial airlines have decided to have some fun with their passengers during their announcements. Here are some real examples of airline crews trying to entertain their passengers with funny announcements:

- From the pilot came this on-board welcome message: "We are pleased to say that we have some of the best flight attendants in the industry. Unfortunately, none of them are on this flight."

- Another pilot announced to the passengers, "Folks, we have reached our cruising altitude now, so I am going to switch off the seat belt sign. Feel free to move about, but please stay inside the plane until we land, since it's a bit cold outside!"

- From the flight attendant giving passengers their basic instructions: "In the event of a sudden loss of cabin pressure, oxygen masks will drop from the ceiling. Stop screaming, grab the mask, and pull it over your face. If you have a small child with you, secure your mask before assisting them with theirs. If you are traveling with two small children, please decide now which one you love more."

- After a really rough landing in Phoenix, the flight attendant got on the PA and said, "Ladies and gentlemen, please remain in your seats until Captain Crash and the crew have brought the aircraft to a screeching halt up against the gate. Once the tire smoke has cleared and the warning bells are silenced, we'll open the door and you can pick your way through the wreckage to the terminal."

- Another flight attendant's comment on a very bumpy landing: "We ask you to please remain seated as Captain Kangaroo bounces us up to the terminal."

- Part of a flight attendant's arrival announcement was, "We'd like to thank you folks for flying with us today. And the next time you get the insane urge to go blasting through the skies in a pressurized metal tube, we hope you'll think of us here at US Airways. Now, last one off the plane gets to clean it."

As much as people complain about airline travel, it's a blessing to be able to go from one location to another so quickly and in relatively comfortable conditions. When the apostle Paul traveled on his missionary journeys—as recorded in Acts—travel was quite difficult and dangerous.

Before we look further into Paul's missionary journeys, let's talk generally about the book of Acts, which is the only book in the history category of the New Testament. The author of Acts was Luke, who also wrote the third Gospel. Notice the connection and continuation that Luke makes in his opening statement of Acts:

> The former account I made, O Theophilus, of all that Jesus began both to do and teach, until the day in which He was taken up, after He through the Holy Spirit had given commandments to the apostles whom He had chosen, to whom He also presented Himself alive after His suffering by many infallible proofs, being seen by them during forty days and speaking of the things pertaining to the kingdom of God.
>
> And being assembled together with them, He commanded them not to depart from Jerusalem, but to wait for the Promise of the Father, "which," He said, "you have heard from Me; for John truly baptized with water, but you shall be baptized with the Holy Spirit not many days from now. . . . You shall receive power when the Holy Spirit has come upon you; and you shall be witnesses to Me in Jerusalem, and in all Judea and Samaria, and to the end of the earth." (Acts 1:1–5, 8)

In the Gospels we see what Christ began to do; in Acts we see what He continued to do by the Holy Spirit. In the Gospels Christ is the risen Savior; in Acts He's the Lord ascending back to heaven. In the Gospels we hear the teachings of Christ; in Acts we see the effect of His teaching on His disciples.

Acts, then, serves as the bridge between the Gospels and the epistles. In the Gospels we have the beginnings of Christianity in Christ—and then in Acts we see how Christianity spreads from Jerusalem to all Judea, Samaria, and across the world. The historical information in Acts gives us the background information for the churches that the epistles were written to, such as the churches at Corinth, Philippi, Ephesus, and so forth.

It's often called "The Acts of the Apostles" to describe the various acts and achievements of the apostles. However, that title is both accurate and also a little bit misleading. This book certainly does describe some of the acts of some of the apostles. At the same time, it also describes the acts of some who were not apostles, such as Stephen, Philip the evangelist, and Mark. Perhaps a better title would be "The Acts of the Holy Spirit." Regardless of which men or women were in action at any given point, the constant thread from chapter 2 onward is the ministry of the Holy Spirit. In fact, the Holy Spirit is mentioned over fifty times in Acts, more than any other New Testament book. Believers are filled with the Holy Spirit and comforted, commissioned, separated, appointed, guided, forbidden, and transported by the Holy Spirit. The Holy Spirit is promised, received, and poured out—but also tempted, resisted, and lied to. The Holy Spirit is the central figure in Acts.

In Acts 1 the disciples get their marching orders, which were really a reiteration of the Great Commission, given by Jesus at the end of Matthew's Gospel, to preach the gospel to the whole world. Then in Acts 2 is the birth of the church, and from there we read how the message and the church spread. Acts covers about thirty years of church history and is really an unfinished book, as the history of the church continues to this day.

The primary apostle in the first twelve chapters of Acts is Peter, but from chapter 13 on the focus is on Paul and his missionary journeys. The gospel message goes first to the Jews, then to the Samaritans, who were half Jew and half Gentile, and then finally to the Gentiles. Paul emerges as the apostle to the Gentiles, while Peter is the apostle to the Jews (see Gal. 2:8).

The message of Acts is the spread of the gospel by the primary method of Paul's three missionary journeys. I once read about a missionary serving in the South Sea islands. When Christmastime was approaching, he spoke to the islanders about the meaning of

Christmas—the birth of Christ. Then the missionary explained the observances of Christmas, including the giving of gifts in celebration of Christ's birth. After hearing all of this, one of the young islanders wanted to give a Christmas gift to the missionary but was very poor.

On Christmas morning, then, the young man knocked on the door of the missionary's hut and presented him with a gift: a rare and beautiful seashell found only at the far end of that island. The missionary was touched and thanked the young man for the beautiful gift as well as for the great distance he had to walk to find that shell. The young native's reply was, "Long walk part of gift." That's a beautiful statement, isn't it?

The same was true of the apostle Paul and his missionary companions, as they willingly exposed themselves to danger, difficulty, and a complete lack of comfort in order to take the gift of salvation to the Gentiles. Here's what Paul's three missionary journeys looked like.

First journey (Acts 13–14): Galatia, for two years

Second journey (Acts 15–17): Greece, for three years

Third journey (Acts 18–21): Asia, for four years

After Paul returned from his third journey, it wasn't long before he was arrested in Jerusalem on false charges. Paul was then transferred to Caesarea on the Mediterranean coast, where he waited two years for a trial. Different governors came and went, and Paul continued to wait, witnessing to anyone who would listen, including King Agrippa.

Finally, when an attempt was made to transfer Paul back to Jerusalem to stand trial there, he learned that some men were going to try to kill him along the way. So Paul used his right of appeal as a Roman citizen to appear before Caesar in Rome. The final two chapters in Acts describe Paul's harrowing voyage by sea from Jerusalem to Rome.

Epistles

That brings us now to our third New Testament category, and by far the biggest grouping: the epistles. There are twenty-one New Testament epistles, or letters. As I mentioned before, this category is subdivided by many into two separate groupings: Pauline epistles (those written by Paul) and non-Pauline or general epistles (those written by other apostles). Paul wrote thirteen of the New Testament letters (possibly fourteen, if he wrote Hebrews).

Some of the epistles were written to specific churches, such as Romans, 1 and 2 Corinthians, Ephesians, Philippians, Colossians, and 1 and 2 Thessalonians. Other letters were written to individuals, such as those to Timothy, Titus, Philemon, and 2 and 3 John. And then other epistles were addressed to groups of people, such as Galatians, Hebrews, James, 1 and 2 Peter, 1 John, and Jude.

Paul's thirteen epistles were written to help believers, including us today, to live out our faith practically and to understand our faith doctrinally. They're called *epistles*, or letters, because they follow the standard form of a letter in the first century: the writer's name and title, the recipient, a greeting, the main body of the letter, and a farewell. Paul also used the normal method of having a scribe, or an *amanuensis*, to write his letters as he dictated them. Paul would usually write the last lines himself and then sign the letter so its readers would know it was authentic.

While all of Paul's letters contain doctrine, instruction, and encouragement, each one has a particular theme and purpose.

- *Romans*—teaching the great truths of the gospel and Christian doctrine. Just about every major doctrine of the Christian faith is presented.
- *1 Corinthians*—correcting a carnal and immature church.
- *2 Corinthians*—defending his apostleship; exhortation to obedience.

- *Galatians*—serious warning against wavering in the faith and being deceived by legalism (Judaizers). Paul's only letter to a group of churches.

- *Ephesians*—the believer's position and privilege in Christ, with three great chapters on doctrine and three great chapters on duty.

- *Philippians*—a very warm letter about maintaining joy in the midst of all circumstances.

- *Colossians*—proclaiming that believers are complete in Christ and warning against heresy.

- *1 Thessalonians*—living in light of Christ's return.

- *2 Thessalonians*—questions about the second coming of Christ.

- *1 Timothy*—instructions for church ministry and conduct.

- *2 Timothy*—continuing the ministry after Paul's death.

- *Titus*—instructions for church ministry and conduct.

- *Philemon*—personal letter to a brother about forgiveness.

It's also worth noting that Ephesians, Philippians, Colossians, and Philemon are known as "the prison epistles." At the end of Acts, Paul is in Roman confinement for about two years, awaiting his trial before Caesar. It was during that confinement that Paul wrote these four letters.

In the same way, 1 and 2 Timothy, along with Titus, are known as the "pastoral epistles." That's because these three letters were written to Paul's two spiritual sons in the faith who would carry on the work of the ministry after his death. Paul instructs and encourages them on the subjects of church organization, discipline, leadership, doctrine, and guarding the church against heresy and rebellious church members.

Now let's talk a little bit about the other non-Pauline (or general) epistles, written by other apostles. None of these eight epistles were written to a specific church. They were all written to various groups of believers, or to Christians in general, while two of them were written to individuals (2 and 3 John). One of these letters, Hebrews, is the only New Testament book whose author is unknown to us. Many believe that Paul wrote Hebrews, while others—myself included—think it was probably someone else. At this point, only God knows who wrote it. If you're ever asked to speak at my funeral service, and you're not sure what to say, just tell them, "At least Jeff finally knows who wrote Hebrews!"

Here's an outline of the non-Pauline epistles:

- *Hebrews*—written to Jewish believers to warn and exhort them against reverting back to the Old Testament covenant but instead going forward by faith in Christ.
- *James*—a very practical letter to believers for living out our faith, written by the Lord's brother.
- *1 Peter*—grace, faith, and hope in times of suffering.
- *2 Peter*—standing firm in our knowledge of the truth.
- *1 John*—living in the light of God's truth; what a genuine believer looks like.
- *2 John*—truth and hospitality; watch out for deceivers.
- *3 John*—truth and hospitality; watch out for troublemakers.
- *Jude*—an exhortation to defend the truth against apostasy with warnings against godless living, written by the Lord's brother.

Prophecy

Revelation is the only New Testament book that focuses primarily on prophetic and future events. It's also the only book that pronounces a particular blessing for reading, hearing, and obeying the message inside (see Rev. 1:3). And then for good measure, it also has the warning of a curse for anyone who might attempt to add to, or take away from, the words of that prophecy (see 22:18–19). But wait—there's more! It's also the only book in the Bible that gives its own natural outline: the things which were, the things which are, and the things which will take place in the future (see 1:19).

Prophecy is a very important part of the Bible, and fulfilled prophecy is one of the major evidences for the reliability of Scripture. How Christians react to Bible prophecy reminds me, in many ways, of the story of the three bears. Some believers are too cold about Bible prophecy, either because they don't care or because they simply don't take the time to understand it as they should. Other believers are too hot about Bible prophecy, either because that's all they want to talk about or because they see a prophecy fulfilled in every news story or world event.

We need to find the balance that's just right—whereby we embrace prophecy and study it but don't become obsessed by it. Remember, about 27 percent of the Bible is prophecy—either past or future. The Bible contains about a thousand prophecies, about half of which have already been fulfilled. That gives us a lot of confidence about the remaining prophecies in Scripture that are yet to be fulfilled—including those in Revelation.

I have to laugh when I hear some people suggest that we can't understand the book of Revelation. The very title means "unveiling," and so God is revealing His future plans to us. And why would God promise a special blessing to the person who reads it and obeys it if it can't be understood! Obviously, we don't understand every detail of Revelation, but I truly believe that the majority of it is straightforward. I like what Vance Havner said: "I do not understand all the details of the Book of Revelation but there is a special blessing promised to all who read, hear, and keep its message, and I don't want to miss that blessing."[3]

I will admit that, as a younger believer, I was intimidated by Revelation. Even as a Bible teacher, I was a bit reluctant to tackle teaching it. Once I finally did, I was immensely blessed and became much more confident that we need the message of Revelation today.

So I taught through Revelation again, and then again, and then the Lord led me to put a book together on Revelation called *Unlocking the Last Days*. If the Lord tarries, I look forward to teaching through Revelation again in the future. According to pastor and prophecy expert Mark Hitchcock, the second coming of Christ is mentioned 318 times in the New Testament; it's mentioned in twenty-three of the twenty-seven New Testament books; and on average, one out of every twenty-five verses directly refers to the second coming of Christ.[4] Just considering those numbers, only an apathetic believer wouldn't be paying attention to their Bible and world events.

Some Questions

As we wrap up this section on the New Testament, let's discuss a few common questions related to the New Testament and the Bible. Let's begin by discussing when the Bible was divided up into chapters and verses.

As the Bible was written, it did not contain chapters or verses. Acts, for example, was written like one long letter. It was an archbishop named Stephen Langton who first began dividing Scripture into chapters, in the early thirteenth century. The Wycliffe Bible, in 1382, was the first Bible to use those chapter breaks. About a hundred years later, a Jewish rabbi divided the Hebrew Old Testament into verses, and another hundred years later, the same was done for the English Bibles.

The Geneva Bible, published in 1560, was the first English Bible to fully use chapters and verses. It also had some notes and maps, so it was also a prototype of the modern study Bible. This whole process was done to help readers find Scriptures more quickly and easily—and it's safe to say that we're all glad they did. It's much easier to find Acts 1:8 than it is to search for the place where Jesus told His disciples that they would receive power when the Holy Spirit comes upon them. Occasionally, we scratch our heads when a chapter break seems to be in an odd place, but overall, the chapter breaks and verses are very helpful.

Another common question we should address is why there are so many different Bible translations. There are as many as fifty different English versions of the Bible. And of those, which ones are the best? Interestingly, the subject of Bible translations is a question for some and a debate for others. There is the "King James Only" group, who insist that the King James Version (KJV) is the only true and authorized version. A few of these folks even consider you a heretic if you're using any other translation! But my response to them is to ask how the church ever survived for over fifteen hundred years, before the KJV came out in 1611.

Don't get me wrong, please. The KJV is great, and my first Bible was a KJV. But many other translations have come out since, and for good reasons. The most obvious is that our language has changed over the years. Let's not forget that when the New Testament was originally written in the first century, it was written in the common language of the people in that day. Our English language has changed more in the past four hundred years than the Greek language has changed in the past two thousand years.

For example, in the KJV James 1:2 reads, "My brethren, count it all joy when ye fall into divers temptations." Don't you find that translation a tad bit confusing? What are "divers temptations"? Is that like a male scuba diver seeing a mermaid and swimming after her? Now, in fairness, there aren't a ton of words like *divers* (which, by the way, means "various") in the KJV. But there are unending uses of words like *ye*, *thou*, and *thy*—and that's simply not the way we talk today. At the church I serve in we use the New King James Version (NKJV), which is very similar to the KJV but with updated words. In my daily devotions I alternate versions, including easy-to-understand versions like the New Living Translation (NLT). There are other easy-to-understand versions, but some are paraphrases, not actual translations. Those paraphrases would include The Living Bible and *The Message*.

So let me try to answer the question of which translation you should use. First of all, common sense dictates that the first Bible translation you should own is the one used by your pastor on Sunday mornings, so that you can follow along. Second, you should also have a translation that helps you best in your daily reading and studies. Some of the more popular translations, along with the KJV and the NKJV, include the New American Standard Bible (NASB), English Standard Version (ESV), New Living Translation (NLT), and the NIV, which is the New International Version (or as some critics like to call it, the "Nearly Inspired Version"). When choosing a translation for yourself, find a passage with several verses you're familiar with. Then read those verses in some of the different translations and see which one works best for you. As a Bible teacher, I have many different translations on my shelf because I like to compare them when I'm preparing to teach a particular passage of Scripture.

Another debate related to translations concerns whether or not the pronouns referring to God should all be capitalized or not. In the NIV, for example, the pronouns referring to God are not capitalized. This becomes a matter of personal conviction and preference. Personally, I dislike it when some translations don't capitalize the deity pronouns. It won't keep me from using that translation, but I don't like it. In my opinion, capitalizing shows reverence for God. Also, it helps the reader to better understand the conversations between Jesus and other people in the Gospels. When words like *He* and *You* are capitalized, we immediately know that they're referring to Jesus and not to someone else.

6

How to Study the Bible

Sometimes, when we travel in foreign countries as Americans, we come across a sign with a message that's lost in translation. That's because other languages often do not translate well into English. For example:

- In a Paris elevator: "Please leave your values at the front desk."
- In an Athens tailor shop: "Order your summer suits now. Because of big rush, we will execute customers in strict rotation."
- In a Hong Kong tailor shop: "Ladies may have a fit upstairs."
- In a Japanese hotel next to the thermostat: "If you want condition of warm in your room, please control yourself."
- In a Copenhagen airline ticket office: "We take your bags and send them in all directions." (Most airlines do!)
- In an Acapulco hotel: "The manager has personally passed all the water served here." (No comment!)

When it comes to Bible study and reading God's Word, perhaps there have been times when you've felt that what you're reading has been lost in translation. If so, take heart! You are not alone. Remember the Ethiopian eunuch in Acts 8? He was returning from religious observances in Jerusalem and was in his chariot, trying to read and understand an Old Testament passage from the prophet Isaiah. When Philip the evangelist approached him and asked, "Do you understand what you are reading?" his humble and honest reply was, "How can I, unless someone guides me?" (Acts 8:30–31).

This brings us to the important and useful subject of how to study the Bible, which is undoubtedly the most practical section of this book.

This subject might sound like it's geared toward newer believers, but I'm quite confident that every Christian can take something away with them from this chapter. Perhaps the best place to begin is with the question of why it's so important for us as believers to study God's Word. In 2 Timothy 3:16–17, we read, "All Scripture is given by inspiration of God, and is profitable for doctrine, for reproof, for correction, for instruction in righteousness, that the man of God may be complete, thoroughly equipped for every good work." We've already discussed how the Bible is inspired, or "God-breathed," but notice how Paul also emphasizes that God's Word is "profitable" to us.

God's Word is profitable, which means that as we spend time reading and studying Scripture, it blesses us with huge spiritual returns. Many people today are looking for good investments with solid returns, and God's Word is the spiritual investment you definitely want. Scripture is profitable for doctrine, reproof, correction, and instruction.

Doctrine—what is right.

Reproof—what is not right.

Correction—how to get right.

Instruction—how to stay right.

110

All of this is for instruction "in righteousness." The Bible doesn't make us righteous; our righteousness as believers has been imputed to us by Christ. But God's Word instructs us on how to walk in that righteousness. The reading, study, and application of God's Word will help mature us in our faith and equip us for every good work.

Several years ago, I came across a thought-provoking article that imagined what it would be like if our Bibles kept a diary. So here is the diary of a Bible (but hopefully not your Bible):

January: A busy time for me. Most of the family resolved to start reading me every day. I was busy for the first two weeks, but now I'm just sitting here.

February: My owner used me for a few minutes the other day. He was having an argument with his wife and was checking for references!

March: Grandpa visited us, and I got to sit on his lap for a full hour as he read me to his grandchildren.

April: I got to go to church for the first time this year . . . on Easter Sunday.

May: I have a few stains on my pages; they put some pressed flowers between my pages.

June: I look like a scrapbook. They stuffed me full of clippings. One of the girls got married.

July: I had a busy day last week. My owner was appointed as the leader of something, so he laid his hand on me and promised he would do a good job.

August: They threw me into a suitcase today. I guess we're going on vacation.

September: Back home again and finally out of that stuffy old suitcase!

October: They used me a little bit today. One of them is sick and I think that the pastor is coming over to pray.

November: Back on the shelf again with lots of company on top of me, including copies of *Sports Illustrated* and *Reader's Digest*. I wish that I could get read just half as much as they do!

December: I think they're going to take me to Christmas service at church.

I wonder, if our Bibles kept a diary, what they would say about us. Let's focus now on how to study the Bible in such a way as to get more out of it.

Strategy Helps

If we're going to succeed in having a more fruitful time in our daily devotions, we need a strategy. It's been well said that if you fail to plan, you plan to fail. So here are some basic tips for improving your devotional time and making your Bible study more fruitful.

1. Commit to daily devotions.

As simple and basic as this sounds, the first and foundational step is that we must commit, by God's grace, to spending time each and every day in God's Word. Under normal circumstances, we wouldn't go through a day without eating food or drinking water, because that would weaken us physically. In the same way, depriving ourselves of spiritual food—God's Word—weakens us spiritually.

And yet, many believers will go for days without drinking a word from Scripture and then wonder why their spiritual life feels so dry! *The Christian who becomes careless in their Bible reading often becomes careless in their Christian living.* I wonder how much time some Christians spend on Facebook compared to their time spent in God's Book.

2. Make a plan.

As the old saying goes, "There's more than one way to skin a cat." By the way, that's not a very nice expression! I'm a dog person myself, but I'm not in favor of skinning any cats. Just recently, my dog walked out front with me to get the newspaper and there was a cat sitting in the front yard. So he ran at the cat full speed, but the cat never budged. He just looked at my dog with an expression that said, *What? You want to mess with* me? We don't have any gangs in our neighborhood, but there are some pretty tough cats!

Now, when I say "make a plan," I recognize that there's more than one way to study God's Word throughout the year. One goal is to read through the entire Bible in a year. If you read for fifteen minutes a day, at average reading speed, you can read the whole Bible in a year. I've done this several times, but I don't do it every year.

Another plan is to read and study the New Testament in a year. The New Testament is less than one-third the length of the Old Testament. So that gives you more time to not only read but to study the New Testament in more depth. I've used this approach many times as well. Another option is reading through the Bible in survey style, which is to review each of the sixty-six books of the Bible from a big picture perspective. You can accomplish that plan in just two months. Websites such as biblegateway.com have survey plans you can use.

A fourth option is a good old-fashioned book study. For example, the New Testament book of Philippians has four chapters, so you might want to study a chapter a week, and after a month you should have a very good understanding of that epistle. There are lots of great study guides to help guide you.

If you've been at this for a long time as a Christian, you might want to try a biographical study, which might take you about four months. This plan allows you to know Bible characters much better. Once again, biblegateway.com offers a biographical reading plan.

Just like the physical food we eat, it's nice to have some variety in our spiritual diet as well. So which is the best Bible reading plan for you? Listen carefully: the best Bible reading plan is the one you actually use! Whichever plan you choose, get in the Word and stay in the Word. If the Bible is going to get into us, we must get into the Bible.

3. Choose a place and time.

We need a more specific strategy than simply planning to read and study each day; we need to have a designated place and an appointed time. For me, it's shortly after I get up in the morning, at the breakfast table, with a hot cup of coffee. Every once in a while I need to rush out of the house very early, so I'll catch up on my reading later in the day, but that's rare for me—maybe four or five times a year. Otherwise, it's every morning, seven days a week, at the breakfast table.

Now maybe you're wired differently and you prefer to do your Bible reading and study in the afternoon or at night. That's perfectly fine, as long as you're consistent with your place and time. Every morning, I have an appointment to meet with God in His Word, and I keep those appointments. Trust me when I tell you that if you don't have an appointed time, your Bible reading will quickly become hit or miss, and probably more miss!

4. Don't just read. Study.

Reading is only the first step in Bible study. Ezra 7:10 talks about how Ezra prepared his heart to study the law of the Lord, and to do it, and to teach others. A couple of things that I like to read every day are my Bible and the newspaper, but there's a big difference between them. I read through the newspaper casually, and I only look at the stories that interest me, but I read and study the Bible thoroughly—book by book, chapter by chapter, and verse by verse. The newspaper informs me, but the Bible transforms me!

It's like the difference between a tourist and an explorer. A tourist visits a place and takes a brief look around at the obvious sights before moving on, but an explorer seeks to uncover details and to make meaningful discoveries. The explorer takes the time to search out much more.

Bible study requires effort on our part, but it's well worth it. Here are some practical questions you can ask yourself as you read and study God's Word:

- What does it say?
- What does it mean?
- How can I apply this in my life?
- What nugget of truth can I chew on today?

Let's take a look at some verses in Proverbs 24. Solomon, the man of great wisdom, is going to give us a lesson on how to study God's Word.

> I went by the field of the lazy man,
> And by the vineyard of the man devoid of understanding;
> And there it was, all overgrown with thorns;
> Its surface was covered with nettles;
> Its stone wall was broken down. (Prov. 24:30–31)

A. What does it say? (Observation)

Solomon went by the property of a lazy person and observed that it was overgrown with weeds and the wall was in disrepair. In other words, the life and property of a lazy person are falling apart. That's pretty straightforward. Now let's read the next verse.

> When I saw it, I considered it well;
> I looked on it and received instruction. (v. 32)

B. What does it mean? (Interpretation)

Solomon is analyzing and evaluating what he sees. He says, "I considered it well; I looked on it and received instruction." So the second step is interpretation; what does it mean? It means that laziness leads to an undisciplined life of poverty.

> A little sleep, a little slumber,
> A little folding of the hands to rest;
> So shall your poverty come like a prowler,
> And your need like an armed man. (vv. 33–34)

C. How can I apply this? (Application)

Solomon understood how this man's laziness brought about his ruin. He made application by recognizing that laziness in his own life could lead to his own deficiency and poverty. This takes us to the fourth step.

D. What nugget of truth can I chew on? (Meditation)

I'm confident that Solomon, in his God-given wisdom, thought about his own life after this experience, perhaps giving thought to personal areas that might have needed attention and discipline.

James reminds us that the unwise person looks into the mirror of God's Word and sees an area that needs attention but then forgets about it as soon as they walk away. So the blessing comes from being doers of the Word, not just hearers or readers (see James 1). In the same way, there's much more to spiritual growth than just reading the Word; no one was ever fed by reading the menu in a restaurant! We need to feed on, chew, and digest the Word.

System Helps

I read about a Russian computer designed to translate English into Russian. It was given the Bible phrase, "The spirit is willing, but the flesh is weak." After the computer translated it into Russian, it was translated back again into English as "The wine is good, but the meat is rotten." The same computer took the phrase "Out of sight, out of mind," and after translating it into Russian, translated it back into English as "invisible idiot."

So how do we keep from misunderstanding and mistranslating the Scripture we read? Here are a few practical tips to help you, for your daily devotions and times of Bible study.

1. Begin with prayer.

The fact that the Bible is God-breathed is called *inspiration*. The help that we need from the Holy Spirit to understand God's Word is called *illumination*. In 1 Corinthians 2:14, Paul writes, "The natural [unsaved] man does not receive [understand] the things of the Spirit of God, for they are foolishness to him; nor can he know them, because they are spiritually discerned." Understanding God's Word begins with being a child of God who has the Holy Spirit living within. It is the Holy Spirit who gives us illumination to understand the Word.

Illumination doesn't mean that we understand every detail in Scripture, nor does it eliminate the need for diligent effort on our part to study Scripture. But it does mean that we should always begin with prayer—inviting the Holy Spirit to give us understanding. In John 14:26, as Jesus was preparing His disciples for His impending departure to heaven, He said to them, "The Holy Spirit, whom the Father will send in My name, He will teach you all things, and bring to your remembrance all things that I said to you."

2. Use a helpful translation.

As I mentioned previously, you should use whatever translation your church uses to follow along on Sundays, but for your own personal devotions and Bible study you might want to use a different translation. If a certain version is difficult for you to use in your devotions, then by all means get yourself a more modern translation. The best translation for you is the one that you understand the best and get the most out of.

3. Use a study Bible.

It's my firm belief that for the average Christian, one of the biggest frustrations in their daily Bible reading and study is coming to words or verses or ideas that are confusing and create questions without handy answers. So please, if you're serious about Bible study, then invest in a study Bible.

Study Bibles provide some commentary and footnotes to help explain the more difficult words or verses. Study Bibles also have maps, charts, and lists, along with introductions to the different books of the Bible. They also provide cross-references so you can look at other verses that have similar meaning or information. Good study Bibles also give you a topical index so that you can search out particular subjects. Some also include a brief doctrine section and other helps such as a concordance or a dictionary.

So your next question, I'm guessing, is, "Which study Bible should I purchase?" That boils down to personal preference, just like the question of which translation is best for you. The wisest way to choose is by comparing some study Bibles against each other. With that said, a few of the most popular study Bibles include, in no particular order:

- *The ESV Study Bible*—this is a very popular study Bible with lots of footnotes and helpful materials.
- *The MacArthur Study Bible*—this has very helpful commentary notes on every page that help explain many of the verses.
- *The Thompson Chain-Reference Study Bible*—this study Bible helps you to follow a particular person, place, or idea throughout the Bible, from beginning to end.

- *The Holman Study Bible*—a sound, middle-of-the-road study Bible that will help you but not overwhelm you.
- *The Transformation Study Bible*—a solid study Bible with commentary notes from Pastor Warren Wiersbe.
- *The Jeremiah Study Bible*—a good study Bible with commentary notes from Pastor David Jeremiah.

The value of a study Bible is that it gives you some commentary, a basic dictionary, background information, and so forth. Buying those resources separately would cost more and be more inconvenient to use. Another piece of information you should keep in mind when choosing a study Bible is that some come in different translations while others don't. So if you're determined to use the NLT, for example, then you would want to make sure that the study Bible you're considering comes in the NLT. Obviously, the ESV Study Bible only comes in the ESV!

4. Eliminate distractions.

The devil is certainly evil but he's not completely stupid. As J. I. Packer pointed out, "If I were the devil, one of my aims would be to stop folks from digging into the Bible."[1] One of the most common ways he does this is by trying to distract us during our devotional and study time. So we need to make every effort to eliminate distractions or deflect the ones that do come up.

If the phone rings, for example, let it go to voicemail or to the answering machine; you can call the person back later. Remember, you have an appointment with God! If it were any other appointment, you wouldn't allow someone to simply call in. Also, don't multitask during your devotions, such as running appliances that will make noise and distract you.

Choose a place and time where you won't get interrupted by your children or the family pet. Another very common distraction that happens to all of us is suddenly remembering something important (email, grocery item, return phone call). When that happens, make a quick note of it and then get right back to your devotions. You can take care of those things you wrote down afterward.

5. Track your progress.

For many of us, tracking our progress is helpful because it motivates us to keep going. For years, I kept a list of my daily Scripture reading so I could track my progress. More specifically, consider keeping a journal of the things that the Lord shows you, or speaks to you each day. For many years, pastor and Bible commentator Warren Wiersbe kept a journal like that. After twenty years, one of his editor friends suggested that he turn those devotional notes into a book, and he did! It was a devotional commentary called *With the Word*.

6. Ask someone to keep you accountable.

This is a very helpful step, especially if you tend to be hit or miss with your devotions and Bible studies. Ask a trusted friend to hold you accountable and to ask you every week where you're reading in your Bible and what you've been learning. Along with that, it's also helpful to have a friend and fellow believer whom you can talk to about what you've been learning, and vice versa. It's always encouraging to share.

7. Ask yourself inductive questions.

As you're reading and studying, ask yourself inductive and investigative questions: who, what, when, where, and why? Asking and answering those basic questions will definitely open up the passage you're reading. I've been a big mystery fan my entire life, so it comes very naturally for me to read, study, and prepare Bible studies with an inductive and investigative mindset.

8. Look for promises, principles, ideas, and commands.

As you're reading and studying, it's very helpful and fruitful to ask yourself these particular questions: Is there a command I need to obey? Is there a promise I can receive? Is there a principle I need to follow? Is there a main idea I need to understand?

9. What's my takeaway?

One of the principles I follow in my own devotions is not to stop reading until that passage of Scripture has spoken to my heart. Otherwise, what's the point? My purpose in reading is to hear from the Lord. I want the Lord to touch my heart, and He's faithful to do so if we pray and seek Him in the Word. When it comes to our devotions and studies, we read the Bible to get the facts, study it to get the meaning, and meditate on it to get the benefit.

One of the great tragedies today is that nine out of ten homes in America have a Bible, and the average household has four Bibles, but the people in those households never read them. My mom and dad used to have a large Bible open and displayed right where you would walk into the house, by their front door, but they never read it. But here's another sad fact: many of the people who do use the Bible give it only a casual reading that essentially bounces off their minds, yielding very little fruit. We want a takeaway from the Lord that will make a difference for that day (like Jacob wrestling with God in Genesis 32).

10. Remember the power of the Word.

In Isaiah 55, we're reminded of the great truth that God's Word will not return void. I love the analogy for God's Word that Isaiah uses:

> For as the rain comes down, and the snow from heaven,
> And do not return there,

> But water the earth,
> And make it bring forth and bud,
> That it may give seed to the sower
> And bread to the eater,
> So shall My word be that goes forth from My mouth;
> It shall not return to Me void,
> But it shall accomplish what I please,
> And it shall prosper in the thing for which I sent it. (Isa.
>   55:10–11)

In my drought-plagued home state of California, we can appreciate how much the rain and snow help to produce flowers, seed, grain, and produce. When the rains and snows fall, there's always a blessing and benefit. In the same way, God's Word comes down to us with spiritual blessings and benefits.

Study Helps

If you are looking for ways to get more out of your devotions and Bible study, I'd like to offer some practical suggestions and tools that can help you.

1. *Audio Bible apps for smartphones.* If you commute, or have the ability to just listen for periods of time, smartphones have access to various free apps that allow you to listen to an audio Bible. So if you're commuting, for example, you can listen to God's Word being read to you. What a terrific way to spend your time in traffic!
2. *Daily Bible reading plans online.* Websites such as bible.org, ESV.org, or biblegateway.com provide many different kinds of free online Bible reading programs.
3. *Daily devotional emails.* Many pastors and ministries offer free daily emails with devotional content. I recommend Pastor Greg Laurie's devotion, available at harvest.org.

4. *Free Kindle Bible reading download.* You can find it at Amazon .com and download it for free for Kindle, Nook, or tablet devices.

5. *Free online commentaries.* Oftentimes, believers are looking for a commentary to help them with their studies but are on a tight budget. If you go to studylight.org, you'll have access to dozens of free commentaries that are very easy to use. I would recommend J. Vernon McGee's "Thru the Bible" and Ray Stedman's commentaries. Both are balanced, biblical, and practical.

The bottom line is that, if you're serious about improving your times of devotions and Bible study, there are plenty of plans and resources to help with that spiritual journey. And most importantly, with a daily intake of God's Word, our spiritual lives will bear fruit. As some godly person said, "Study the Bible to be wise; believe it to be safe; and practice it to be holy."

7

How to Teach the Bible

A young man attending seminary was suddenly called upon by his professor, without warning, to walk up to the front of the class and deliver a brief three-point Bible devotion. The nervous young man walked forward and said to the rest of the class, "My text for this brief devotion will be Luke 19—the story of Zacchaeus, the tiny tax collector who met Jesus. My three points are as follows: (1) Zacchaeus was up a tree, and so am I. (2) Zacchaeus went out on a limb, which is where I'm at right now. (3) Zacchaeus made haste to come down, which is what I will now do." And with that, the young man quickly returned to his seat.

Teaching the Word of God is a serious responsibility, and it's a joyful undertaking, so it's good to learn about preparing and presenting a Bible study. I have many different responsibilities as a pastor, but my main calling and joy is teaching God's Word. In my life, it's been an ongoing process of trial and error, personal study and growth, and complete dependence upon God. So it's my desire to try and help others as much as I can.

The three biggest influences in my teaching ministry as a pastor have been Greg Laurie, Warren Wiersbe, and Chuck Swindoll.

- *Greg Laurie* has taught me to keep it simple and understandable, to be relevant, and to preach the gospel. I started attending Harvest Christian Fellowship in late 1980, so I've been sitting under Pastor Greg's teaching now for more than three decades! He is a very gifted communicator who connects with all people. And I've never met a pastor who is as passionate and committed to the gospel and seeing people saved as Greg. He has, by far, been my greatest influence.

- *Warren Wiersbe* has been another huge influence in my ministry life, teaching me the importance of application and balance in every area of ministry. I first met Warren at The Cove Training Center in Asheville, North Carolina, back in the early 1990s. I even had the opportunity to visit with him in his home in Lincoln, Nebraska. The first commentary I ever owned was a BE Series commentary. I have several dozen of his books in my library and have read them all—some of them several times. What I've learned from Wiersbe, both in person and through his books, is immeasurable.

- *Chuck Swindoll* has taught me to have passion and persuasion in my teaching. I've had the opportunity to meet him a handful of times, and he's the real deal. I've grown greatly through reading many of his books and have learned a lot of lasting lessons from him about leadership and ministry. Swindoll is a great role model for teaching and for ministry.

God has used, and continues to use, other pastors to influence and encourage my teaching.

Let me share three things with you before we continue:

1. *I don't have all the answers.* I'm not an expert. I have been teaching God's Word for some thirty years, so hopefully I

can simply pass some things on to you that I have learned over those years. I never feel worthy or sufficient to teach God's Word, but I also know that I do so by His grace and empowering, and I'm very grateful that He allows me this blessing.

2. *It's an ongoing process.* You never arrive at the point where you have mastered the act of teaching; there's always room for improvement. To this day, I still read books on preaching and listen to good preaching. I never stop trying to become better in my ministry of teaching God's Word.

3. *This is not an exhaustive study of how to teach the Bible.* There's so much to learn on this subject that we could spend months looking at it—indeed, many Bible college courses do. My goal is simply to give you some of the basic mechanics and principles.

I'm dividing this chapter up into three segments: the perspective, the preparation, and the presentation.

The Perspective

First, let's talk about what the act of teaching is. The primary New Testament Greek word for *teach* and *teaching* is *didasko* (e.g., Matt. 4:23), which means "to give instruction." Of course, we're not teaching subjects such as medicine, mathematics, or Greek mythology but rather the holy Word of God. To paraphrase Warren Wiersbe, it's the communication of God's truth, by God's servant, to God's people.

The purpose of teaching the Bible is to explain God's Word in a clear and simple manner. One of my favorite definitions of teaching comes from a New England preacher of the late 1800s, Phillips Brooks, who described teaching as "truth through personality." That's a good definition because it reminds us that it's

God's truth, and it comes through the personality of the particular person who is teaching. When we think about teachers such as Greg Laurie, Alistair Begg, James MacDonald, Chuck Swindoll, and John MacArthur, we acknowledge that all of them are excellent Bible teachers but each has a different personality.

That leads us to another consideration: Who can and should be teaching? That's an important question, and there are several elements that need to be considered.

1. Those who are gifted.

Teaching God's Word is listed as being a gift of the Spirit in passages such as Romans 12:7. I understand that, in the beginning, it's hard to know whether or not you are gifted. I faced that same dilemma when I began teaching a midweek class in 1984. If you have the strong desire and the opportunity, then I think it's good to try it and see.

There is a warning in James 3:1 that says, "My brethren, let not many of you become teachers, knowing that we shall receive a stricter judgment." However, I would point out that those words specifically apply to the people in the official positions of teaching in the church—the main pastors and teachers. The bottom line is that not many are called to teach in that capacity, but there are lots of ministry opportunities for lay teachers.

If you're honest with yourself, and in tune with the Holy Spirit, you'll know pretty quickly if you are called to teach or not. And the rest of us will also know! If you are not gifted in the area of teaching but persist in it, it will become a miserable experience both for you and your listeners.

2. Those who are Bible students.

To become a teacher of the Word, you must first be a student of the Word! If your devotional life is hit and miss, then do yourself and everyone else a favor and forget about any silly notions of becoming a Bible teacher. In the words of Jesus, "If the blind leads the blind, both will fall into a ditch" (Matt. 15:14).

When I went into ministry, God gave me a particular verse that I've hung on to, and it's 2 Timothy 2:15, when Paul told Timothy, "Study to show yourself approved to God, a workman that needs not to be ashamed, rightly dividing the word of truth" (AKJV). Teachers need to be diligent Bible students, hard workers, and careful handlers of God's Word. So if you're not already reading and studying diligently, then please forget about teaching.

3. Those who have a good understanding of Scripture.

It's dangerous to start teaching the Bible before you have a solid foundation of what the Bible is all about. Don't get me wrong; I'm still learning the Bible, and that will never stop on this side of heaven. But it's imperative to have a solid working knowledge of Scripture, both Old and New Testaments.

A teacher needs to understand the theme and message of Scripture, and how all sixty-six books of the Bible work together. Teachers also need to understand the categories and themes of the Old and New Testaments, such as we've looked at in previous chapters.

4. Those who have a basic knowledge of doctrine and theology.

Doctrine describes the teachings and truths of Scripture, while *theology* refers to the study of God. Once again, I'm not suggesting that we all must be theologians or Bible scholars. But I am saying that we need to have a solid understanding of these things. Teaching the Bible is about teaching doctrine and theology.

5. Those who are not new believers.

A teacher of God's Word should not be someone new in the faith. The reason for this should be obvious: a new believer does not have a solid grasp and understanding of Scripture, doctrine, and theology. In the area of church leadership, one of the requirements is that they "not [be] a novice," according to 1 Timothy 3:6, and that certainly applies to a teaching ministry as well.

When I first began to teach, I had been a Christian for about four years. During those four years I studied God's Word fervently, attending many different studies or services every week. Even after four years of reading and studying God's Word, when the Lord started knocking on the door of my heart to teach, I hardly felt prepared. I took classes through a Bible school, read many books, and applied myself to learning.

When Paul was converted to the faith in Acts 9, God called him to become a preacher and a teacher to the Gentiles. But first Paul spent three years in Arabia, where he received many of his revelations and instructions from the Holy Spirit in preparation for his ministry (see Gal. 1:17–18). The other apostles also had their three years of walking with Jesus, receiving hands-on training.

6. *Those who have an active and consistent prayer life.*

A strong prayer life is essential to a strong teaching ministry. Alan Redpath used to say, "A prayerless preacher will make for a successful failure." Teaching requires dependence upon God through each step of the process. So if you don't have a strong prayer life, you'll definitely struggle! A. W. Tozer said, "No one should stand before God's people who has not first knelt before God."

7. *Those who love God and love His people.*

It's not enough to love to teach God's Word; we must love the people we're teaching. Vance Havner was right in saying, "A lot of preaching misses the mark because it proceeds from the love of preaching, not love of people."[1] As Paul noted, if we have not love, then we've become "sounding brass or a clanging cymbal" (1 Cor. 13:1).

Warren Wiersbe has said, "Love makes truth palatable, while truth makes love practical."[2] God's desire is to provide His people with teachers and leaders who have a heart like His. Our motive for teaching must never be for recognition, ego, or self-esteem. Our motive must be to honor God and to instruct His people.

8. Those who take Bible teaching seriously.

You might think that every Christian would take Bible study seriously, especially if they want to teach. But the reality is that some teachers are lazy and sloppy, and it shows. There are no shortcuts or tricks when it comes to Bible study preparation. I can listen to a Bible study and tell if the teacher has spent time preparing or if he or she simply threw something together—and I think you can as well.

As I already mentioned, Bible study preparation is hard work, and if it's not, then it's not really Bible study preparation. Don't get me wrong: it's enjoyable, but it requires diligence, prayer, research, study, and lots of time, if done correctly. On average, it takes me twelve to fifteen hours to prepare a one-hour Bible study. Some people might need less or more time, so it's reasonable to say that a one-hour message would require somewhere between ten and twenty hours of preparation.

The person who scares me is the one who says it only took an hour to prepare a sixty-minute message! That's like saying you cooked a twenty-five-pound turkey in the oven for sixty minutes. (Remind me not to come to your house for Thanksgiving!) There are exceptions like Charles Spurgeon, who used to prepare his Sunday morning message in a few hours on Saturday night and prepare his Sunday evening message in a few hours on Sunday afternoon! But the Spurgeons of the world are few and far between. When you start preaching like Spurgeon, then you can start preparing like Spurgeon!

In my opinion, it's a sin to throw a Bible study together. In fact, I've never done it and I refuse to do it. The Word of God is holy, and God's people are holy. Therefore, the preparation for teaching must also be holy, not haphazard.

So if you believe that you are called by God to teach His holy Word, then check yourself against these perspectives. If you believe yourself to be on par with all of these things, then by all means, proceed. If there are any conflicts or concerns, then please be completely honest with yourself and honest with your church.

Tools of the Trade

As I share with you some of the essential tools of the trade, let me just acknowledge that I'm a book guy, meaning I have lots and lots of books in my library. Some of you will gravitate more to computer Bible programs, like the Logos Bible software. That's great, and most of the study books I tell you about are included in that software. So whether you have these tools on your computer or on your shelf, here are a few recommendations that I consider essentials.

- *Bible Concordance* (Strong's)—This easy-to-use tool allows you to look up an English word from the Bible, find the corresponding Greek or Hebrew word, learn the basic meaning, and also see where that word is used elsewhere in the Bible. I use this tool in every study. Not many of us are fluent in understanding Greek and Hebrew, but that's OK, because tools like the *Strong's Concordance* allow us to get the correct meaning of a word in its original language.
- *Dictionary of Old Testament and New Testament Words* (Vine's)—This dictionary allows you to look up those same

Greek and Hebrew words but then gives you more detail and a fuller explanation of what that word means, along with other similar words.

- *Willmington's Guide to the Bible*—This is part handbook, part commentary, part doctrine, and much more. (It's the Costco of books!)
- *Bible handbook* (Halley's or Unger's)—A Bible handbook gives you the background information and history for each book of the Bible.
- *Bible dictionary* (Unger's or Nelson's).
- *Bible encyclopedia* (Baker or Zondervan)—Bible encyclopedias give you added information on the people and places of the Bible.
- *Quote books.*
- *Commentaries.*
- *Books of illustrations.*
- *Books of theology/doctrine.*

The Preparation

How should we go about preparing our Bible study before we teach it?

1. Prayer

The preparation process should always begin and end with prayer. I have seen two extremes in Bible study preparation that are both dangerous. The first extreme is that the Bible study is prepared with little or no prayer. Most of us have heard the old phrase "When all else fails, pray." That's not only bad advice; it's bad Bible study practice! Spurgeon said, "All our libraries and studies are mere emptiness compared with our prayer closets. We grow, we wax mighty, and we prevail, in private prayer."[3]

The other extreme comes when some teachers pray and pray but spend little time on actual sermon preparation. Then when the time comes to present their message, they presume God will simply provide their sermon supernaturally. I've heard some teachers defend this method and explain that they are operating by faith, but it was D. L. Moody who said, "I used to think that I should close my Bible and pray for faith, but then I came to see that it was in the studying of the Word that I was to get faith."[4]

Proper Bible study preparation requires a combination of prayer and diligent preparation. And the process should definitely begin and end with prayer. It helps us to recognize that, in the end, it's God's Spirit who will teach and communicate to the hearts of the people through us.

What are some of the things we should be praying about?

THE MESSAGE

First, pray about the message—either for what the message will be, or, if you have the text, then for the message that will come from the text. Let me pause to briefly mention that there are different types of messages, including expository (verse by verse, chapter by chapter), topical, and devotional. If you are in need of preparing a topical study, or perhaps a short devotion, you need to pray about what message and passage to teach. As you pray over that, you should definitely consider who your audience will be.

One of the best places to find the subject for your next topical study or devotion is your own devotional time. In other words, what has the Lord been showing you in your personal quiet time? Or what truths from Scripture have excited you lately? Select something from your devotions that God has impressed upon your heart. Then prepare and preach the message God gives you. This again underscores the necessity for teachers to maintain a faithful and fruitful daily devotional time.

If you're teaching through a book, you already have your text. As you begin praying about your message, you can read through the passage several times and allow God's Spirit to illuminate the main theme or idea. In the preparation process, then, devote some time to focused prayer and then open up the Word and start digging in!

THE HEART

Now let's talk about prayer for the heart. As Warren Wiersbe has said, "The teacher, as well as the sermon, must be prepared."[5] We need to make certain that there is no unconfessed sin or unbiblical attitude in our hearts. Handling the Word of God as a teacher is a holy endeavor. We also want to pray that God would first touch our own hearts with His message in a powerful way. If the message doesn't excite you, it won't excite anyone else!

THE TEXT

We also need to pray for the text. In some cases, we may be given a topic to speak on for some specific event such as a retreat or small gathering, but we must still prayerfully choose the Bible text. One way to do this is by finding several Bible passages that cover that particular topic. Then pray over them and let God's Spirit highlight one of those texts in your heart.

THE AUDIENCE

One more area of prayer is for the audience. We want to pray for those who will be hearing our message and ask God to prepare their hearts to receive His Word. In order for teaching to be effective, we need anointed listeners as well as anointed teachers. If you have been teaching for a while, you've probably had the experience after a study of someone sharing with you how God really spoke to them about a particular situation or need. I find that happening regularly. Obviously we have no prior knowledge of their situation; it's the Holy Spirit speaking to their hearts.

2. Reading

Now let's talk about the importance of reading in the preparation process.

REPETITION

My first suggestion would be to read through your text several times. You may think it's crazy, but reading it through ten times or more will really help you. When you do that, certain words, points, thoughts, and ideas begin to jump off the pages. Just when you think you really know the passage, the next reading will reveal something new.

It's also a must to keep a notepad and a pen handy so you can write those things down. Look for repeated words, phrases, and images in the text. *Don't trust your memory!* If you don't write things down as you receive them from the Lord, you'll stand a good chance of forgetting them. Sometimes the Lord gives me some of those wonderful thoughts and ideas while I'm out walking and I have to stop to type them on the notepad app on my phone!

Another approach I personally use in my Bible study preparation is to look for questions or controversies that might exist in the passage. Now, don't misunderstand me; I don't try to create questions or controversies but I do look for the ones that already exist. I always try to put myself in the pew and look for the questions I would be asking if I were listening to the message. It doesn't help the audience when the teacher explains the obvious and ignores the difficult.

Another good question to ask in your study preparation is: What information or insights can I share that the majority of my audience doesn't already have? Once again, I'm not looking for obscure or novel things; I'm looking for fresh information and insights that will open up the passage and help the people—the Sherlock Holmes approach!

RELATED SCRIPTURE

Next I would suggest you read related verses and passages. In other words, if your Bible contains other Scripture references in the margins, that means those verses are somehow related, either in topic or in context, to the verses you are reading. You should always check those cross-references because often you'll gain additional insights.

Also, if another Scripture passage covers the same theme or topic elsewhere, turn there and spend some time reading it. For example, if you were studying Psalm 51 and David's confession of sin with Bathsheba, you should also read and study Psalm 32, which is the sequel of the same confession. The same principle applies to stories found in multiple Gospels.

COMMENTARIES

The next step is to read commentaries. There are two main reasons for using commentaries. The first is to make sure that your ideas and insights are doctrinally correct. You may think you have discovered a wonderful insight only to learn in the commentaries that your insight does not fit the word, verse, or passage. If that happens, throw that idea away and forget about it. Remember, we need to "rightly divide the word of truth."

The second reason for using commentaries is to glean additional ideas and nuggets. This helps to strengthen your study. I've heard some people boast that they never use commentaries for study preparation, but I'm not impressed. In fact, it appears to be a matter of pride! All of the wonderful truths and insights we can find in commentaries were given by the Holy Spirit to His people. Why would we ignore those valuable blessings from the Lord?

Now, on the flip side of that, we must also guard against turning our Bible study into a regurgitation of commentaries. As someone once said, you can milk a lot of cows but you need to make your own butter! Or take pollen from different flowers and then make your own honey. That is to say: do a lot of reading but then build your own message. One way to help guard yourself in this area is to read several different commentaries. In other words, milk a lot of cows and pollinate a lot of flowers!

Above all else, let the Holy Spirit be your first commentator. In other words, pray and read on your own first, and allow God's Spirit to speak to your heart. Then, after you've done that thoroughly, you can go to the commentaries for additional insights. This is very important and helps to make it your own message.

There is something else I want to say about commentaries that I think will really help you: use a variety. Different commentaries have different emphases. For example, commentaries by John MacArthur, James Boice, or R. Kent Hughes have a strong emphasis on interpretation. Other commentaries have more of a devotional emphasis, such as those by Alan Redpath or F. B. Meyer. Finally, there are commentaries that emphasize practical application, such as those by Warren Wiersbe, John Philips, and J. Vernon McGee.

You could use ten different commentaries, but if they all emphasize interpretation, then your studies will be very dry. In my own teaching, I find that after the first couple of weeks in a new series, I've narrowed it down to four or five commentaries that I use for the rest of the series, and they offer me the variety I'm looking for.

On a side note, whenever I'm teaching a book of the Bible or a series, those study books come off my shelves and don't go back until the series is over. They stay on my desk, close at hand, the entire time.

OTHER SCRIPTURE VERSIONS

It's also helpful to read other versions of the Bible for clarity and new insights. If you're teaching from the New King James Version, it's helpful to read your text in a couple of other versions, like the New International Version or New Living Translation. This practice helps to open up the meaning of the text. I would strongly suggest, however, that you always teach using the same translation. People get frustrated if you keep changing translations on them.

3. Research

BACKGROUND

First off, we need to research the background of the passage. Often we fail to grasp the main meaning or theme of the passage because we didn't research the background. I once heard John MacArthur say something along the lines of, "If you present a good introduction and background into any book of the Bible, then that book will, in turn, preach itself." That's definitely true. If you're teaching systematically through a book of the Bible, then the first study should include a solid background introduction. The same goes for topical studies.

I always like to invest a lot of extra study into the historical background, setting, and culture of a book, or the subject of a new series. Take the four Gospels, for example. As we talked about earlier, Matthew was written to the Jews, emphasizing Jesus as a king; Mark was written to the Romans, emphasizing Jesus as a servant; Luke was written to the Greeks, emphasizing Jesus as the Son of Man; and John was written to a wide audience, including the unsaved, emphasizing Jesus as God.

When we explain the background, many of the verses and passages make sense and come to light because the audience understands where, when, why, or how they were written. Oftentimes the commentaries themselves will give you some background information. Also, I strongly suggest using Bible handbooks or surveys for that type of information (such as Halley's, Unger's, or Willmington's).

CONTEXT

Another important step in the preparation process is to research the proper context of the passage. What is the verse saying in the context of the other verses around it? For example, in Matthew 13, Jesus shares several parables. In one of those parables, He compares the kingdom of heaven to the leaven that a woman uses in her baking. Now I've heard some teachers speak on that parable, claiming that leaven is a symbol of evil in the Bible; therefore, the leaven Jesus is speaking of describes evil influence in the kingdom.

But in the context of that entire chapter, everything else Jesus compares the kingdom of heaven to—a mustard seed, a treasure hidden in a field, a pearl of great value, and so forth—is always positive and represents the permeating effect of the kingdom. So, in the proper context, this leaven represents God's kingdom spreading and influencing all that it comes in contact with. This is all part of "rightly dividing the word of truth."

We should also spend some time researching the key words in the passage. Take, for example, the word *hate* that Jesus uses in Luke 14:26, saying that genuine disciples must hate their father and mother. As we research that word using *Strong's Concordance*, we discover that the Greek word, *miseo*, means both "to hate" and "to love less." So Jesus was saying that if we're truly His disciples, then our love for Him must be supreme—and by comparison, our love for everyone else is less. This is where a combination of a *Strong's Concordance* and *Vine's Expository Dictionary of New Testament Words* really helps.

Other Sources

Something else I like to do is to research news articles, stories, illustrations, quotes, and so forth. All of these types of things can really help strengthen a Bible study. If I were to compare the preparation of a Bible study to something, then without hesitation I would compare it to preparing a meal. A Bible study and a meal both need to be well-planned, well-prepared, balanced, nutritious, and satisfying. The introduction is the appetizer. The message is the meal. The outline is the recipe. The different main points are the different courses. The quotes and illustrations are the seasonings and spices that add flavor. The conclusion is the dessert.

Now let me say a few words about quotes, illustrations, and humor. I like using good quotes. The right quote can really help a study, because after you spend some time explaining something in your study, it can express the entire point or application in a single sentence. In fact, I like to refer to quotes as "one-sentence sermons." I can talk about sin and the consequences of sin for several minutes, and then use a quote such as "You can choose your own sins, but you cannot choose the consequences" to drive home the point with a single sentence.[6] If someone can say it better than I can, then I like to quote them! Now, when using quotes, it's good to give proper credit to the person who said it. Sometimes we simply don't know who said it, and life goes on. But when we do know, we should acknowledge that person by name.

When it comes to using stories and illustrations as seasonings, we don't want to overdo it by substituting stories for sermons or illustrations for illumination! Too much seasoning spoils the meal. I've heard messages made up of stories and silly jokes and very little Bible study. That's dishonoring to the Lord and is a dereliction of teaching.

Now let's talk about illustrations for a moment. I think that illustrations play an important role in a Bible study. I can be talking about a spiritual point, and then if I'm able to use an illustration that makes it clearer in the minds of the audience, it becomes like a window that lets the light into a room.

If you're wondering where to get good illustrations, my answer would be the Bible and life. Sometimes, the best illustrations are other stories in the Bible, and the Old Testament is often a great source of illustration for the New Testament. But another source is life itself. When I first began teaching I was heavily dependent upon illustration books, but now I rarely ever use them. That's because they're not personal and often are outdated and therefore unhelpful.

Several years ago I read a book called *Preaching with Fresh-ness*, and it really helped me to see how many great illustrations are happening to us and around us on a daily basis if we know how to look for them. It's not a book filled with illustrations but rather a book on how to see them for yourself. So I find most of my illustrations in the Bible or in life, as well as in the books I read, the newspaper, the nightly news, and so forth.

Let me share a few quick pointers:

- *Get the facts and details right.* If you share something with incorrect information, and people realize it, it's not only embarrassing but also undermines your credibility as a teacher. People think, *If he's not getting that story right, then I wonder if he's actually getting the passage right.* If you're unsure about something, get the facts—or else don't use it!
- *Use personal stories when possible.* You've experienced it and you have all the facts. Also, it allows you to be more than just a teacher; you become a real person whom the audience can relate to on a personal level.
- *Never base your sermon on an illustration.* Always base it on the Scriptures. Remember: quotes and illustrations are like the seasoning to the meal; they're not the main course.

Let me say a word about humor in the study. I enjoy humor, as I think most people do. There is a place for humor in the study, if handled tastefully and correctly. Laughter is a universal language and humor can be an effective way to connect with the audience. Having no humor is tolerable, but it can also make the teacher and the message sound overly somber and serious. The joy of the Lord is our strength! But at the same time, when the speaker is not naturally funny but tries to be funny, it comes off as awkward and even distracts from the message—so above all else, be yourself!

In my opinion, Greg Laurie is exceptionally good at throwing a little humor into his message to "let the air out of the room" at the proper time. In other words, when the subject is serious, there can be some tension that builds, and well-placed humor or wit can bring some needed relief. There is a difference between being funny or witty and being silly. There's no place for silliness in Bible study. Just as illustrations and quotes should be like the seasonings and spices we add to the main meal, humor can be like sugar. There's a place in the recipe for some sugar to sweeten things, but too much of it will ruin the taste.

OTHER TOOLS

One last thing we can research is other tools and helps. It could be a theology book, a word study book, or a pronunciation guide. Another good research tool, used carefully and wisely, is the internet. I have found a lot of information very quickly by searching the internet. Whether it's a news story, information about a person, or trying to nail down a certain quote, the internet can be very helpful. (Be sure to check the validity of your internet stories before using them. Sites like snopes.com or urbanlegends.com can be good for this.)

4. Outlining/Organizing

Finally, let's discuss the value of outlining our studies.

THE NEED

Recognize the need for outlining. An outline for a study is like a recipe for a meal or a blueprint for a building. It's difficult to proceed without one. Outlining your studies is beneficial for several reasons.

First, outlining your study makes it much easier to prepare it. If you've outlined your Bible passage, you have a much better idea where you're going and how you're going to get there. It helps you to focus in on where you're at. Second, outlining your study makes it much easier to teach and makes it simpler to present your message in a clear and organized manner.

Third, outlining your study makes it a lot easier for your listeners to understand and receive it. Many people like to take notes, so if we've outlined our message and give it point by point, it is easier for them to do so. And the easier it is to take notes on a study, the better they will be able to retain the information they've been given. Oftentimes, people will not remember everything you taught but they may remember your outline and your main points.

Fourth, outlining your study makes it much easier to pace your study. One of the most difficult things to do, especially for newer teachers, is to keep your study within a certain timeframe. Outlining your study will help you to stay on track time-wise. So for example, if you have a forty-minute slot to teach and you have three main points, then you know you need to keep each point at about ten minutes each, on average, which will leave you an additional ten minutes for your introduction and conclusion.

The Main Theme

Something else we should do within the outline of our studies is to recognize the main theme. This is called "the propositional statement." You should be able to state the main point or theme of your message in a single sentence. If you can't do that, then you don't really have a clear and firm handle on the passage. I've heard studies that made several good points and had interesting facts. But afterward I was left to wonder what the main point of the message was.

The Main Points

Finally, we want to recognize the main points. Once again, I've listened to studies, as you have, where the teacher gave thirty or forty minutes of pretty good running commentary. But in the midst of that running commentary they never established any main points for me to hang my hat on. I believe that most studies should have main points, though I have heard some great messages that had no set of points. Occasionally I find myself teaching without a set of points, but that's rare for me, and the majority of the time I have main points.

In summary, here is what my preparation process looks like:

1. I pray.
2. I read the text repeatedly, taking notes on what the Lord shows me.
3. I do additional research on words, names, places, phrases, and so forth.
4. I title and outline my study.
5. I read and mark the commentaries.
6. I type my study out (mine are word for word).
   - Introduction
   - Main body of the message
   - Conclusion and final application
7. I review it repeatedly, making cuts, changes, and adding highlights.

The Presentation

As we come now to our third section, we're going to talk about how to present the message. However, there are several elements about the presentation that overlap with preparation, so let's talk a little about both.

1. Teach Expositionally

Expositional teaching, in simple terms, refers to expounding and explaining the Bible text. John MacArthur put it this way: "By expositional teaching, we mean preaching in such a way that the meaning of the Bible passage is presented entirely and exactly as it was intended by God."[7] That is a holy responsibility that comes with the stewardship of being a Bible teacher. There are four main steps in which expositional teaching should be constructed, if it is to be done correctly.

Observation—What does the text say?

Interpretation—What does the text mean?

Illustration—What does this truth look like?

Application—How do we apply this truth in our lives?

First of all, we approach the passage by asking ourselves the question: What does the text say? We call this *observation*. We're not asking ourselves what we think the text means to us but what the text actually says—and what it doesn't say!

Second, we need to address the question: What does the text mean? We would call this *interpretation*. The first question gives us the facts, while the second question gives us the meaning.

When God's Word says something it only means one thing, and while a passage may have many different applications, it only has one intended meaning. Both observation and interpretation must be accomplished through prayer and diligent Bible study—including reading, research, and using study tools such as commentaries, dictionaries, handbooks, and concordances.

The third step in expositional teaching is when we address the question: What does this look like? We call this third step *illustration*. In other words, using a story or anecdote to help illustrate the meaning of the text. This helps to make the message more relevant and practical for the audience.

The fourth step in expositional teaching is for the teacher to ask and answer the question: How do we apply this truth in our lives? We call this *application*. Proper Bible teaching will never be complete until we talk about how to apply these truths personally. Otherwise our Bible study becomes nothing more than a stale lecture.

When you put these four steps together, you have the basis for expositional teaching, which in my opinion is the best way to teach

God's Word. If you use only one or two of these steps, your study is not going to accomplish its goal. That is to say, I've heard studies that were almost all application. But how can you make good application out of Scripture when you're not even sure what the text really says or means in the first place?

I've also heard messages that were all interpretation, without illustrations or application, and they quickly became boring and lifeless lectures. Application is not incidental to good expository preaching; it's essential! It takes observation, interpretation, illustration, and application to make a study expositional and meaningful.

Now let's talk about the format of the study. What I'm about to share with you will sound very simple, but it's the key that helps unlock putting a study together.

2. Teach with a Format

Warren Wiersbe says, "God is not the author of confusion, but some teachers are, and they do it in God's name!"[8] Some teachers present a Genesis 1:2 type of message: "without form, and void!" Messages should be prepared and presented with a basic format. And it's a format that probably all of us have used in different ways and at different times in our lives. It's the same format for writing a letter or a formal email. That format includes an introduction, a body, and a conclusion. Or to put it in terms of preparing and serving a meal, it is an appetizer, main course, and dessert.

THE INTRODUCTION

First there is the introduction. It was Dietrich Bonhoeffer who said, "The first minutes in the pulpit are the most favorable, so do not waste them with generalities, but confront [your audience] straight off with the core of the matter."[9] The purpose of the introduction in a study is to briefly tell your audience where you are taking them in that particular message.

Before you simply dive into a passage of Scripture, people need to have a sense of where you're going. The introduction lays the grid for each message. In terms of a book or newspaper article, the introduction is referred to as "the hook." Studies show that when the speaker begins to address the audience, they have about three to five minutes before the audience decides if they're going to tune in or tune out. The introduction is critical in connecting with your listeners. Once you've lost the audience, it's tough to get them back.

A word of caution: while it is unwise to begin a study without a good introduction, it is also unwise to make your introduction too long. That will also cause people to start tuning out. So tell people where you're taking them, then get behind the wheel and start driving the bus! Otherwise, people will grow weary of waiting for you to actually start the engine.

In my opinion, you should try to keep your normal Bible study introductions to about five minutes. The exception would be when you're beginning a brand-new series, and you want to put forth all of the important background information. But even then, use a hook, get people's attention, tell them briefly about the new series, and then move forward with that background information.

If you are teaching chapter by chapter through a book of the Bible, or message by message through a series, you may become tempted to skip introductions. In other words, it becomes easy to simply say, "Today, we pick up where we left off last week." The trouble with that is you will have different people coming in and out each week. So the person who didn't hear your study last week instantly feels disconnected. But at the same time, don't turn every introduction into a twenty-minute rehash either. That will bore all of the other people to death.

The best strategy is always to give each study its own fresh and brief introduction. Even if you're teaching through a particular book of the Bible, let each chapter or message stand on its own subject, with its own title and points. At the same time, as you teach that message, keep it connected to the theme and to the main flow of that book. Your goal is that, by the end of any given series, someone could listen to any single message from the middle of that series and it would be complete with its own personal application, but at the same time they could listen to every message in that series and feel its connection and continuity.

One very important part of the introduction is the title. Like every other part of the message, the title is significant. A good title sets the tone for the sermon. A good title should make you want to listen to the message. Chuck Swindoll shares his example of preaching on David's sin with Bathsheba, asking which of these two titles sounds more interesting: "David's Great Sin" or "Autopsy of a Moral Failure"? It's not just the words but what those words communicate. The word *autopsy* reveals that the speaker is going to dissect the inner problems that led to David's great sin and therefore has more promise of being an interesting message. The title should, in about seven words or less, prepare the audience for what they're going to hear.

When Swindoll was going to speak on the life of Samson, he felt that the study itself was going to be a little heavier than normal, so he decided to go with a lighter title: "Samson: A He-Man with a She-Weakness." When I visited Swindoll's church in Fullerton many years ago, he was starting a new series on the Ten Commandments that he was calling "Grace Etched in Stone." Those are great message titles from a very gifted communicator.

Now, a couple of words of warning about message titles: (1) Don't overpromise and then underdeliver! A title like "How to Make Every Problem Disappear" is simply too good to be true. That title is guaranteed to disappoint. (2) Don't let the title become the best part of your message. There's nothing worse for an audience than to get excited about a promising title only to hear a boring message that makes them feel like they were misled.

Sometimes introductions come easily and sometimes they're the hardest part of the message preparation. If you're struggling with your introduction but are ready to begin writing your message, then get started with the message and come back to the introduction later on. That's not always easy to do, but it's better than sitting in front of the computer for an hour staring at a blank screen with the cursor just pulsating in front of your eyes. Clearly I am speaking from experience!

And let me be honest and transparent about this: if I don't have my introduction dialed in, I can't move on with the rest of the message, no matter how hard I try. Perhaps my mind is too structured and rigid; I have to complete each step before I can move on to the next. That can sometimes become a struggle for me.

The Body

Then comes the second part of the study: the body. It's the main course! In my opinion, the body of every good message should be organized and outlined with specific points. As I mentioned earlier, outlining your message with main points accomplishes several helpful things. It's easier to prepare. It's easier to teach. It's easier for listeners to receive and to retain. It's easier to track your time.

The body of the message is where you take your chapter or verses and group them into main points. The purpose of the message body is to teach and apply Scripture to life. And along the way, we also talk about history, geography, and theology.

The Conclusion

Then comes the third and final part of the message: the conclusion. Once again, in terms of a meal, it's the dessert. The main purpose of the conclusion is twofold.

First, you want to bring a sense of closure to the message. Most of us have probably seen a movie that ended so abruptly there was no sense of closure, and it was kind of frustrating. In the same way, ending a message too abruptly, without a proper conclusion, can actually harm an otherwise good message.

Second, and more importantly, the conclusion is where we make our final, overall application. There should be application throughout the main message, but then, specifically, the conclusion is where we wrap everything up. Like the introduction, the conclusion should not be too lengthy. We've all heard messages that sounded like they were coming in for a landing when the teacher suddenly decided to keep talking for another fifteen minutes. That can also leave a sour taste on an otherwise good message.

So when you prepare and present your messages—whether it's a fifteen-minute devotion or a sixty-minute Bible study—always format it with an introduction, a body, and a conclusion. If you were to look at any of my teaching notes, you would see that exact format on every study. And by that, I mean that in my own Bible study notes, I actually type those headings into every message: introduction, message, and conclusion. If you consistently struggle with putting your messages together, then I suspect this is the area you may be overlooking in your preparation process.

3. What to Aim For

As teachers, we need to know what we're aiming for. As the old saying goes, "If you aim at nothing, you're bound to hit it."

First, we're aiming for the head. This would be the doctrinal side of the study. We want to reach the mind of the listener first by telling them what the text says. This would be *instruction*.

Second, we want to aim for the heart. This would be the devotional side of our message. We want to touch the heart of the listener. This happens by telling them what the text means. This would be *illumination*.

Third, we want to reach the hands of our audience. This would be the duty side of the study. We're now referring to how to apply the text. This would be *inspiration.*

Every good and well-rounded Bible study should aim for the head (doctrine), the heart (devotion), and the hands (duty). I'm sure you've heard messages that are all doctrine and no duty . . . or studies that are all hands and no heart. Unless there is a proper balance, the message will fail and fall short.

4. What to Teach With

POWER

Let's talk about teaching with power. We must teach our studies in the power of God's Spirit. This is accomplished in two ways. First, we pray and ask God to empower our words. As Paul said in 1 Corinthians 2:4, "My speech and my preaching were . . . in demonstration of the Spirit and of power." Before every study, I always take the time to pray for God's power and anointing upon that message. Second, Hebrews 4:12 reminds us that, "The word of God is living and powerful, and sharper than any two-edged sword." The reason some messages lack power is simply because there's way too much fluff and not enough Scripture. Some teachers share a verse or two and then spend the remainder of their time telling stories, illustrations, and jokes.

Several years ago, there was a speaker who had been invited to share at our church's married couples' conference. He was energetic, charismatic, funny, and a good communicator. But for both of his Saturday morning sessions, he used very little Scripture. He never even brought a Bible up to the podium with him. In the end, it was like filling up on cotton candy.

It was Thomas Brooks who said, "He is the best preacher, not that tickles the ears, but that breaks the heart."[10] Spurgeon compared the Word of God to a lion, and he exhorted teachers to simply "let the lion out of the cage!"[11] Let Scripture and the exposition of it dominate the study, and use other things sparingly.

PASSION

Teaching also needs to be done with passion. As Chuck Swindoll well said, "There is absolutely nothing sacred or spiritual about boring teaching!"[12] If the study doesn't excite you, it certainly won't excite your listeners either! Teaching is not taking Bible verses and then simply restating them. That's not teaching; that's torture.

It was D. L. Moody who said, "The best way to revive a church is to build a fire in the pulpit."[13] Now let me balance this out by saying that passion is not being loud, obnoxious, or theatrical. Teachers are not performers. We're handling the holy Word of God. The right kind of passion comes from within, from personal conviction and experience, and not by trying to act excited, like when you get a weird birthday present.

PEACE

There also needs to be peace. Many teachers get a little nervous before a study, and that's OK. That nervousness reminds you that you're dependent upon God. But as we pray and diligently prepare our studies, there should also be a supernatural peace from God. I have good news for you: the people listening to you want you to do well and are pulling for you.

PRESENCE

We need to have a sense of God's presence. As Moses said to God in Exodus 33:15, "If Your Presence does not go with [me], do not bring [me] up from here." God is with you, and He certainly doesn't want you to fail.

5. Teach Systematically

The word *systematic* refers to being methodical, orderly, and well-organized. Our teaching should be chapter by chapter and verse by verse. Systematic Bible teaching has many positive benefits. For one, you know where you're going in your study every week. As Haddon Robinson has said, "Only a genius can think up enough original material that is fresh and stimulating" each week.[14]

Systematic and expositional Bible teaching keeps teachers from hiding in their comfort zone. In other words, if you're doing a lot of topical messages, you'll have the tendency to just teach on your favorite subjects, in the areas that you feel comfortable with. Systematic and expositional teaching keeps us from neglecting "the whole counsel of God." As I go through different books of the Bible, it forces me to deal with subjects that I'm less familiar with and promotes personal growth in my own life and ministry—and the listeners are getting the whole counsel of God.

6. Teach with Accuracy

Let's start with your text. Never bend, twist, mistranslate, or manhandle a Bible verse or text just to make it fit into what you want it to say. A teacher's responsibility is to "rightly divide the word of truth" (see 2 Tim. 2:15), not to force our message onto some Bible text.

Be careful with Scripture references. Avoid quoting a Scripture until you're sure the verse is correct and you know where it's at in the Bible. We all make innocent mistakes and mix up our references, which happens when we trust our memories. So I suggest making a practice of adding the Scripture references into your notes. Even if you don't give the reference, you'll have it later if someone asks you for it.

Watch your quotes. By this, I mean use quotes accurately and correctly. And as I already shared, give credit where credit is due. Don't forget that quotes and illustrations are seasonings, not the main meal, and we should only sprinkle them here and there. Similarly, be careful with illustrations and stories. Share them correctly, use them carefully, and don't twist facts and information just to make the story sound more exciting. (That's called lying.)

Work on your pronunciation of words. It can be funny once in a while when you encounter those almost-impossible-to-pronounce words, but when teachers take the time to learn the correct pronunciation for the names of people and places in the Bible, it sends a signal to the listeners that they've given their best effort in preparation.

7. Pearls, Points, and Pet Peeves

Let's finish with some of my personal thoughts on teaching. I apply these things to myself as a teacher. Many of these I've already touched on, so I'll try to keep it brief.

- *Start praying, keep praying, and don't stop praying.* Adam Clarke said, "Study yourself to death, and then pray yourself alive again."[15]
- *Study diligently, work hard, and give 100 percent effort.* Martin Luther described his Bible study process like this: "First I shake the whole tree, that the ripest apples may fall. Then I climb the tree and shake each limb. Then I shake each branch and each twig. Then I look under every leaf!"[16] If you want to be a good teacher, you have to learn to be a good student who studies hard.
- *Always give some helpful application.* Listening to a message with no application is like eating a meal and still feeling hungry; it's not satisfying. In your messages, always answer the question "So what?" Tell your listeners how they can apply these things in their lives.
- *Be passionate and excited about your study.* If teaching is truly your spiritual gift, then you're going to get excited about it. If you're not excited, I promise your audience won't be excited either.
- *Learn from others but develop your own style.* Try to learn from other good teachers but don't copy or imitate them. Be yourself. If you speak and act like a different person while

teaching, then people will see you as being insincere. Trust that God knew what He was doing when He made you the way you are!

- *Build a good library*. Every teacher needs tools, and books are an investment, not an expense. If you're called into an ongoing teaching ministry, then keep on building up a good library. Start with the basic tools, such as a Bible dictionary, a handbook, a concordance, good theology books, sermon books, and, of course, commentaries.

- *Use Scripture like a scalpel, not a sword*. As teachers, we need to use tact in our teaching. The Word of God is called a sword, but if we're not careful, we can end up cutting off the ears of our listeners, like Peter in the Garden of Gethsemane (see Matt. 26:51). If the Scriptures, spoken truthfully, offend people, that's one thing. But if I offend people because I'm insensitive or obnoxious, then God help me. Speak the truth in love.

- *Talk to your audience at their level and not in such a way as to try to impress people*. Ecclesiastes 12:10 says, "Indeed, the Teacher sought to find just the right words to express truths clearly" (NLT).

- *Teach using notes*. I admire pastors who teach without notes, but they are the exception, and I believe that the negatives of not using notes far outweigh any positives. For example:

  1. There's too much to remember and to trust our memories to.

  2. Your notes help you to keep your flow and train of thought.

  3. After spending hours of research and preparation, why take the chance of forgetting something important or critical to the study?

  4. After all of the work I've put into those studies, I don't want to lose that valuable information. With notes I can refer back to it later.

- *Trim the fat from your studies.* In the final stages of your Bible study preparations, look over your message and cut out any repetitious statements or words, like trimming the excess fat from a steak. As George Burns well said, "The secret of a good sermon is to have a good beginning and a good ending, then having the two as close together as possible."[17]

- *Make a beeline for Jesus and the cross.* When all is said and done, it's all about Jesus and it's all about the cross. Don't ever preach a message without making that connection.

- *Be practical in your teaching.* For example, don't just tell people that worrying is a sin; give them biblical and practical ways to deal with worry when it comes, like praying, worshiping, and remembering Scripture.

- *If you make fun of anyone, let it be yourself.* It keeps you from sounding negative and makes you more real to the audience.

- *Keep your study within your timeframe.* Better to leave them wanting more than wishing you had stopped a while ago! Or as the proverb says, "The mind cannot retain what the seat cannot endure." So if you're asked to give a fifteen-minute devotion, then give a fifteen-minute devotion, not a thirty-five-minute message with seven points!

- *Avoid repeated words that are irritating*, such as "of course," "and," or "OK?"

- *Don't be monotone.* In real-life conversations, we emphasize the exciting and important things and we talk softly about the somber things.

- *Words are your tools, so choose them carefully and well.* Mark Twain wrote that "the difference between the right word, and the almost right word, is the difference between a lightning bug and lightning."[18] Words are our tools, so I spend extra time in my message prep and review, choosing the right ones.

- *Preach to be faithful, not to be popular.* At an early time in his ministry, G. Campbell Morgan felt like something was missing in his preaching. So he went into his study and called out to God in prayer to show him what needed to change. In that still, small voice, God spoke to Morgan's heart and revealed that he was preaching to be popular rather than being faithful. Morgan states that, after hearing God's voice, he took all of his clever outlines and feel-good sermons from his files and threw them into the fireplace. When G. Campbell Morgan passed away in May 1945, he was known as "The Prince of Expositors." John Wesley was quoted as saying, "Once every seven years I burn all of my sermons; for it is a shame if I cannot write better sermons now than I did seven years ago."

- *Love God and His people more than you love teaching.* To love to teach is good—to love the people we are teaching is paramount. Paul wrote in 1 Corinthians 13, "Though I speak with the tongues of . . . angels . . . and [have] all knowledge . . . but have not love, I am nothing" (vv. 1–2).

- *Strive to keep improving.* Like the apostle Paul, our attitude should be, "It's not as though I've arrived or have been perfected" (see Phil. 3:12). Read good books on preaching, listen to podcasts of good sermons, and keep evaluating your preaching and how you can improve it.

- *Preach with authority.* The preacher's authority doesn't come from having a great speaking voice or by using clever words— it comes from rightly dividing the Word of truth!

- *Do everything for God's glory.* Preach to honor God's Word and to exalt Him. It's not about us and it never will be—it's about Him and His glory. If I get a compliment after a message, I desire to hear, "God ministered to my heart through that message," or "I feel closer to Jesus," as opposed to someone saying, "Good message, Pastor."

PART 2

BOOKS OF THE BIBLE

Ever since I committed my life to Christ in 1980, I have had a strong appetite for the Word of God. In addition to all the great truths and principles found in Scripture, I really enjoy what might be termed as the nuggets or gems in God's Word. These will oftentimes come in the form of insights, reflections, observations, parallels, quotes, and so forth. That is along the lines of what this second section is all about—insights and information into all sixty-six books of the Bible.

These types of insights are much more than mere novelty; they have helped me to have a greater appreciation and understanding for the richness and depth of God's Word. My hope is that they will do the same for you.

GENESIS

Important Information

Author: Moses
Themes: Origins; Man's Sin and God's Salvation
Category: The Law

Fascinating Facts

1. Genesis tells us about the beginning of everything (life, sin, salvation, judgment, marriage, family, government, and so forth) except God Himself.
2. Genesis records the life of Enoch, one of only two people in the Bible who did not physically die (Elijah is the other).
3. Genesis contains the record of seven men who all lived to be over nine hundred years old (5:5, 8, 11, 14, 20, 27; 9:29).
4. Genesis tells us about the longest life on record: Methuselah at 969 years (5:27).
5. Genesis records the first death and murder, that of Abel (4:8).
6. Genesis covers a longer time period than any other book in the Bible, 2,350 years, which is longer than the rest of the books of the Bible put together.
7. Genesis lays out the basic foundation for all of the great doctrines of Scripture.

8. Genesis opens with a garden and closes with a grave; it begins with creation and closes with a coffin.

9. Genesis records the only instance in Scripture in which God rested (Gen. 2:2; also quoted in Exod. 20; 31; and Heb. 4).

10. Genesis records the first appearance of Satan in human history (3:1).

11. One-half of the great heroes of faith listed in Hebrews 11 lived during the time of Genesis.

12. Genesis gives us the first reference to the gospel of Jesus Christ (3:15).

Quotable Quotes

The narrative is so simple, so much like truth, so consistent everywhere within itself, so correct in its dates, so impartial in its biography, so accurate in its philosophical details, so pure in its morality, and so benevolent in its design, as amply to demonstrate that it never could have had an earthly origin. —Adam Clarke

The book of Genesis is probably the most important book ever written. . . . If the Bible were somehow expurgated of the book of Genesis (as many people today would prefer), the rest of the Bible would be incomprehensible. It would be like a building without a ground floor, or a bridge with no support. —Henry M. Morris

Every single biblical doctrine of theology, directly or indirectly, ultimately has its basis in the book of Genesis. —Ken Ham

Notable Notes

Genesis 3 is one of "the three great third chapters" of the Bible. The other two are John 3 and Romans 3. All three of these "third chapters" speak of the "three Rs": ruin, redemption, and regeneration.

Christ Connections

Christ can be found in Genesis as:

Creator

Seed of the Woman

Ark of Salvation

EXODUS

Important Information

Author: Moses
Themes: Redemption, Deliverance
Category: The Law

Fascinating Facts

1. In Exodus, we see the birth of the nation of Israel.
2. In Exodus, we have the beginning of Israel's Passover and its subsequent observation (ch. 12).
3. In Exodus, we also see the beginning of the tabernacle, the priesthood, and the yearly festivals.
4. Exodus gives us the beginning of the law, highlighted by the ten commandments.
5. Exodus gives us the clearest picture of God's salvation in the Old Testament.

6. In Exodus, there are perhaps more symbols of Christ than in any other Old Testament book, such as: Moses, the Passover lamb, the tabernacle, and the ark of the covenant.

7. Eleven chapters of Exodus (more than one-quarter of the book) are devoted to instructions about the tabernacle.

8. In Exodus, we see many miracles and miraculous events, highlighted by the parting of the Red Sea.

9. Exodus presents a contrast in tens: ten plagues and ten commandments.

10. The ten plagues in Exodus, performed by God through Moses, served as a challenge to numerous false gods of Egypt.

11. In this book, Moses led the exodus from Egypt and was a type of Christ; in the Gospels, Jesus spoke of His exodus on the Mount of Transfiguration and Moses appeared next to Him (Luke 9:31).

12. Exodus records the first great praise songs in the Bible (ch. 15), led by Moses and his sister Miriam.

Quotable Quotes

Exodus stands at the heart of the Old Testament as the greatest example of the saving acts of God before Christ. —*Talk Thru the Bible*

It took one night to take Israel out of Egypt, but forty years to take Egypt out of Israel. —George H. Morrison

The life of Moses presents a series of antitheses. He was the child of a slave, and the son of a queen. He was born in a hut, and lived in a palace. He inherited poverty, and he lived in royalty. He was the leader of armies, and the keeper of flocks. He was the mightiest of warriors, and the meekest of men. He was educated in the court, and dwelt in the desert. He had the wisdom of Egypt, and the faith of a child. He was fitted for the city, and wandered in the wilderness. He was tempted with the pleasures of sin, and endured the hardship of virtue. He was backward in speech, and talked with God. He had the rod of a shepherd, and the power of the Infinite. He was a fugitive from Pharaoh, and an ambassador from heaven. He was the giver of the Law, and the forerunner of grace. He died alone on Mount Nebo, and appeared with Christ on the Mount of Transfiguration. No man assisted at his funeral, yet God buried him. —H. I. Haldeman

Notable Notes

In Revelation 15 reference is made to the saints in heaven singing the "Song of Moses" for their deliverance and victory. That song, which is recorded in Exodus 15, supplies the lyrics to a song that God's people will sing together in heaven.

Christ Connections

Christ can be found in Exodus as:

Passover Lamb

Deliverer

High Priest

LEVITICUS

Important Information

Author: Moses
Themes: Holiness, Worship, Communion
Category: The Law

Fascinating Facts

1. No other book in the Bible contains as many direct messages from God as Leviticus does (such as 1:1; 4:1; 11:44).

2. Leviticus speaks more about holiness than any other book of the Bible.

3. It is the first of only three books in Scripture that begins by stating that God is speaking (see also Numbers; Joshua).

4. In Leviticus, the Holy Spirit is never mentioned by name, though all of the other books of the Pentateuch refer to Him.

5. The New Testament quotes or refers to Leviticus more than one hundred times.

6. The words *holy*, *blood*, *priest*, and *sacrifice* appear more times in Leviticus than in any other book of the Bible.

7. Leviticus covers a time period of only one month (Exod. 40:17; Num. 1:1) and records no geographical movement in the history of Israel.

8. Even though the title "Leviticus" means "pertaining to the Levites," there is only one casual mention of the Levites in this book (25:32).

9. Levi, from whom the Levites descended, was the third son of Jacob and the great-grandfather of Aaron, Moses, and Miriam.

10. In chapters 11–15 alone, the word *unclean* appears more than one hundred times.

11. The two main symbols of evil in Scripture are referred to in this book: leprosy and leaven.

Quotable Quotes

Holiness is the Grand Theme of the book of Leviticus. A Holy God is seen providing a Holy Savior who through the power of the Holy Spirit enables the believer to worship God in the Beauty of Holiness. —W. G. Heslop

Leviticus stands in the same relation to Exodus that the Epistles do to the Gospels. —C. I. Scofield

Considering that it embraces the history of only one month, this may claim to be the most remarkable book in the Old Testament. —Joseph Parker

The holiness of God shines like a white, fearful light upon the whole book. —G. Campbell Morgan

Notable Notes

In Leviticus 23, Moses makes mention of the three great feast days: Passover, Pentecost, and Tabernacles. Passover reminds us of Jesus Christ, our Passover Lamb, whose blood cleanses us from sin; Pentecost reminds us of the Holy Spirit being poured out upon believers at Pentecost, when the church was born; and the Feast of Tabernacles reminds us of the Father and how He provided for and protected His people in the wilderness. Therefore, in these three great feasts, we see a picture of the Trinity: Father, Son, and Holy Spirit.

Christ Connections

Christ can be found in Leviticus as:
    High Priest
    Sacrifice

NUMBERS

Important Information

Author: Moses
Themes: Our Service and Walk; Consequences of Unbelief
Category: The Law

Fascinating Facts

1. Several of the events described in Numbers are used in the New Testament to warn believers about the consequences of sin and unbelief (such as 1 Cor. 10; 1 Pet. 2; Jude).

2. The sin of Balaam (chs. 22–25) is mentioned by three different New Testament writers: Peter, Jude, and John.

3. It is the second of only three books in Scripture that begins by stating that God is speaking (see also Leviticus; Joshua).

4. It is the first book of the Bible to record a detailed census (chs. 1; 26).

5. The word *wilderness* is used forty-five times in this book.

6. The raising up of the brass serpent in Numbers 21 is one of the clearest Old Testament pictures of Jesus hanging on the cross and of people being saved by faith (John 3:14).

7. Numbers records several instances of rebellion against God's ordained leadership (14:2; 16:2; 16:41; 20:2; 21:4).

8. Numbers records God's selection of Joshua to succeed Moses (27:18–23) and to lead the people into the Promised Land.

9. Numbers explains the Nazirite vow (ch. 6), the red heifer sacrifice (ch. 19), and the institution of the six cities of refuge (ch. 35).

10. Numbers 20 records the deaths of both Miriam and Aaron.

Quotable Quotes

The faithfulness of God is clearly seen in the fact that three million men, women, and children enter into, and pass through, a sterile desert without a drop of water, a loaf of bread, or a blade of grass! An army of three million men, women, and children enter into and pass through a trackless, pathless, uncharted desert without a guide, compass, chart, map, footstep, finger post, or stop and go sign . . . without a grocery store, bakery, meat market, surgeon, doctor, butcher, undertaker, drug store, or hospital. Think about the faithfulness of God. —W. G. Heslop

The story of Numbers is of deep interest . . . every careful reader of the New Testament Scriptures knows that Numbers is there repeatedly quoted. —Arno C. Gaebelein

[Numbers] is a story at once depressing and inspiring; according as we look at the shameful unbelief of man, or at the unfailing love of God. . . . There is no royal road into blessing; where the people of God fall they must rise; where they deny they must confess, and to the point from which they wander from God must they return; blessing can be found only where it was lost. This, in the main, is the subject of Numbers. —W. Graham Scroggie

Notable Notes

In Numbers 20, Miriam dies, Moses loses his entry into the Promised Land, and Aaron dies. The law (Moses), the priesthood (Aaron), and prophecy (Miriam) could not bring us into the Promised Land, but Jesus (Joshua) could!

Christ Connections

Christ can be found in Numbers as:
Pillar of Cloud/Fire
Tabernacle
Smitten Rock
Star out of Jacob

DEUTERONOMY

Important Information

Author: Moses
Themes: Obedience to God; God's Love for His People
Category: The Law

Fascinating Facts

1. Deuteronomy contains the longest recorded farewell speech in the Bible, given by Moses in chapters 31–33.

2. Jesus quoted from Deuteronomy three times in the wilderness to defeat Satan's temptations (Matt. 4:1–11) and also to sum up the law (Matt. 22:37).

3. Deuteronomy 33:16 contains the only Old Testament reference to God in the burning bush (Exod. 3).

4. Deuteronomy is quoted or alluded to more than ninety-five times in seventeen different books of the New Testament.

5. Deuteronomy makes the first mention of death by hanging on a tree (21:22–23).

6. Deuteronomy has been nicknamed "The Gospel of Love," and the word *love* is used some twenty-one times in this book.

7. Deuteronomy makes at least 250 references to its four preceding books, and is itself referred to over 350 times in the rest of the Old Testament.

8. Moses is the only person in Scripture who is said to have been buried by God Himself (34:6).

9. This book contains the great prediction of the coming Prophet (Messiah/Christ) in Deuteronomy 18:15–19.

10. Of all of the books of the Pentateuch, the prophets most used and quoted from Deuteronomy in their books.

11. Moses repeats the phrase "the LORD your God" to the people more than 250 times in Deuteronomy.

12. Jesus quoted more from the book of Deuteronomy than from any other book of the Pentateuch.

Quotable Quotes

The book of Deuteronomy is the book which demands obedience. Obedience is the keynote of almost every chapter. It is the great lesson of the book. Obedience in the spirit of love, flowing from a blessed and enjoyed relationship with Jehovah, is the demand made of His people. —Arno C. Gaebelein

It may be safely asserted that very few parts of the Old Testament Scriptures can be read with greater profit by the genuine Christian than the book of Deuteronomy. —Adam Clarke

Moses, at the close of his life, looked upon a new generation, a new land, a new life, a new leader, and so there was the need for this new revelation of the Divine "love," nowhere mentioned until now, though much illustrated. . . . It is probably true that

Deuteronomy is the most spiritual book in the Old Testament.
—W. Graham Scroggie

Notable Notes

According to Deuteronomy 34, Moses died just outside the Promised Land and was not allowed to enter in. However, Moses did eventually make it in. Later on, in the Gospels, Moses is seen inside of the Promised Land on the Mount of Transfiguration, talking with Jesus and Elijah (see Matt. 17:3; Luke 9:30–31).

Christ Connections

Christ can be found in Deuteronomy as:
    Prophet like Moses
    Law Giver

JOSHUA

Important Information

Author: Joshua
Theme: Possessing Our Inheritance
Category: History

Fascinating Facts

1. The name of Moses appears fifty-seven times in the book of Joshua, showing that even though Moses had died, his words and works had not been forgotten.

2. The book of Joshua begins and ends with death (1:1; 24:33).

3. The message of Joshua is to the Old Testament what the message of Ephesians is to the New Testament: possessing our inheritance.

4. In Joshua 6:26, a remarkable threefold prophecy is made about the city of Jericho, which was fulfilled some five hundred years later (1 Kings 16:34).

5. The great event in Moses's life was the passage through the Red Sea, and the great event in Joshua's life was the passage through the Jordan River.

6. In Joshua, we read of four incredible miracles that took place: the crossing of the Jordan, the fall of Jericho, the "selective" hailstones, and the sun standing still.

7. Rahab, whose story is recorded in chapters 2 and 6, is the first known Gentile who was converted under Mosaic Law.

8. The word *land* is used over eighty-five times in this book, while the words *inheritance* and *inherit* appear over sixty times, emphasizing Israel's possession of the Promised Land.

9. Joshua refers to nine memorials of stones or altars to commemorate important events.

10. Joshua is the third of only three books in Scripture that begin by stating that God is speaking (see also: Leviticus; Numbers).

11. Joshua is the first book of the Bible named after its main character.

12. Joshua records one of the best-known and best-loved Bible stories: the fall of Jericho.

Quotable Quotes

The book of Joshua records one of the most interesting and important portions of Israel's history. It is the capstone to the books of Moses, the foundation of those which follow. Omit Joshua, and there is a gap left in the sacred history which nothing could supply. —A. W. Pink

As I have studied Joshua, I have become convinced that this is a message very much needed in our time. We have many professing Christians in our day . . . but we do not seem to have many Joshuas. We do not have many who, without trying to be novel or spectacular, determine to obey the law of God in every particular and then actually do obey it throughout a lifetime of faithful service. —James Montgomery Boice

I think the church needs the message of the book of Joshua more than ever before. . . . The book of Joshua tells us how to be victorious soldiers and how to claim our rich spiritual inheritance in Jesus Christ. It tells us how to be strong and courageous as we face our enemies and march forward to claim new territory for the Lord. —Warren W. Wiersbe

Notable Notes

Rahab, the prostitute turned convert (ch. 2), has several special distinctions in Scripture: hers was the first recorded conversion of a woman in the Bible; she is one of only four women referred to by name in the genealogy of Jesus (see Matt. 1); and she is one of only two women mentioned by name in Hebrews 11, the great "Hall of Faith."

Christ Connections

Christ can be found in Joshua as:

    Captain of Our Salvation

    Victorious Leader

JUDGES

Important Information

Author: Unknown
Theme: Israel's Compromise and God's Compassion
Category: History

Fascinating Facts

1. Judges is one of four Old Testament books with an unknown author (see also Ruth, Esther, and Job).
2. The time of Judges has been called "the Dark Ages" of Israel's history.
3. Judges contains the oldest known parable in the world (9:8–15).
4. Judges contains the record of the first female leader of Israel, Deborah (ch. 4).
5. Judges records one of the worst stories of depravity found in Scripture (chs. 19–21).
6. Judges tells the story of thirteen different "judges" or "deliverers," four of whom are listed in the "Hall of Faith" in Hebrews 11:32.
7. In Judges, various forms of the word *deliver* occur some forty-eight times.
8. Judges contains one-fourth of the Old Testament references to the "Angel of the Lord," who is undoubtedly Christ Himself.
9. Judges tells of the strongest man recorded in history: Samson.
10. Judges tells of the first Nazirite recorded in history: Samson.

11. Judges contains the first two recorded suicides in Scripture: Gideon's son Abimelech (9:54) and Samson (16:30).

12. Judges records the only instance in Scripture in which someone (Eglon) is called "a very fat man" (3:17).

Quotable Quotes

As we cannot obliterate the tragic record [of Judges], let us be quick to learn from it; for although it is such a pathetic anticlimax to the book of Joshua, it is nevertheless one of the richest books in Scripture in the salutary lessons and examples which it contains. —J. Sidlow Baxter

The book of Judges is perhaps less studied and quoted from than most other historical books of Scripture . . . but even the most neglected parts of the Lord's garden will be found to yield flowers of heavenly fragrance. —Luke H. Wiseman

Judges, more than any other book of the Bible, illustrates the way God works through ordinary people to accomplish His purposes. —Cyril J. Barber

Notable Notes

This seventh book of the Bible records seven distinct cycles, which include: seven apostasies of Israel, their seven subjections to seven heathen nations, seven pleas for rescue to God, and seven deliverances.

Christ Connections

Christ can be found in Judges as:
    Judge and Law Giver
    Deliverer

RUTH

Important Information

Author: Unknown
Theme: God's Plan of Redemption
Category: History

Fascinating Facts

1. The book of Ruth is the only instance in Scripture in which an entire book is devoted to the history of one woman.

2. Ruth is the second of four Old Testament books with an unknown author (see also Judges, Esther, and Job).

3. Ruth is the first of only two books in the Bible named after a woman (see also Esther).

4. Ruth is one of only four women referred to by name in the genealogy of Jesus, as recorded in Matthew 1.

5. Ruth contains the second recorded conversion of a Gentile in Scripture (the first was Rahab's; see Josh. 2).

6. The book of Ruth gives us an illustration of the family marriage duty/custom of that day (Deut. 25:5–10).

7. The book of Ruth begins with a series of funerals and ends with a wedding. It opens with a famine and closes with a family.

8. The name of David is mentioned for the first time in Scripture, in Ruth 4:17.

9. The Hebrew word *ga'al*, translated "redeem" and "redeemer," is found thirteen times in this book.

10. The book of Ruth is read annually by orthodox Jews on the Feast of Pentecost, because Ruth's betrothal took place during harvest season when Pentecost is observed.

Quotable Quotes

After reading Judges . . . Ruth is like a lily in a stagnant pond. Here, instead of unfaithfulness, is loyalty; and instead of immorality, is purity. Here, instead of battlefields are harvest fields, and instead of the warrior's shout is the harvester's song. —W. Graham Scroggie

What Venus is to statuary and the Mona Lisa is to paintings, Ruth is to literature. —John MacArthur Jr.

It seems incredible that this beautiful love story could occur during the dark days of the judges, but such is the grace of God. We are living in trying days today; yet God is at work in His world, getting a bride for His Son and accomplishing His eternal purposes. Never permit the bad news of man's sin to rob you of the good news of God's love and grace. —Warren W. Wiersbe

Notable Notes

Dr. Samuel Johnson, the great literary authority of the eighteenth century, once read the story of Ruth to his friends in a London club. After he had finished reading it, his listeners thought it had just recently been written and they were loud in their praises for its simple beauty. Dr. Johnson then informed his listeners, to their surprise, that he had just read the book of Ruth, taken from the book that they all despised: the Bible!

Christ Connections

Christ can be found in Ruth as:

Kinsman Redeemer

Lover

Protector

1 SAMUEL

Important Information

Authors: Samuel, Nathan, and Gad
Theme: The Establishing of the Kingdom of Israel
Category: History

Fascinating Facts

1. 1 Samuel records the name of God as "Lord of Hosts" for the first time in Scripture (1:3). It is the first of 281 Old Testament occurrences.

2. 1 Samuel contains two of seven suicides recorded in Scripture, and the only back-to-back suicides (31:4–5).

3. Samuel was the last judge of the 350-year period of the judges.

4. Samuel anointed Israel's first two kings: Saul (10:1) and David (16:13).

5. 1 Samuel is the first biblical book to use the word *anointed* (2:10), which is the origin of the word *messiah*.

6. 1 Samuel gives us the original title by which the prophets were known: *seer*, meaning "to see" (9:9).

7. 1 Samuel contains the first mention of a school of prophets, which most believe was founded by Samuel (10:5; 19:20).

8. 1 Samuel opens up with the birth of Samuel, Israel's last judge, and closes with the death of Saul, Israel's first king.

9. 1 Samuel contains the only biblical references of the ill-fated name *Ichabod*, which means "Where is the glory?" (4:21; 14:3).

10. The word *prayer* is used over thirty times in this book.

11. One of the greatest examples of friendship found anywhere in Scripture, that of David and Jonathan, is recorded in 1 Samuel 18.

12. 1 Samuel describes the largest man found in Scripture, Goliath, who was at least nine feet nine inches tall (17:4)!

Quotable Quotes

It is astonishing how full this book is of prayer. Indeed, it could be viewed as a treatise on prayer vividly illustrated from life. The very name of Samuel means "asked of God," and it is a monument to a prayer presented and granted. Here we see prayer offered at all times. Therefore, we take the chief message of the book to be the place for, and the power of prayer in all experiences of life. —Robert Lee

For sheer interest, 1 Samuel is unsurpassed. Not only does it record eventful history; it is eventful history interwoven with the biographies of three colorful personalities—Samuel, Saul, and David. —J. Sidlow Baxter

"Behold, I have played the fool." This is the whole story of man. —G. Campbell Morgan

Notable Notes

The story of the witch at En Dor, whom Saul consulted in chapter 28, has intrigued and puzzled students for years. It is the only instance in Scripture in which God allowed the actual spirit of one of His people to ascend out of the earth and to speak "from the dead."

Christ Connections

Christ can be found in 1 Samuel as:

Anointed Prophet and Priest

True Claimant to the Scepter of Judah and Throne of David

2 SAMUEL

Important Information

Authors: Nathan and Gad
Theme: The History of David's Kingdom
Category: History

Fascinating Facts

1. 2 Samuel is devoted almost entirely to the history of David as king.

2. David's name appears 280 times in 2 Samuel and 1,118 times total in Scripture, second only to the name of Jesus.

3. 2 Samuel gives us the first instance in which a ruler was compared to a shepherd (5:2).

4. 2 Samuel contains two notable parables; in particular, Nathan's parable that exposed David's sin (12:1–12; 14:1–20).

5. In 2 Samuel, David claims divine inspiration of his writings (23:2).

6. 2 Samuel is a powerful picture of the New Testament truth stated in James 1:15 about the effects of sin.

7. 2 Samuel records the establishment of Jerusalem as the Holy City of God.

8. While Samuel's name appears at least 130 times in 1 Samuel, it does not appear once in the book of 2 Samuel.

9. The books of 1 and 2 Samuel were originally one single book in the old Hebrew Bible that was simply called the book of Samuel.

10. David, the son of Jesse, is the only person in the Bible to bear that name, which means "beloved."

Quotable Quotes

The story of the second book of Samuel is one of triumph and tragedy, the rise and decline of King David, the triumph of his public life and the tragedy of his private one. —Eric W. Hayden

The book [of 2 Samuel] teaches us first that God's opportunity is created by the attitude of man towards Him; and secondly, that man's opportunity is created by the attitude of God towards him. —G. Campbell Morgan

The Bible never flatters its heroes. . . . As we consider the record of Bible characters, how often we find ourselves looking into a mirror. We are humiliated by the reminder of how many times we have failed. Great has been our stubbornness but greater still has been His faithfulness. Nowhere is this more true than in the story of the life of David. —Alan Redpath

Notable Notes

In 2 Samuel 3:1–5, six of David's sons are named, and each one was born to a different wife! Unlike most of the other future rulers of Israel, David's sins never included idolatry. However, they did include polygamy.

Christ Connections

Christ can be found in 2 Samuel as:
    Son of David
    Greater David

1 KINGS

Important Information

Author: Probably Jeremiah
Theme: Sin Brings Division
Category: History

Fascinating Facts

1. 1 Kings opens and closes with death: it opens with the death of David (2:10) and closes with the death of Ahab (22:37).

2. 1 Kings opens with Israel as one kingdom and closes with Israel as two kingdoms.

3. 1 Kings records the shortest reign of any earthly king, which was seven days for King Zimri (16:15).

4. Solomon was wiser than anyone who has ever lived (4:31). He spoke 3,000 proverbs and wrote 1,005 songs (4:32).

5. 1 Kings contains Scripture's first record of a bodily resurrection from the dead (17:22).

6. The building of the first of three temples is recorded in 1 Kings.

7. Solomon was the foremost polygamist in the Bible, with seven hundred wives and three hundred concubines (11:3).

8. 1 Kings records the first instance of someone kneeling in prayer, Solomon (8:54).

9. The word *king* appears some 250 times in this book.

10. 1 Kings contains the first recorded instances of someone taking hold of the horns of the altar for refuge and protection (1:50; 2:28).

11. Israel's land size was the largest ever during the reign of Solomon (4:24).

12. Two well-known female characters from 1 Kings, Jezebel and the queen of Sheba, are referenced in the New Testament to make important spiritual points (Matt. 12:42; Rev. 2:20).

Quotable Quotes

These books [1 and 2 Kings] present God as sovereign over all man's affairs, God as faithful to His people, and man as responsible for his actions. —Richard I. McNeely

These are the two most important books of history in the world. Every day expeditions are digging up the records of history about which nothing has been written outside the books of the Kings. —Henrietta C. Mears

The best part of a good story is its conclusion. The reason is that a story is like a giant puzzle. Story elements—exciting action, conflicts between characters, lovely landscapes—sketch in "pieces" of the scene. Only at the end, however, when the last "piece" falls into place, does the whole finished picture appear. First Kings provides the preliminary pieces of Israel's life under the monarchy. —Robert L. Hubbard Jr.

Notable Notes

The wealth of King Solomon was staggering. It included billions of dollars in gold, forty thousand horses, fourteen hundred chariots, an extensive fleet of ships, and an ivory throne overlaid in gold and surrounded by twelve statues of lions!

Christ Connections

Christ can be found in 1 Kings as:

The Only Perfect King
Greater Solomon
Builder of God's Temple

2 KINGS

Important Information

Author: Probably Jeremiah
Theme: Sin Brings Discipline
Category: History

Fascinating Facts

1. 2 Kings records the longest reign of any earthly king, fifty-five years for King Manasseh (21:1).

2. 2 Kings references the only naturally bald man in Scripture, Elisha (2:23).

3. 2 Kings records one of only two people in the Bible who did not die, Elijah (2:11; see also Enoch in Gen. 5).

4. 2 Kings records the account of the only woman who ever ruled Judah, a wicked and murderous woman named Athaliah (ch. 11).

5. During the period of 2 Kings, the following prophets all prophesied: Amos, Hosea, Obadiah, Joel, Isaiah, Micah, Nahum, Habakkuk, Zephaniah, and Jeremiah.

6. 2 Kings records two of the three bodily resurrections found in the Old Testament (4:34–35; 13:20–21).

7. Half of 2 Kings deals with the life and ministry of just one man, Elisha the prophet.

8. In 2 Kings, we read that a king "did evil in the sight of the Lord" twenty-one times, and only eight times do we read that any king "did what was right in the sight of the Lord."

9. 2 Kings covers a time period of about 270 years, or more than twice the period of time in 1 Kings.

10. 2 Kings records the two instances in which God parted the waters of the Jordan River.

11. There is not a single instance of failure recorded in the ministry of Elisha.

12. In 2 Kings 19–20, the prophet Isaiah is referred to some thirteen times.

Quotable Quotes

As Elijah's mighty works were very much the glory of the former book, towards the latter end of it, so were Elisha's the glory of this one, towards the beginning of it. These prophets out-shone their princes; and therefore, as far as they go, the history shall be accounted for in them. —Matthew Henry

In the days when Josiah carried out his reformation, the book of the Law was found. Mark the significance of this fact that it had to be found! Moreover, its teaching so astonished Josiah that he halted in the middle of his work to enquire from the prophetess Huldah. The people had so forgotten the law of their God that, when it was found, they were absolutely unfamiliar with it. —G. Campbell Morgan

The second book of Kings has been much more extensively confirmed and illustrated through recent research than any other book of the Old Testament. This is due to the fact that the annals of Assyria and of Babylon, covering the same period of 2 Kings, have been so largely recovered . . . could there be any fuller proof of reliability? —John Urquhart

Notable Notes

When Elijah prepared to depart for heaven in 2 Kings, his servant and succeeding prophet, Elisha, asked that a double portion of his spirit be upon him (2:9). As it turned out, Elisha did indeed perform twice as many miracles as his mentor, Elijah. The only other person in Scripture who did more miracles than Elisha was Jesus!

Christ Connections

Christ can be found in 2 Kings as:

    The Only Perfect King
    Man of God
    Word of God

1 CHRONICLES

Important Information

Author: Ezra
Theme: A Spiritual Perspective
Category: History

Fascinating Facts

1. 1 Chronicles contains the shortest verse in the Old Testament (1:25) and one of the strangest verses (26:18).

2. 1 and 2 Chronicles make more mention of nonbiblical books (twelve) than any other books in the Bible (i.e., book of Nathan, book of Gad).

3. 1 and 2 Chronicles review the history of man from Adam to Cyrus, covering a period of about 3,500 years.

4. 1 Chronicles contains the only recorded instance of someone sitting down while praying (17:16).

5. 1 Chronicles contains far more listings of genealogies than are found in any other book of the Bible.

6. 1 Chronicles 21:1 refers to Satan by name for the first time in Scripture.

7. 1 Chronicles is not directly quoted anywhere in the New Testament.

8. The first nine chapters of 1 Chronicles are the most extensive listings of genealogies in the Bible.

9. "Seek the Lord" is a recurring statement and theme in 1 Chronicles.

10. The name David is recorded more than 180 times in this book.

Quotable Quotes

The history of the chosen people is related afresh in a new manner, and from a new standpoint. While the same events are recorded, they are viewed from a different standpoint. In Samuel and Kings we have the facts of history; here we have the divine words and thoughts about these facts. In the former books they are regarded from a man's standpoint; here they are viewed from a divine standpoint. —E. W. Bullinger

The book of Chronicles is occupied from beginning to end with magnifying God, and giving Him His right place in Israel. —Robert Lee

First impressions can be misleading. In the case of Chronicles they usually are. . . . What seems at a casual glance to be a re-telling of Samuel/Kings turns out to be something more than a mere repeat. . . . Its object is the fostering of a right relationship between God and His people. —Michael Wilcox

Notable Notes

The familiar story of David numbering the tribes and bringing grave consequences upon the people as a result of his sin is recorded in chapter 21. The threshing floor of Ornan that David bought and where he offered a sacrifice was located on Mount Moriah. This was the same place where Abraham offered up his son Isaac (Gen. 22:2), and where Solomon later built the temple (2 Chron. 3:1). The Jews believe that the altar of burnt offering in the temple at Jerusalem was situated on the exact site of the altar on which Abraham intended to sacrifice Isaac. Today a Muslim mosque, the Dome of the Rock in Jerusalem, is situated on this site.

Christ Connections

Christ can be found in 1 Chronicles as:

The Reigning King

2 CHRONICLES

Important Information

Author: Ezra
Theme: God Keeps His Word
Category: History

Fascinating Facts

1. 2 Chronicles records the largest army actually ever assembled: one million soldiers (14:9).

2. 2 Chronicles records the youngest king who ever ruled, Joash, who was only seven years old (24:1).

3. 1 and 2 Chronicles heavily emphasize the various elements of worship: the temple, its services, priests, Levites, singers, musicians, and so on.

4. 2 Chronicles opens with the building of the first temple and closes with the decree to rebuild the second temple.

5. 2 Chronicles is not directly quoted anywhere in the New Testament.

6. 2 Chronicles 33 records the conversion of Israel's most wicked king, Manasseh.

7. 2 Chronicles is the last book of the Hebrew Bible.

8. 2 Chronicles ends with Judah going into their Babylonian captivity. After their restoration from that captivity, Judah never worshiped idols again!

9. The closing verses of 2 Chronicles (36:22–23) are also the opening verses of Ezra (1:1–3).

10. In 2 Chronicles, the word *house*, referring to the house of the Lord, is mentioned nearly 150 times.

Quotable Quotes

1 and 2 Chronicles are the "epitome of the Old Testament." —Jerome

Put all this together, and the truth of the Word of God will appear, those who honor Me I will honor, but those who despise Me shall be lightly esteemed. —Matthew Henry

The message of Chronicles is "messianic"; that is, it looks forward to the coming King who will rule over God's people forever. . . . In the New Testament, we learn that this King's name is Jesus. —John Sailhamer

Notable Notes

Second Chronicles 32 records the story of Hezekiah's tunnel. The king wanted to have water provisions available for the city in the case of an outside siege or attack. This 1,700-foot-long tunnel brought water from the Gihon Spring in the Kidron Valley to Jerusalem. In 1880 a young boy discovered the old tunnel while he was playing in the water. The tunnel still functions today, and if you visit Jerusalem, you can walk inside of it.

Christ Connections

Christ can be found in 2 Chronicles as:

The Perfect King

Priest

Prophet

EZRA

Important Information

Author: Ezra
Theme: The Word of the Lord
Category: History

Fascinating Facts

1. The book of Ezra records no miracles.

2. Ezra was one of the last Old Testament authors.

3. Ezra is one of two books in the Bible that carries a significant amount of original material in Aramaic (see also Daniel).

4. The book of Ezra records the building of the second temple of God in Jerusalem.

5. The book of Ezra is never quoted anywhere in the New Testament.

6. Ezra records the first two of three returns of Jewish exiles from Babylon to Jerusalem.

7. Ezra is the only scribe to author a book of the Bible.

8. Ezra is the only book that begins with virtually the same final words of another book (compare 2 Chron. 36:22–23 with Ezra 1:1–3).

9. Ezra has the unusual feature of having an almost sixty-year break between its two main divisions (chs. 1–6; 7–10).

10. Ezra 7:21 contains all of the letters of the alphabet except the letter *j*.

11. The name of Jerusalem appears some forty-seven times in this book.

12. Jewish tradition and the Talmud claim that Ezra was responsible for helping to put the Old Testament canon together.

Quotable Quotes

That the book of Ezra contains much-needed truth for the present time is my firm belief. —H. A. Ironside

The book of Ezra is a work of so simple a character as scarcely to require an "introduction." It is a plain and straightforward account of one of the most important events in Jewish history—

the return of the people of God from the Babylonian captivity. . . . No book of Scripture has fewer difficulties or obscurities. There is no miracle recorded in it, hence its historical truth is admitted almost universally. —*The Pulpit Commentary*

Ezra is often called "the Father of Judaism." . . . The rabbinic tradition praised Ezra highly; he is mentioned often in the Talmud. He was considered a man of the Torah, as was Moses. It was observed that if Moses had not preceded him, Ezra would have received the Torah straight from Yahweh. Further, whereas God had given the Torah to the people through Moses, at a later time, when the Torah was largely forgotten, Ezra acted to reestablish it in the Jewish community. —Fredrick Carlson Holmgren

Notable Notes

Ezra has been called, next to Moses, "The Second Lawgiver," because he brought the Law of Moses back to the people. In addition, the book of Ezra has been called "The Second Great Exodus." Just as in the book of Exodus Israel left slavery in Egypt to go and worship the Lord in their new homeland, so, too, in the book of Ezra God's people left captivity in Babylon to go and worship the Lord in their homeland.

Christ Connections

Christ can be found in Ezra as:
    Faithful Scribe
    Builder and Restorer of the Church

NEHEMIAH

Important Information

Author: Ezra and/or Nehemiah
Themes: Prayer and Perseverance
Category: History

Fascinating Facts

1. Nehemiah contains the longest prayer in the Old Testament (9:5–38).
2. Nehemiah begins and ends with prayer and throughout the book is filled with twelve instances of prayers.
3. Chronologically, Nehemiah is the last historical book of the Old Testament.
4. Nehemiah was the most autobiographical of the historical writers.
5. Nehemiah's life is one of the very best examples of spiritual leadership in the Bible.
6. The decree of King Artaxerxes in Nehemiah 2:8 is the beginning of Daniel's famous seventy weeks (Dan. 9:25–27).
7. The person of Nehemiah is not mentioned anywhere else in Scripture outside of this book.
8. Nehemiah is never quoted anywhere in the New Testament.
9. The prophet Malachi was a contemporary of Nehemiah's and helped to rebuke the sins of the people in Jerusalem.
10. Nehemiah prayed and fasted for four months and then led in the difficult task of rebuilding the wall around Jerusalem in only fifty-two days (6:15)!
11. The word *build* is used nearly two dozen times in this book.

Quotable Quotes

Let us learn this lesson from Nehemiah: you never lighten the load unless you first have felt the pressure in your own soul. You are never used of God to bring blessing until God has opened your eyes and made you see things as they really are. There is no other preparation for Christian work than that. Nehemiah was called to build the wall, but first he had to weep over the ruins. —Alan Redpath

[Nehemiah's] achievements were as outstanding as his gifts. He rebuilt the ruined wall of Jerusalem in fifty-two days, when nobody else thought it could be rebuilt at all. . . . He takes his place, by right, as it seems to me, with the greatest leaders of God's people in the Bible story—with Moses and David and Paul. Nehemiah was truly a marvelous man. —J. I. Packer

May God, who raised up Nehemiah, raise up many like him in our day. The church has seldom been in greater need of such leaders. —James Montgomery Boice

Nehemiah, although an ordinary man underneath, emerges as one of the most significant leaders in history. He was highly motivated to do a job for God that had many difficult circumstances surrounding it. —Charles R. Swindoll

Notable Notes

In the book of Joshua, Joshua was called by the Lord to bring down a wall around Jericho. In the book of Nehemiah, Nehemiah was called by the Lord to raise up a wall around Jerusalem. Both were godly men and godly leaders, but were called to opposite tasks.

Christ Connections

Christ can be found in Nehemiah as:
  Rebuilder of the Broken Walls
  Governor of the Church
  Restorer and Protector

ESTHER

Important Information

Author: Unknown
Theme: The Providence of God
Category: History

Fascinating Facts

1. Esther is the third of four Old Testament books whose author is unknown (see also Judges, Ruth, and Job).

2. Esther is the second of only two books in the Bible named after a woman (see also Ruth).

3. Esther is the first of only two books in the Bible that does not mention God by name or the title of "Lord" (see also Song of Solomon).

4. Esther is the one book in the Bible devoted entirely to the providence of God.

5. Esther is the only book that gives us the origin of the Feast of Purim (ch. 9), or that even mentions this festival.

6. Esther contains the longest single verse in the Bible, ninety words (8:9).

7. The book of Esther is never quoted or alluded to in the New Testament.

8. Esther's story takes place in Persia and gives us a window into the customs and culture of the Persian empire.

9. The book of Esther contains no recorded miracles and yet the entire story, knit together, is a very miraculous story.

10. The book of Esther is a clear illustration of God's promise made to Abraham and his descendants in Genesis 12:3, "I will bless those who bless you, and I will curse him who curses you."

11. Reference to "the Jews" is made forty-three times in this book.

Quotable Quotes

An alternative title for the book of Esther might well be "The Romance of Providence," for providence might be said to be the key word by which to remember the main theme and teaching. God is certainly out of sight, hidden, unrecognized, but He is all the time at work, completing His plan and purpose for individuals, nations, and the universe. —A. T. Pierson

Esther could be compared to a chess game. God and Satan (as invisible players) moved real kings, queens, and nobles. When Satan put Haman into place, it was as if he announced "Check." God then positioned Esther and Mordecai in order to put Satan into "Checkmate!" —John MacArthur Jr.

If the name of God is not here, His finger is. —Matthew Henry

Tucked away in the Bible in an obscure corner of the Old Testament is the little book of Esther. . . . It is a gripping tale, but one might rather expect to find it in the pages of *Reader's Digest* than the Bible. —Ray C. Stedman

Notable Notes

When the book of Esther is read every year at the Feast of Purim, and the name of Haman is read, the people respond by stomping their feet on the floor and saying, "Let his name be blotted out! The name of the wicked will rot!" Oftentimes the children will have special Purim rattles and will shake them every time they hear Haman's name read. Then, at the end of the reading, the people say, "Cursed be Haman; blessed be Mordecai!"

Christ Connections

Christ can be found in Esther as:

Our Mordecai

Our Advocate

JOB

Important Information

Author: Unknown
Themes: Man's Suffering, God's Sovereignty
Category: Poetry/Wisdom

Fascinating Facts

1. Job is considered by many to be the oldest book of the Bible and, very possibly, the oldest book in the world.
2. Job is the fourth of four Old Testament books in which its author is unknown (see also Judges, Ruth, and Esther).

3. The book of Job refers to Satan by name more times than any other book in the Bible (fourteen times).

4. The book of Job uses the name of "Almighty" (Shaddai) for God more times than any other book in the Bible (thirty-one times).

5. Job is the only book in the Bible that makes references to what many believe were the dinosaurs, *behemoth* and *leviathan* (40:15; 41:1).

6. Job contains the only recorded conversation in Scripture between God and Satan in heaven (1:6–12; 2:1–6).

7. Job is the one book in the Bible largely devoted to the subject of human suffering.

8. Job contains far more archaic language than any other book in the Bible, because it is an ancient book.

9. Sixteen times in this book, Job asks God the question, "Why?"

10. In Job 38–41, God confronts Job with at least seventy-five questions of His own!

11. The book of Job is directly quoted twice in the New Testament (Rom. 11:35; 1 Cor. 3:19), and both Ezekiel (14:14) and James (5:11) refer to the person of Job.

12. The final five chapters of Job give us a significant overview of God's creation.

Quotable Quotes

Though the book is ancient, its insights are remarkably modern, and its message is needed more today than ever before. —Henry M. Morris

[Job is] more magnificent and sublime than any other book of Scripture. —Martin Luther

I call this book, apart from all theories about it, one of the grandest things ever written with pen. . . . There is nothing

written, I think, in the Bible or out of it, of equal literary merit.
—Thomas Carlyle

The book of Job is perhaps the greatest masterpiece of the
human mind. —Victor Hugo

Notable Notes

The book of Job contains an intriguing recurrence of the numbers
seven and three: seven sons and three daughters; seven thousand
sheep and three thousand camels; three friends who sat with Job
for seven days; and so on.

Christ Connections

Christ can be found in Job as:
   Ever-Living Redeemer

PSALMS

Important Information

Author: David and Others
Theme: Praise and Worship
Category: Poetry/Wisdom

Fascinating Facts

1. Psalms is the longest book in the Bible.
2. Psalms contains the longest chapter (119) and the shortest
   chapter (117) in the Bible.

3. Psalms is the most quoted Old Testament book in the New Testament, and Psalm 110:1 is the most quoted Old Testament verse in the New Testament.

4. Psalm 117 is the middle chapter of the Bible (out of 1,189 total).

5. Psalms is the most Messianic of the Old Testament books.

6. Jesus quoted from Psalms at the beginning and at the end of His ministry (John 2:17; Luke 23:46).

7. Almost every psalm contains some note of praise to God.

8. Psalm 23 is one of the most familiar, best-known, and well-loved passages of Scripture.

9. No other book of the Bible is so filled with devotional material and expressions as Psalms.

10. Every great doctrine in the Bible is taught, expressed, or implied in Psalms.

11. One hundred of the 150 psalms identify the author's name.

12. Of the 150 psalms in this book, about half identify David as the writer.

13. Every attribute or characteristic of God's divine nature is found in the Psalms.

14. The word *praise* is used over 175 times throughout Psalms.

15. The book of Psalms is the best example in the Bible of the nature of Hebrew poetry.

16. In Psalms, the word *salvation* is found over sixty times, more than twice that of any other book in the Bible.

17. Psalms is the only book in the Bible that begins with the word *blessed*.

18. Psalms has more authors than any other book in the Bible.

19. Psalms is the only book of the Bible quoted by Satan (in Matt. 4:6 Satan quotes Ps. 91:11–12).

Quotable Quotes

In this book of Psalms the tempted and the tested gain fortitude from pilgrims of yesterday, whose feet have bled along the same thorny pathway. —J. Sidlow Baxter

Although all Scripture breathes the grace of God, yet sweet beyond all others is the book of Psalms. History instructs, the Law teaches, Prophecy announces, rebukes, chastens, Morality persuades; but in the book of Psalms we have the fruit of all these, and a kind of medicine for the salvation of men. —Ambrose of Milan

Moses gave to the Israelites the five books of the Law; and David gave them the five books of the Psalms. —ancient Jewish statement

He that would be wise, let him read the Proverbs; he that would be holy, let him read the Psalms. —R. Steele

Notable Notes

C. H. Spurgeon's greatest written work was undoubtedly *The Treasury of David*, his extensive commentary on the book of Psalms, which took him over twenty years to research and write. It sold over 148,000 copies while Spurgeon was still alive! After completing it, Spurgeon said, "A tinge of sadness is on my spirit as I quit *The Treasury of David*, never to find on this earth a richer storehouse. . . . Blessed have been the days spent in meditating, mourning, hoping, believing, and exulting with David."

Christ Connections

Christ can be found in Psalms as:

   Our Shepherd

   All in All

   Beloved of God

   Our Rock and Fortress

PROVERBS

Important Information

Author: Solomon
Theme: The Wisdom of God
Category: Poetry/Wisdom

Fascinating Facts

1. Proverbs is one of three books written by Solomon, whom the Bible calls the wisest man to ever live (1 Kings 3:12).

2. The author of Proverbs, Solomon, wrote 3,000 proverbs and compiled 1,005 songs (1 Kings 4:32).

3. Proverbs contains the longest introduction of any Old Testament book.

4. In Proverbs, the words *wise* and *wisdom* are used at least 125 times.

5. There are at least eighteen references in Proverbs to "the fear of the LORD," which is the beginning of wisdom (9:10).

6. In the New Testament, Proverbs is quoted more than twenty times.

7. Fewer than eight hundred of Solomon's three thousand proverbs are found in this book.

8. Proverbs is one of just a few books in Scripture that clearly describes its purpose (1:2–6).

9. The title of "Lord" (Jehovah) is never used in any of Solomon's three books, though "God" is used over eight times in this book.

10. Proverbs is perhaps the most practical book in the Bible for everyday living, touching on nearly one hundred topics.

11. Proverbs, more than any other book in the Bible, addresses youth with instruction and direction.

12. Proverbs contains the most graphic and comprehensive description of the ill effects of alcohol found anywhere in Scripture (23:29–35).

Quotable Quotes

The book of Proverbs is about godly wisdom, how to get it, and how to use it. It's about priorities and principles, not get-rich-quick schemes or success formulas. It tells you, not how to make a living, but how to be skillful in the lost art of making a life. —Warren W. Wiersbe

A proverb is a wise saying in which a few words are chosen instead of many, with a design to condense wisdom into a brief form both to aid memory and stimulate study. . . . Only profound meditation will reveal what is hidden in these moral and spiritual maxims. —A. T. Pierson

The book of Proverbs is the kind of biblical fare you should indulge in often, but not in large doses. The "stuff" of Proverbs has already been distilled so that its advice comes to us in highly concentrated form. These sage tidbits have been boiled down, trimmed, honed, polished, and sharpened to where a little goes a long way. —Robert L. Alden

Notable Notes

It has been pointed out in Jewish thinking that Solomon wrote three books at three different points in his life. He wrote Song of Solomon as a young man in love. Then he wrote the book of Proverbs as a middle-aged man in wisdom. Finally, he wrote Ecclesiastes as an older man in his later years after learning many of life's lessons the hard way.

Christ Connections

Christ can be found in Proverbs as:

Wisdom of God

ECCLESIASTES

Important Information

Author: Solomon
Theme: The Meaning of Life
Category: Poetry/Wisdom

Fascinating Facts

1. Ecclesiastes is one of three books written by Solomon, the wisest and wealthiest man who ever lived (see also Proverbs and Song of Solomon).

2. Ecclesiastes is the most philosophical of all the books in the Bible.

3. Ecclesiastes is the only book aimed directly at the question of the meaning of life.

4. In Ecclesiastes, the word *vanity* is found thirty-seven times.

5. In Ecclesiastes, the phrase "under the sun" appears twenty-nine times.

6. Ecclesiastes contains virtually no history and no significant stories or parables.

7. Ecclesiastes is more pessimistic in perspective than any other book in the Bible.

8. Ecclesiastes contains the most picturesque description of old age in Scripture (12:1–7).

9. Ecclesiastes contains a remarkable number of scientifically accurate statements.

10. The word *wisdom* is used twenty-eight times in this book.

Quotable Quotes

It is the message that everything on earth, even at its best, is fleeting and unsatisfying, and that the heart of man was made for God and will not find rest and satisfaction till it finds realization in Him who is changeless, absolute, and permanent. —Merrill F. Unger

You do not have to go outside the Bible to find the merely human philosophy of life. God has given us the book of Ecclesiastes, the record of all that human thinking and natural religion has ever been able to discover concerning the meaning and goal of life. —Henrietta Mears

Whether prose or verse, I know nothing grander in its impassioned survey of mortal pain and pleasure, its estimate of failure and success; none of more notable sadness; no poem working more indomitably for spiritual illumination. —Ray C. Stedman

Notable Notes

Ecclesiastes is a part of the Old Testament books of the Megilloth, or "scrolls," which includes Ruth, Esther, Song of Solomon, and Lamentations. These books were read both publicly and privately at the various Jewish feasts. Publicly, the rabbis would read from these five books in the synagogue on five special occasions during the year: Ruth was read at Pentecost, Esther at Purim, Ecclesiastes at Tabernacles, Song of Solomon at Passover, and Lamentations in remembrance of Nebuchadnezzar's destruction of Jerusalem.

Christ Connections

Christ can be found in Ecclesiastes as:

Wisdom of God

Preacher

Son of David

King of Jerusalem

SONG OF SOLOMON

Important Information

Author: Solomon
Theme: Marital Love
Category: Poetry/Wisdom

Fascinating Facts

1. The Song of Solomon is the only book of the Bible that is completely devoted to the subject of marital love.

2. Song of Solomon is the second of only two books in the Bible that does not mention God by name or use the title of "Lord" (see also Esther).

3. The Song of Solomon is never quoted or alluded to in the New Testament, nor is it quoted in the other books of the Old Testament.

4. Song of Solomon is one of three books written by Solomon, the wisest and wealthiest man who ever lived (see also Proverbs and Ecclesiastes).

5. The Song of Solomon refers to twenty-one different varieties of plants, fifteen species of animals, and fifteen geographic locations.

6. The Song of Solomon is one of two books in Scripture that has routinely been labeled by nonbelievers as fictional and not factual (see also Jonah).

7. The Song of Solomon was one of the most challenged books for inclusion into the Old Testament canon of Scripture.

8. The Song of Solomon records nearly fifty words that are not found anywhere else in Scripture.

9. The Song of Solomon has thirty-two occurrences of the word *beloved*.

10. The Song of Solomon was sometimes referred to as the "Canticles," which is the Latin word for "songs."

Quotable Quotes

The Song occupies a sacred enclosure into which none may enter unprepared . . . the holy of holies, before which the veil still hangs to many an untaught believer. —C. H. Spurgeon

Solomon calls this book "the Song of Songs." In the temple there was a holy of holies; Jesus stands among men as the King of kings; in the universe there is a heaven of heavens. And among the poetical books of the Word of God there is a song of songs. —John Phillips

It is well that Ecclesiastes is followed by the Song of Solomon, for the one is the complement of the other. In Ecclesiastes we learn that without Christ we cannot be satisfied, even if we possess the whole world—the heart is too large for the object. In the Song of Solomon we learn that if we turn from the world and set our affections on Christ, we cannot fathom the infinite preciousness of His love—the Object is too large for the heart. —Robert Lee

Notable Notes

The Song of Solomon has been the favorite book of the Bible with some of the most famous men of God. That list includes C. H. Spurgeon, D. L. Moody, and Hudson Taylor.

Christ Connections

Christ can be found in Song of Solomon as:

Perfect Lover and Bridegroom

King of Peace

ISAIAH

Important Information

Author: Isaiah
Theme: The Salvation of God
Category: Major Prophet

Fascinating Facts

1. The book of Isaiah is a picture of the entire Bible in miniature form, containing sixty-six chapters (compare with sixty-six books of the Bible) and with two main sections, one of thirty-nine chapters and one of twenty-seven chapters (compare with thirty-nine books of the Old Testament and twenty-seven books of the New Testament).

2. The reference to God as the "Holy One of Israel" is used over thirty times in the book of Isaiah.

3. Isaiah contains the longest name or word found in Scripture, the name belonging to the son of Isaiah, Mahershalalhashbaz (8:1).

4. Isaiah is the most-quoted Old Testament prophet in the New Testament.

5. The prophet Isaiah is mentioned by name twenty-one times in the New Testament.

6. Isaiah contains the only Old Testament prophecy of the virgin birth of Christ (7:14).

7. Isaiah contains more references to the coming Savior than any other book of the Bible.

8. Isaiah was married to a woman who also prophesied (8:3).

9. Isaiah was the most evangelical of all the prophets.

10. The name Isaiah means "Salvation of God," and the word *salvation* is found nearly thirty times in the book, second only to the book of Psalms.

11. Isaiah is the longest prophetic book of the Old Testament.

12. Isaiah presents more insights into the nature of God than any other book of the Old Testament.

13. When Jesus began His public ministry, He quoted from chapter sixty-one of Isaiah in fulfillment of that prophecy (Luke 4:18).

14. In Isaiah, the phrase "For the mouth of the Lord has spoken it" is found three times (and nowhere else) in Scripture.

15. Isaiah prophesied during the reigns of five kings of Judah: Uzziah, Jotham, Ahaz, Hezekiah, and Manasseh.

16. Isaiah is one of two Old Testament books (see also Ezekiel) that records the origin of Satan's fall (14:12–14).

17. Isaiah 53, the key chapter in this book, is quoted or alluded to more than eighty-five times in the New Testament.

18. Isaiah contains the only reference in Scripture in which the "seraphim" angels are mentioned specifically by name (6:2, 6).

19. There are seven things that are called "everlasting" in Isaiah: salvation, light, joy, strength, kindness, covenant, and judgment.

20. Only in Isaiah is Satan called "Lucifer," which means "bright one" or "bearer of light" (14:12).

21. Zion is mentioned more times in Isaiah than in any other book of the Bible.

Quotable Quotes

Isaiah was a princely character, a wise and patriotic statesman, a gifted poet, and a divinely inspired prophet. He may not have been of noble birth, as some have supposed; but his heroic courage, his spotless purity, his sympathy with the poor, his hatred of sham and pretense, his exalted ideas and his unfailing faith in God gave him a more royal rank than any kingly pedigree could have conferred. —Charles R. Erdman

Never perhaps has there been another prophet like Isaiah, who stood with his head in the clouds and his feet on the solid earth, with his heart in the things of eternity and his mouth and hands in the things of time, with his spirit in the eternal counsel of God and his body in the very definite moment of history. Truly, Isaiah may be called the dean of prophets. —Jan Valeton the Younger

Hardly anyone would question the claim that Isaiah is a prince among prophets. His eloquence is very evident. His major theme is Yahweh's sovereignty. He has at his command a vocabulary richer than that of any prophet, even more comprehensive than that of the book of Psalms. —H. C. Leupold

Notable Notes

Tradition says that Isaiah was martyred by being placed inside of a hollow log and sawn in two. The wicked King Manasseh ordered this because Isaiah spoke against some of the king's acts of idolatry. If this is true, then the author of the book of Hebrews may have had Isaiah in mind in Hebrews 11:37 when he referred to the martyrs of the Christian faith who were "sawn in two."

Christ Connections

Christ can be found in Isaiah as:
    Messiah
    Holy One of Israel

Prince of Peace
Salvation, Righteousness, and Comfort
Judge

JEREMIAH

Important Information

Author: Jeremiah
Theme: The Judgment of Judah
Category: Major Prophet

Fascinating Facts

1. Jeremiah is the only major or minor prophet to author more than one book (see also Lamentations).
2. Jeremiah was the only prophet ever instructed by God not to pray for his own nation (ch. 7).
3. The book of Jeremiah is quoted at least seven different times in the Old and New Testaments.
4. Jeremiah's calling included remaining unmarried (16:2), and he was the only man in the Bible who was told not to marry.
5. Jeremiah makes reference to Babylon (God's instrument of judgment) over 160 times, more than the rest of Scripture combined.
6. Jeremiah was the most despised and persecuted Old Testament prophet.
7. Jeremiah was the only prophet to give us an eyewitness account of Jerusalem's destruction (ch. 39).

8. Jeremiah records more about his own personal life than any other prophet.

9. Jeremiah's life spanned the reigns of at least five kings in Judah: Josiah, Jehoahaz, Jehoiakim, Jehoiachin, and Zedekiah.

10. Jeremiah 52 is almost identical to 2 Kings 24:18–25:30.

11. Jeremiah, like the apostle Paul, was set apart before birth to serve God in a special way (Jer. 1:5; Gal. 1:15).

12. The name of God as "Lord of Hosts" is found some eighty times in this book.

13. *Backsliding* is a key word in Jeremiah, used some thirteen times.

Quotable Quotes

Jeremiah is the most misunderstood of all the great men of history. To be one of the healthiest of men and to be thought morbid, to be one of the strongest and to be thought weak, to be one of the bravest and to be thought faint-hearted, to be a titan and to be thought a pigmy, has been his hard fortune. —Ballantine

The book of Jeremiah is one of outstanding fascination for the Bible student for it clearly reveals the life and character of the writer, the prophet himself. . . . Perhaps in the life of suffering we see in Jeremiah a man most near to the Man of Sorrows, the Lord Jesus Christ Himself. —Eric W. Hayden

Jeremiah was the prophet of Judah's midnight hour. —J. Sidlow Baxter

Notable Notes

No other Old Testament prophet of God probably suffered as much as Jeremiah did during his forty years of ministry. He often found himself standing alone and opposed by people, false prophets, princes, and priests. He was mocked, whipped, accused, threatened, despised, hated, rejected, imprisoned, and cast into a pit. He never appears to have been free from trials and troubles during his ministry. No wonder he is well-remembered as the Weeping Prophet, and as such, was a type of Christ.

Christ Connections

Christ can be found in Jeremiah as:

Righteous Branch

The Lord Our Righteousness

LAMENTATIONS

Important Information

Author: Jeremiah
Theme: Lament over Jerusalem's Destruction
Category: Major Prophet

Fascinating Facts

1. Lamentations is the only book in the Bible filled primarily with laments.

2. Jeremiah was the only prophet to give us an eyewitness account of Jerusalem's destruction.

3. Jeremiah is the only major or minor prophet to author more than one book (Lamentations and Jeremiah).

4. Jeremiah, who wrote this great lament over Jerusalem, is oftentimes referred to as the "Weeping Prophet."

5. Lamentations is perhaps the most heartbreaking of all the books in the Bible, as it records the funeral of the holy city.

6. Lamentations contains five complete poems, one for each chapter, and four of them are acrostics.

7. Lamentations is the only book of the major and minor prophets that does not explicitly identify its author.

8. Every year in Israel, Lamentations is read publicly to recall the destruction of Jerusalem by Nebuchadnezzar and the Babylonians.

9. The actual destruction of Jerusalem, which is lamented in this book, is detailed in four Old Testament passages: 2 Kings 25; 2 Chronicles 36; and Jeremiah 39 and 52.

10. Lamentations, more than any other book of the Bible, reveals the suffering heart of God over sin.

Quotable Quotes

There is nothing like the Lamentations of Jeremiah in the whole world. There has been plenty of sorrow in every age, and in every land, but such another preacher and author, with such a heart for sorrow, has never again been born. —Alexander Whyte

The touching significance of this book lies in the fact that it is the disclosure of the love and sorrow of Jehovah for the very people whom He is chastening—a sorrow wrought by the Spirit in the heart of Jeremiah. —C. I. Scofield

It is a cloudburst of grief, a river of tears, and a sea of sobs.
—J. Sidlow Baxter

It is the wailing wall of the Bible. —J. Vernon McGee

Notable Notes

Below the hill now known as Golgotha and Calvary, just outside of Jerusalem, there is a dark incline known as "Jeremiah's Grotto." This is believed to be the location where the rejected prophet sat and observed the ruins of Jerusalem while writing the book of Lamentations. If this is true, then it is significant that Jeremiah's Grotto is located so close to the spot where the rejected Savior died for the sins of His people some six hundred years later.

Christ Connections

Christ can be found in Lamentations as:

  Man of Sorrows

  Weeping Prophet

EZEKIEL

Important Information

Author: Ezekiel
Theme: The Glory of the Lord
Category: Major Prophet

Fascinating Facts

1. Ezekiel is one of only two people in the Bible who was commanded by God to eat a scroll (John was the other; see Rev. 10:9–10).

2. Ezekiel, more than any other prophet, was called upon by God to act out his divine messages (see, for example, 3:26; 4:9).

3. The book of Ezekiel contains more dates than any other Old Testament prophetic book and is therefore well-documented.

4. The book of Ezekiel contains well over sixty occurrences and/or variations of the phrase "then they will know that I am the LORD."

5. In Ezekiel, the prophet is called "son of man" over ninety times by God, a title that Jesus used for Himself about eighty times in the Gospels.

6. Nothing else is recorded in Scripture about Ezekiel outside of his book.

7. Ezekiel and Daniel were both captives in Babylon together, and Daniel is referred to three times in this book (14:14, 20; 28:3).

8. Ezekiel, more than any other prophet, received his messages in visions.

9. Ezekiel is one of two Old Testament books (see also Isaiah) containing passages that describe the fall of Satan (ch. 28), to which Jesus apparently made reference in Luke 10:18.

10. Ezekiel places great emphasis upon the personal responsibility of sin (18:4, 20–32).

11. In Ezekiel, there are at least twenty-five references to the Holy Spirit.

12. Ezekiel speaks more about Israel's days back in Egypt than any other prophet, and is the only one to speak of Israel's

idolatry in Egypt and how close they were to being judged there (20:8).

13. In Ezekiel, a key phrase is "the glory of the LORD," which is used fourteen times in the first eleven chapters.

14. Ezekiel's ministry opens with a heavenly vision of God and closes with an earthly vision of God.

15. It is stated seven times in the book of Ezekiel that "the hand of the LORD" was upon the prophet.

Quotable Quotes

Ezekiel was a captive and in the land of a stranger. God opened heaven and gave him visions and revelations of His word and will. The hour of greatest need is the hour of Divine Presence, and Divine Strength. In the most hopeless hour of life, in the darkest and dreariest of days, in the loneliest moments of human miseries, God will be at hand to strengthen and to save. —W. G. Heslop

Of all the prophetic books, Ezekiel is the one that has been neglected most. Many persons are repelled by the marvelous vision of the opening chapter and, finding it too difficult to understand, proceed no further; and so they lose the blessing that they would otherwise gain. —H. A. Ironside

The visions of glory Ezekiel had belong to some of the greatest recorded in the Word of God. —Arno C. Gaebelein

Notable Notes

Because Ezekiel was a younger contemporary of the prophet Jeremiah by at least twenty years, he seems to have patterned his ministry style after Jeremiah's or may have even been his disciple. There are several points of Ezekiel's teachings that find their origin in Jeremiah's writings. Ironically though, there is no mention of Jeremiah anywhere in the writing of Ezekiel.

Christ Connections

Christ can be found in Ezekiel as:
> Four-Faced Man
> Son of Man Sent to Rebellious Israel

DANIEL

Important Information

Author: Daniel
Theme: The Sovereignty of God
Category: Major Prophet

Fascinating Facts

1. Daniel is the only Old Testament book that references Gabriel and Michael, the only two holy angels whose names are known to us (8:16; 10:13).

2. Daniel is one of two books in the Bible that carries a significant amount of material in Aramaic, one of the three languages used for writing the Bible (see also Ezra).

3. Daniel never claimed to be a prophet and is nowhere spoken of as such in the Old Testament, yet Jesus called him a prophet (Matt. 24:15).

4. Daniel uses the phrase "Most High" some fourteen times in this book.

5. Daniel records more about the coming antichrist and the tribulation period than any other Old Testament book.

6. No failure on Daniel's part is ever recorded in Scripture.

7. The information contained in nine of Daniel's twelve chapters revolves around various dreams and visions.

8. In Daniel 11, there are more fulfilled prophecies recorded than in any other chapter of the Bible.

9. The book of Daniel contains more fulfilled prophecies than any other book in the Bible.

10. Daniel contains the only occurrences of the word *messiah* in the Old Testament (9:25, 26).

11. Daniel 12:1–4 is one of the most distinct passages of the Old Testament regarding the resurrection.

12. There are a number of miraculous events recorded in Daniel, including visions, interpretation of dreams, and deliverances from death.

13. Daniel spoke and wrote while in exile, as did Ezekiel and John (see Revelation).

14. Daniel's name appears some seventy-five times in this book.

Quotable Quotes

The book of Daniel with its great prophecies, fulfilled and unfulfilled, is one of the most important portions of God's Holy Word. No other book has been so much attacked as this prophetic book. For almost 2,000 years, wicked men, heathen philosophers, and infidels have hammered away against it; but the book of Daniel has proven to be an anvil upon which the critic's hammers have been broken into pieces. —Arno C. Gaebelein

Outstanding among the books of the Old Testament is the book of Daniel . . . a mighty tonic to faith in the absolute sovereignty of God throughout the entire earth. —Lehman Strauss

Daniel's book has a theme of such simplicity that the most brilliant minds in the world have been unable to grasp it. It is just this: God is in charge. No one understood that better than Daniel. Centuries ago he deciphered some strange signs written by an unseen hand. Today, more than any time in history, we should be able to look at our perplexing planet and say that we, too, are able to see the handwriting on the wall. —David Jeremiah

Notable Notes

There are three great "ninth chapters of prayer" in the Old Testament. They include Ezra 9, Nehemiah 9, and Daniel 9. In all three chapters, these men of purity and integrity included themselves in the sins of the people they were praying for, in spite of the fact that no failure is ever recorded about any of them!

Christ Connections

Christ can be found in Daniel as:

    Fourth Man in the Fiery Furnace

    Smitten Stone That Fills the Earth

    King of Kings

HOSEA

Important Information

Author: Hosea
Themes: Israel's Unfaithfulness; God's Faithful Love
Category: Minor Prophet

Fascinating Facts

1. Hosea is one of only two prophets from the northern kingdom of Israel whose writings are found in Scripture (see also Jonah).

2. Hosea is mentioned nowhere else in the Old Testament except in the first two verses of his book, but he is referenced by Paul in the New Testament (Rom. 9:25).

3. More than any other Old Testament prophet, Hosea's personal circumstances mirrored his prophetic message.

4. In Hosea, the prophet makes some 150 statements concerning the sins of Israel.

5. The book of Hosea is quoted or referred to many times in the New Testament.

6. In Hosea, references to harlotry are made some fourteen times, emphasizing Israel's unfaithfulness to the Lord.

7. The book of Hosea contains many metaphors, imageries, and allegories.

8. Hosea probably ministered longer than any other prophet, living well into his nineties (1:1).

9. Hosea was one of the last prophets to bring the Word of the Lord to the northern kingdom before its overthrow.

10. The book of Hosea, along with Deuteronomy and the Gospel of John, ranks as one of the greatest books in the Bible on the love of God.

Quotable Quotes

No other messenger gives so complete an outline of the ways of God with His earthly people as does Hosea, even Daniel not excepted. —H. A. Ironside

The language of the book is plain and frank. There is no way to tone it down. To do so is to lose the force of its message. Bear in mind that it is God's Word. Desperate circumstances call for strong measures. —K. Owen White

Perhaps no book of the Bible reveals more clearly than this of Hosea, the travail of God over His wayward people.... No prophet sounded more profound depths of anguish in proclaiming the warning of impending judgment than Hosea; none pleaded with an apostate people more poignantly. — Herbert F. Stevenson

Notable Notes

Hosea's marriage to a prostitute named Gomer has been one of the most debated events recorded in Scripture. Some believe that the circumstances were merely allegorical and did not actually take place. Others believe that the two were married and that Gomer became a prostitute only after her marriage to Hosea. Still others believe that Hosea married Gomer not realizing she already was a prostitute. Finally, there are those who argue that Hosea knowingly married Gomer the harlot in obedience to God's direct command, to illustrate the unfaithfulness of Israel as a nation and its sin against God.

Christ Connections

Christ can be found in Hosea as:

Patient Bridegroom

Healer of the Backslider

JOEL

Important Information

Author: Joel
Theme: The Day of the Lord
Category: Minor Prophet

Fascinating Facts

1. It is believed that Joel was the first prophet, major or minor, to write his words.

2. Joel is one of two books in the minor prophets that deals almost exclusively with the coming Day of the Lord (see also Zephaniah).

3. Joel is quoted by Peter during the apostle's famous sermon on the day of Pentecost (Acts 2:16–21).

4. In the book of Joel, disaster is a recurring theme: locusts, famine, fire, and so on.

5. In Joel, while the warning of judgment for sin is clear, there is no mention of any specific sins.

6. Joel gives us the grandest description in all of literature of a locust invasion.

7. Joel gives us the first reference in Scripture to the outpouring of the Holy Spirit upon all flesh (2:28–29).

8. In Joel, the range of prophecies extend from the prophet's own day until the end of time.

9. In Joel, the phrase "Day of the Lord" is used five times, more often than in any other book of the Bible.

10. Joel makes many references to nature and agriculture.

Quotable Quotes

It seems strange that so few of God's people read and prayerfully study these great prophetic visions. Of all generations we are the most privileged living in these significant days, standing on the threshold of the fulfillment of these predictions. We behold in our day how everything is shaping for the great events with which this present age will close. The study of the sublime, God-breathed utterances of Joel is indeed of great value and help to those who truly wait for His Son from heaven. —Arno C. Gaebelein

As we meditate on this marvelous disclosure in God's Word, we are driven to the question, How far off can it be? Not very far! —Charles L. Feinberg

Joel, like most of the Old Testament prophets, consists largely of vivid poetry. . . . Joel moves his readers from horror and hopelessness to mourning and repentance, dread and awe, joy and assurance, hope and expectation. . . . Obviously one needs to approach the book with imagination and sensitivity for its poetic features. —Thomas J. Finley

Notable Notes

The book of Joel presents a literal and devastating swarm of locusts with prophetic implications. In doing so, Joel bridges the book of Exodus, with its literal swarm of locusts that came in the form of the eighth plague from God against the Egyptians (Exod. 10), and the book of Revelation, with its prophetic description of demonic "locust-like" creatures that will torment mankind for five months during the tribulation period (Rev. 9).

Christ Connections

Christ can be found in Joel as:

> Baptizer with the Holy Spirit
>
> Deliverer
>
> Judge

AMOS

Important Information

Author: Amos
Theme: A Coming Judgment for Sin
Category: Minor Prophet

Fascinating Facts

1. Amos carries one of the clearest examples of the constraint of the divine calling to be found anywhere in Scripture (7:14–15).

2. Amos is the only Old Testament prophet who was from one portion of the divided kingdom and was called to prophesy to the other portion.

3. The book of Amos is one of the clearest and most articulate cries for justice and righteousness in all of the Bible.

4. Amos makes many references and allusions to previous history and to the Pentateuch.

5. The only Old Testament occurrences of the name Amos are found here in his book.

6. Amos, a sheepherder and fruit grower by trade, makes many references to nature and the wilderness (such as 3:4–5; 5:8).

7. Amos 9 contains some of the greatest prophecies of Israel's future restoration found anywhere in the Bible.

8. Amos was the only prophet to state his occupation before asserting his divine calling (7:14).

9. Amos's familiar statement, "for three transgressions . . . and for four," is repeated seven times in this book.

10. Like many of the unschooled New Testament disciples (Acts 4:13), Amos was called by God into full-time ministry without any formal training.

11. Amos is quoted in the New Testament books of Matthew, Acts, and Romans.

Quotable Quotes

It is ever God's way to prepare His servants in secret for the work they are afterwards to accomplish in public. Moses at the backside of the desert; Gideon on the threshing floor; David with his "few sheep" out upon the hillside; Daniel's refusing to be defiled with the king's meat; John the Baptist in the desert; Peter in his fishing boat; Paul in Arabia; and Amos following the flock and herding the cattle in the wilderness of Tekoa—all alike attest this fact. It is important to observe that only he who has thus learned of God in the school of obscurity is likely to shine in the blaze of publicity. —H. A. Ironside

From the obscurity of a shepherd's role Amos stepped out for a few brief moments upon the stage of history, to go down in its annals as one of its first and great reformers. —Homer Hailey

The book of Amos is one of the most readable, relevant, and moving portions of the Word of God. But in much of church history (until very recent times) little or no attention has been paid to it. Why? It is because the book speaks so powerfully against social injustices and religious formalism, and many who would otherwise read the book have been implicated in such sins and are condemned by it. —James Montgomery Boice

Notable Notes

In the very first verse of Amos's book, the prophet makes reference to an earthquake that took place two years later. That earthquake must have been of considerable magnitude and consequence, because the prophet Zechariah refers to it again some 250 years later (Zech. 14:5). The Jewish historian Josephus also referred to it in his writings (*Antiquities*), attributing the cause of the quake to God as a punishment for King Uzziah's usurpation of the temple and priesthood (2 Chron. 26:16).

Christ Connections

Christ can be found in Amos as:
  Burden-Bearer
  Heavenly Bridegroom
  Judge

OBADIAH

Important Information

Author: Obadiah
Theme: The Judgment of Edom
Category: Minor Prophet

Fascinating Facts

1. Obadiah is the shortest and smallest book in the Old Testament, containing just twenty-one verses.

2. Obadiah is never quoted or alluded to in the New Testament.

3. Obadiah is a book with just one theme: the destruction of Edom.

4. The only biblical reference to the prophet Obadiah is found here in the very beginning of this book (v. 1).

5. Obadiah was the first prophet to mention the Day of the Lord (v. 15).

6. Obadiah is the only book in the Old Testament with just a single chapter.

7. Obadiah was one of the earliest of the writing prophets.

8. There are at least a dozen other men named Obadiah in the Old Testament, but apparently none of them are this prophet (v. 1).

9. The words *Esau* and *Edom* are found nine times in this book.

10. Obadiah illustrates the biblical truth that "pride goes before destruction" (Prov. 16:18).

Quotable Quotes

This is the shortest of all the books of the Old Testament, the least of those tribes, and yet it is not to be passed by or thought meanly of, for this penny has Caesar's image and superscription upon it; it is stamped with a divine authority. —Matthew Henry

The prophecy of Obadiah is a classic warning against anti-Semitism. The nation that curses and persecutes the Jew will inevitably reap what it sows. The nation that harbors and protects the Jew will surely enjoy the blessing of God. —John Phillips

One clear light ever burns ahead, leading us upward and onward; it is perfectly expressed in the closing words of Obadiah, "The kingdom shall be the Lord's." —G. Campbell Morgan

Notable Notes

Obadiah's prophecy was the end result of an ongoing feud that began hundreds of years before that time, in the womb of Isaac's wife Rebekah (Gen. 25:20–23). She gave birth to twin boys, Esau and Jacob, whose descendants were bitter rivals throughout the years. Edom, the descendants of Esau, acted very cruelly toward their brethren Israel (Jacob) and it led to their total extinction as a race of people. As God foretold to Abraham, "I will bless those who bless you, and I will curse him who curses you" (Gen. 12:3).

Christ Connections

Christ can be found in Obadiah as:

Savior

Judge

Executor of Divine Retribution

JONAH

Important Information

Author: Jonah
Theme: God's Universal Concern for the Lost
Category: Minor Prophet

Fascinating Facts

1. Jonah is one of only two books in the Bible that ends with a question mark (see also Nahum).

2. Jonah was the only prophet whose ministry was exclusively to the Gentiles.

3. Jonah is the only prophet whose experience Jesus likened to Himself (Matt. 12:40).

4. Jonah was the only prophet who tried to run away from God's commission.

5. Jonah was the only prophet who tried to conceal his message.

6. More than any other Old Testament book, Jonah demonstrates God's compassion and concern for all mankind.

7. Everything and everyone in the book of Jonah obeys the Lord (the storm, the fish, the wind, the Ninevites, the plant, the worm, and so forth) except Jonah.

8. Eight hundred years after Jonah fled from Joppa and from his mission to preach to the Gentiles, another Jewish preacher named Peter was commissioned at Joppa to also preach to the Gentiles (Acts 10).

9. There are some ten miracles recorded in this brief book.

10. Some Bible students believe that Jonah actually died inside the great fish and was raised from the dead, making him a more literal type of Christ.

11. Jonah is one of two books in Scripture that has routinely been labeled by nonbelievers as allegorical and not factual (see also Song of Solomon).

12. The book of Jonah is, in several instances, a recorded conversation between God and this prophet.

13. Jonah is one of only two prophets from the northern kingdom of Israel whose writings are found in Scripture (see also Hosea).

Quotable Quotes

By picking Jonah from among all of the other available types of death and resurrection with which the Old Testament abounds, Jesus raised the book of Jonah out of the realm of doubt and speculation, above all questions of fiction or parable, and established the book as infallibly inspired, and the events in the book as an actual, literal account of a historic experience and event. —M. R. DeHaan

If the story of Jonah and the whale is a myth, then so is the story of the resurrection. —John E. Hunter

The author of the book of Jonah strikes the high-water mark of Old Testament theology. In large-heartedness, in love of mankind, and in the appreciation of the character of God, this little book stands preeminent as the noblest, broadest, and most Christian of all Old Testament literature. It contains one truth far in advance of Jonah's age, a truth which will never pass out of date so long as men have human hearts, and prize the gospel. —George L. Robinson

Notable Notes

In February 1891, the whaling ship known as *The Star of the East* was hunting off the Falkland Islands. When a whale was spotted, smaller boats were lowered to harpoon the mammal. One of those smaller boats was capsized, and a sailor named James Bartley disappeared without a trace. After the whale was killed, the crew began the long process of removing the blubber from the whale. The next day, the sailors heard intermittent sounds from the stomach of the whale, and upon cutting the stomach open, discovered their lost sailor! Though initially unconscious, within three weeks he was well enough to return to his ship duties.

Christ Connections

Christ can be found in Jonah as:

Foreign Missionary

One Greater than Jonah

MICAH

Important Information

Author: Micah
Theme: Judgment Is Coming
Category: Minor Prophet

Fascinating Facts

1. Micah was the only prophet whose ministry was directed at both kingdoms, Israel and Judah.

2. Micah was the last prophet to speak to the northern kingdom (Israel) before its fall.

3. Micah is the only prophet to foretell the actual birthplace of the Messiah, and he did so seven hundred years beforehand.

4. The book of Micah contains several important prophecies within its seven brief chapters.

5. Micah was one of the leading prophets to speak against social injustice, and is oftentimes called "the prophet of the poor."

6. Micah was a contemporary of Isaiah, Hosea, and Amos.

7. Micah bears several similarities to the book of Isaiah, and has been referred to as "a miniature Isaiah" and "Isaiah in shorthand."

8. In Micah, the word *hear* is found some nine times.

9. The book of Micah is considered by many as the most eloquently written of the minor prophets.

10. Micah is one of the few prophets referred to by name in the book of another prophet (see Jer. 26:18).

Quotable Quotes

In Micah's case the message of judgment was heeded, repentance followed, and the disaster was postponed for a century. Hosea and Amos were ignored. Jeremiah was imprisoned. But here was one prophet who was listened to and whose preaching therefore changed history. In coming to Micah we should be encouraged that one man did make a difference. —James Montgomery Boice

Micah was the first of all the prophets to focus men's eyes upon Bethlehem as the birthplace of a coming Deliverer; a yeoman at that! —George L. Robinson

The world will never find its true order and its peace until all other governors—whether emperors, kings, or presidents—have kissed the scepter of the King of kings and reign under His control. That is the great message of Micah. —G. Campbell Morgan

Notable Notes

Micah is quoted elsewhere in Scripture on three significant occasions. A hundred years after his ministry, his words were quoted by the elders of Judah in Jeremiah 26:18, and, as a result, Jeremiah's life was spared! Micah's words were also quoted by the priests and scribes to King Herod in Matthew 2:6, in response to the king's inquiry of where the Messiah was to be born. Finally, Jesus Himself quoted from Micah's words in Matthew 10:35–36 as He sent out His disciples to minister.

Christ Connections

Christ can be found in Micah as:

Messenger with Beautiful Feet

Rejected King

NAHUM

Important Information

Author: Nahum
Theme: Judgment and Destruction of Nineveh
Category: Minor Prophet

Fascinating Facts

1. The book of Nahum picks up where the book of Jonah left off.

2. Nahum is one of two minor prophets whose book is devoted exclusively to the story of Nineveh (see also Jonah).

3. Nahum is never quoted or alluded to in the New Testament.

4. Nahum is one of only two books in the Bible that ends with a question mark (see also Jonah).

5. There are almost fifty references made to nature in Nahum.

6. Only here does the word *book* occur in the title of a prophecy (1:1).

7. Nahum not only predicted the demise of the city of Nineveh but also the manner in which it would fall (1:8).

8. The only reference to the person of Nahum in the Bible is Nahum 1:1.

9. Nahum quotes Isaiah in Nahum 1:15, and some believe that Nahum may have been a disciple of Isaiah (Isa. 8:16).

10. The New Testament city of Capernaum means "city of Nahum," and it is therefore believed by some that Nahum was from the area of Capernaum in Galilee. ·

11. The book of Nahum is our greatest source of biblical information on the fall of Assyria.

Quotable Quotes

The real value, as I see it, of studying a book like Nahum, is that the true wonder of the Bible begins to shine through even those parts of it which seem so utterly at variance with what we have grown to think of as Christian truth. —A. E. Gould

This little book ranks amongst the finest things in Hebrew literature. In poetic fire and sublimity, it approaches the best work of Isaiah. —G. G. Findlay

Nahum's mighty intellect, his patriotism and courage, his rare, almost unequaled, gift of vivid presentation . . . indeed he looms as one of those outstanding figures in human history who have appeared only at rare intervals. —Walter A. Maier

Notable Notes

In Nahum 3:11, the prophet predicted that Nineveh would "be hidden." And sure enough, the destruction of Nineveh was so complete that Alexander the Great marched his troops right over the same desolate ground and didn't even realize that there had once been a great city there! It wasn't until 1842 that archaeologists finally discovered the site and location that was once Nineveh.

Christ Connections

Christ can be found in Nahum as:

Avenger
Stronghold in Day of Trouble
Prophet of Comfort and Vengeance

HABAKKUK

Important Information

Author: Habakkuk
Theme: Judgment against Unrighteousness
Category: Minor Prophet

Fascinating Facts

1. Habakkuk 2:4 is quoted in three different books of the New Testament (Romans, Galatians, and Hebrews).

2. Though a brief book, Habakkuk is quoted or referred to a number of times in the New Testament.

3. The book of Habakkuk is, in its entirety, a recorded conversation between God and this prophet.

4. Habakkuk 3 is recognized as a great psalm of praise, virtually unmatched anywhere else in Scripture.

5. Almost nothing is known about the prophet Habakkuk except his name, which means "embraced by God."

6. Habakkuk is the only Old Testament prophet who primarily directs his words to God rather than to others.

7. In Habakkuk 2, the prophet utters five "woes" against the Chaldeans.

8. Habakkuk and Jeremiah were the last prophets to speak to the southern kingdom of Judah before its captivity by the Babylonians.

9. Habakkuk sees one of the greatest manifestations of God's glory recorded in the Old Testament (3:3–15), reminiscent of Moses at Sinai (Exod. 19) and Isaiah in the temple (Isa. 6).

10. From what is recorded in Habakkuk 3:19, we learn that this prophet was involved in temple worship and therefore was most likely from the tribe of Levi.

Quotable Quotes

Habakkuk is the inspired authority for the fundamental doctrine of justification by faith, and the certainty of judgment to come for those who reject the testimony of the Holy Ghost as to the Lord Jesus Christ. —H. A. Ironside

When you live by faith, you aren't worried about the things that go on in the world. You may be burdened. It doesn't mean that we shouldn't be concerned about crime and injustice, but we don't lose our faith because of it. We don't become discouraged and despondent and give up. The main message of Habakkuk is that the just shall live by faith. —Warren W. Wiersbe

It's a beautiful gem of a book written by the prophet who started out wrestling with God and ended up worshipping Him. —Jon Courson

Notable Notes

Habakkuk 2:4, "But the just shall live by his faith," was the biblical doctrine quoted by the apostle Paul in the New Testament books of Romans and Galatians that liberated Martin Luther's heart, turned his life around, and eventually propelled him into the Protestant Reformation. For this reason, Habakkuk has been called "the grandfather of the Reformation." Those same words from Habakkuk 2:4 also had a profound impact in the life of John Wesley.

Christ Connections

Christ can be found in Habakkuk as:

God of My Salvation

Judge of Babylon

Rewarder of Those Who Seek Him

ZEPHANIAH

Important Information

Author: Zephaniah
Theme: The Day of the Lord
Category: Minor Prophet

Fascinating Facts

1. Zephaniah was one of the last prophets to warn Judah before its captivity and is sometimes referred to as "the eleventh-hour prophet."

2. Zephaniah was evidently the great-grandson of King Hezekiah (1:1) and, therefore, the only prophet descended from royalty.

3. Zephaniah does something very unusual in his opening words, as he traces his ancestry back four generations.

4. The only reference to the person of Zephaniah in the Bible is Zephaniah 1:1.

5. Zephaniah refers to Jerusalem in such a way as to indicate that the prophet was a resident of the very city he was condemning (1:4, 10).

6. Zephaniah is one of two minor prophets who deal almost exclusively with the coming Day of the Lord (see also Joel).

7. Zephaniah opens and closes his book by declaring that God was speaking (1:1; 3:20).

8. Zephaniah refers or alludes to the coming Day of the Lord some twenty-three times.

9. Zephaniah's preaching undoubtedly contributed greatly to the reforms in Israel that took place under King Josiah (see 2 Chron. 34–35).

10. The clearest picture in the Bible of the Day of the Lord was given by Zephaniah.

Quotable Quotes

Love seeks the best interests of the beloved. That is what this little book of Zephaniah is all about—the dark side of love. . . . The Father is never more close to you, my friend, than when He is reaching in and taking out of your heart and life those things that offend. —J. Vernon McGee

Perhaps no prophet gave a more definite declaration of the terrors of the divine judgment against sin than did Zephaniah, and this is emphasized by his ignoring utterly the reforms which he saw and knew to be insincere on the part of the people. —G. Campbell Morgan

No hotter book lies in the Old Testament. —George Adam Smith

Notable Notes

Zephaniah was a contemporary of the prophet Jeremiah, and while both men carried similar messages and spoke to the same people and in the same place, their personalities were quite different. Jeremiah was known as the "Weeping Prophet," being sensitive and sympathetic. Zephaniah, on the other hand, was about as straightforward and forthright as any prophet of God. God used both men to help bring renewal and reform in the days of godly King Josiah.

Christ Connections

Christ can be found in Zephaniah as:
    Lord Mighty to Save
    Executor of Judgment

HAGGAI

Important Information

Author: Haggai
Theme: Putting God First
Category: Minor Prophet

Fascinating Facts

1. Haggai is the only book in the Bible that is two chapters long.

2. Haggai is the second shortest book in the Old Testament (Obadiah is the shortest).

3. Haggai the prophet was a contemporary of Zechariah, and both of them are named in the book of Ezra.

4. Haggai's prophecies are more precisely dated than any others in Scripture.

5. Haggai was the first prophet to be heard after the Babylonian captivity.

6. Haggai's total prophetic ministry lasted less than four months.

7. Haggai uses the phrases "says the LORD" and "LORD of hosts" a dozen times each.

8. Haggai's brief prophecy includes at least seven questions.

9. Haggai was one of just a few prophets who saw immediate results after his preaching—in this case, just twenty-three days later (1:15)!

10. Haggai 2 contains one of the most remarkable prophecies of the coming Messiah (vv. 6–9).

11. Haggai is quoted on only one occasion in the New Testament (Heb. 12:26).

12. The prophet Haggai is the only man in Scripture who bears that name.

Quotable Quotes

[Haggai's] words are all the working out of one idea—the unprofitableness, on the whole and in the long-run, of a godless life. —Alexander Maclaren

Haggai himself seems to have almost finished his earthly course, before he was called to be a prophet; and in four months his office was closed . . . yet in his brief space he first stirred up the people in one month to rebuild the temple. —E. B. Pusey

The brief record of Haggai's ministry does . . . show him as a man of conviction. He has the unique place among the prophets of having really been listened to and his words obeyed. . . . Though his words were plain and not poetic, he had one major point to make; and he made it forcefully and well. —Robert L. Alden

Notable Notes

Haggai the prophet was a contemporary of the Chinese philosopher Confucius. Haggai's ministry was also in close proximity to the spiritual leader Buddha, in India, who preached his first sermon within a year after Haggai's prophecy.

Christ Connections

Christ can be found in Haggai as:
   Prophet, Priest, and King
   Builder of the House of the Lord

ZECHARIAH

Important Information

Author: Zechariah
Theme: Israel's Future Blessing
Category: Minor Prophet

Fascinating Facts

1. The name of God as "LORD of hosts" is found some fifty times in this book.
2. Zechariah is the longest book of the minor prophets.
3. Zechariah contains more Messianic prophecies than any other book in the Old Testament except Isaiah.
4. Zechariah is quoted or referred to at least forty times in the New Testament.
5. Zechariah is quoted from or alluded to by other books in Scripture more than any other Old Testament book.
6. Zechariah makes more references and allusions to the coming Messiah than all of the other minor prophets combined.
7. Zechariah saw at least eight different visions in one single night (1:7–6:8).
8. There are at least two dozen men in Scripture who bear the name of Zechariah, including the author of this book.
9. Zechariah uses the phrase "the Word of the LORD" some fourteen times.
10. In Zechariah, the city of Jerusalem is named more than forty times.
11. The book of Zechariah has been called "the Apocalypse of the Old Testament."

12. The book of Zechariah contains more references to angels than almost any other book of the Old Testament.

Quotable Quotes

The book of Zechariah is the most Messianic, the most truly apocalyptic and eschatological, of all the writings of the Old Testament. —George L. Robinson

The book of the prophet Zechariah is not much studied nor adequately understood in our day . . . yet the book as a whole can be studied with great profit and to the strengthening of one's faith. The New Testament makes repeated use of the book. So should we. —H. C. Leupold

While most Christians are aware of the great messianic prophecies in Isaiah, few are cognizant of the fact that Zechariah is rich with predictions of Christ as well—of both His first and second comings. —Harold L. Willmington

Notable Notes

The book of Zechariah makes some amazing and important prophecies concerning the Messiah. Some of those Old Testament prophecies are only found in Zechariah, and they include Christ's triumphal entry into Jerusalem on the back of a donkey (9:9), the betrayal of Christ for thirty pieces of silver (11:12), and the usage of those thirty pieces of betrayal money to purchase a potter's field (11:13).

Christ Connections

Christ can be found in Zechariah as:
Righteous Branch
Yahweh's Servant

Smitten Shepherd
King-Priest

MALACHI

Important Information

Author: Malachi
Theme: A Warning to Backsliders
Category: Minor Prophet

Fascinating Facts

1. Along with Obadiah, Malachi is the most obscure Old Testament prophet. His only reference is in 1:1, and it contains no family or geographic history.
2. Malachi was the last prophet to write in the Old Testament.
3. The statement "thus says the LORD of hosts" is recorded some twenty times in Malachi, emphasizing that it was God's message.
4. Malachi lists more questions per verses than any other book of the Bible, with some twenty-seven questions in just fifty-five verses.
5. Malachi is the only prophet who concludes his book with judgment.
6. Malachi, the last book of the Old Testament, and Revelation, the last book of the New Testament, both end with warnings.
7. In Malachi, well over three-quarters of the verses are spoken by God, the highest percentage of all the prophets.

8. Malachi records the most familiar passage on tithing found in the Old Testament (3:8–10).

9. Malachi closes his book with a look backward at Moses and a look forward to Elijah (4:5–6).

10. Malachi lists the last Old Testament Messianic prophecy (4:2).

11. Malachi is the last message from God to His people for four hundred years.

12. Portions of Malachi are written in the form of a debate, unlike any other book of the Bible.

13. Malachi is one of the most argumentative books of the Bible.

Quotable Quotes

I think that none of the messages of these Minor Prophets fits the present age as exactly as does this of Malachi. —G. Campbell Morgan

The more I read this book, the more I see the present generation illustrated in vivid colors. The people concerned were not the heathen or pagan tribes of those days, but the priests and the people of God. The Bible is here showing that before the darkness falls there is dissension, and before the silence there is sacrilege. —John E. Hunter

God and Malachi wanted a righteous nation, a pure and devoted priesthood, happy homes, God-fearing children, and a people characterized by truth, integrity, generosity, gratitude, fidelity, love, and hope. —Robert L. Alden

Notable Notes

At the end of Malachi, there is a promise that God will one day send forth Elijah the prophet (Mal. 4:5–6). In recognition of that promise, when the Jewish people observe the Passover Seder meal, the door is left ajar, an extra place setting is fixed, and an extra glass of wine is set there. That glass is called "Elijah's cup," and it is set out in anticipation of Elijah's return. In Matthew 17:10–13, Jesus states that Elijah had already come, in the person of John the Baptist. However, many recognize that God also stated that Elijah himself would return just before the Day of the Lord. Therefore, many believe that he will return as one of the two witnesses referenced in Revelation 11.

Christ Connections

Christ can be found in Malachi as:

Sun of Righteousness

Messenger of the New Covenant

Refiner and Purifier of His People

MATTHEW

Important Information

Author: Matthew
Theme: Christ the Messiah-King
Category: Gospel

Fascinating Facts

1. Matthew makes first mention of the church in the New Testament (16:18), and makes the only reference to it in the Gospels.
2. Matthew uses the term *King* more times than any other New Testament book.
3. Matthew contains the shortest prayer in the Bible: "Lord, save me!" (14:30).
4 Matthew is one of two Gospels that contain the only recorded earthly conversation between God and Satan in Scripture (ch. 4).
5. Matthew refers to more Old Testament books than any other New Testament book.
6. Matthew's Gospel contains the most complete record of what Jesus said, with His spoken words found in about 60 percent of its total verses.

7. Nowhere in the four Gospels do we find a single recorded word that Matthew himself spoke.

8. Matthew uses the phrase "the kingdom of heaven" over thirty times in his Gospel, a phrase found nowhere else in the New Testament.

9. Matthew records three miracles by Jesus found nowhere else: the healing of the two blind men (ch. 9), the deliverance of the demon-possessed man (ch. 9), and the coin in the mouth of the fish (ch. 17).

10. Matthew contains one of the only two genealogies of Jesus (ch. 1), and it traces His lineage back to Abraham.

11. Only in Matthew's Gospel do we have the record of the visitation by the Magi to the Christ child (ch. 2).

12. In Matthew's genealogy of Jesus, there are references to four Old Testament women with tainted pasts: Tamar (harlot), Rahab (prostitute), Ruth (Moabitess), and Bathsheba (adulteress).

13. The Gospel of Matthew records five major discourses of Jesus.

14. Matthew's Gospel is by far the most Jewish of the four Gospels.

15. Only Matthew refers to himself in Scripture as a "tax collector" (10:3)—the other Gospel writers refer to him as Levi.

Quotable Quotes

Matthew was the most widely read Gospel in the early church. The patristic writers quoted from it more than from any of the others. It greatly influenced the thinking of early Christians. —D. Edmond Hiebert

Matthew is the gospel written by a Jew to Jews about a Jew. —*Talk Thru the Bible*

No gospel is more instructive to those who are the Lord's disciples and who are called to represent Him in the world. The lessons on discipleship are life-changing for the reader, as they were for the eleven who were Jesus's first followers. Thus, with all its great themes of majesty and glory, rejection and apostasy, the book of Matthew lacks no practicality. Woven through all that is the constant thread of revealed instruction for those who are His representatives among men. —John F. MacArthur Jr.

Notable Notes

There are several unique dreams recorded in the Gospel of Matthew. In chapter 1 is Joseph's dream in which an angel explains Mary's pregnancy to him, thereby averting a divorce. In chapter 2 is Joseph's dream in which an angel warns him to flee from Herod with Mary and the Child into Egypt. Later on, in another dream, an angel tells Joseph he can return to Israel from Egypt. In the same chapter, in still another dream, God instructs Joseph to relocate to Galilee. Finally, in chapter 27, there is the dream of Pilate's wife, who tells her husband that Jesus is a just man and that Pilate should have nothing to do with Him.

Christ Connections

Christ can be found in Matthew as:

    Son of David

    Head of the Church

    Savior

MARK

Important Information

Author: John Mark
Theme: Christ the Servant
Category: Gospel

Fascinating Facts

1. Mark is the shortest and most graphic of the four Gospels.
2. Mark was the first of the four Gospels to be written.
3. Mark's Gospel is one of action, and the word *straightway* (or *immediately*) is recorded more than forty times.
4. Mark's Gospel records about eighteen of Jesus's many parables.
5. Over one-third of Mark's Gospel focuses on the final eight days of Jesus, from Palm Sunday to Resurrection Sunday.
6. Mark's Gospel contains very few Old Testament references.
7. Mark's Gospel records fewer of Christ's teachings than any of the other three Gospels.
8. Only in Mark's Gospel are we told that Jesus was a carpenter (6:3).
9. Because only Mark's Gospel records the story of the young man who fled away naked, many believe that it is a reference to Mark himself.
10. Mark's Gospel includes half of Jesus's recorded miracles (eighteen), and he devotes more space, proportionately, to miracles than the other Gospels.

11. Mark's Gospel was written to a Roman audience and mind-set, and the last human to speak in this Gospel is the Roman centurion who proclaimed Jesus to be the Son of God (15:39).

12. Mark was not one of the main disciples, and the acceptance of his Gospel account stems from the knowledge that Peter supplied Mark with much of the information used in writing this Gospel.

Quotable Quotes

There is a freshness about this gospel. . . . Here we find rapid action, vivid detail, picturesque language. Many a preacher might be jolted out of his rut—another word for long grave—by letting the impact of Mark really hit him. —Ralph Earle

This gospel emphasizes what Jesus did rather than what He said. —Charles C. Ryrie

This gospel has the charm of two personalities who contributed to its contents, Peter and John Mark. Both were vivacious and versatile and have preserved the portrait of Jesus with the freshness of the morning. —A. T. Robertson

Notable Notes

Since Simon Peter refers to John Mark as "Mark my son" in his first epistle (1 Pet. 5:13), many people believe that Mark was converted and discipled under Peter's ministry. If this is true, something else these two held in common was their well-known moments of failure. Peter's came when he denied the Lord three times (Matt. 26), while Mark's came when he abandoned Paul and Barnabas during their first missionary journey (Acts 13:13). The lives of both men remind us that the Lord is a God of second chances.

Christ Connections

Christ can be found in Mark as:

Suffering Servant of Yahweh

Mighty King

LUKE

Important Information

Author: Luke
Theme: The Humanity of Christ
Category: Gospel

Fascinating Facts

1. Luke, the author of this book, is the only known Gentile author of Scripture (Col. 4:10–14), and wrote more words of the New Testament than anyone else.

2. Luke is the longest Gospel, and the longest book in the New Testament, with 1,151 verses.

3. Luke's account is the most extensive and precise of the four Gospels (1:1–3).

4. Luke and Matthew contain the only recorded earthly conversation between God and Satan in Scripture (ch. 4).

5. Luke's Gospel contains one of just two genealogies of Jesus (ch. 3), and it traces His lineage back to Adam.

6. Luke is the only Gospel that tells us about the salvation of the dying thief who was crucified with Jesus.

7. Luke's Gospel gives us the most complete account of Christ's birth, childhood, and ancestry.

8. Luke's Gospel is the only New Testament book that references the name of Gabriel the angel (1:19, 26), and one of only two books in the Bible that does so (see also Dan. 8:16).

9. More than one-half of the material in Luke's Gospel is found in no other Gospel.

10. Luke has been called "The Gospel of Womanhood" because he emphasizes the role of women, referring to them some forty-three times.

11. Luke's Gospel contains five great hymns or songs and three angelic benedictions (chs. 1–2).

12. Luke's account is the most literary and classical in style and language of the four Gospels.

13. Luke's Gospel uses the phrase "Son of Man," which was Jesus's most commonly used designation for Himself, at least twenty-five times.

14. Luke's Gospel records twenty-two parables, seventeen of which are found only in his account.

15. Luke was a physician (Col. 4:14); therefore, he uses many medical terms in his writing.

16. Luke's Gospel is the most socially minded of the four Gospels, with more recorded instances of Jesus's dealings with the poor, strangers, and so on.

17. Unlike the other Gospel writers, Luke places emphasis upon the activity of the Holy Spirit in the ministry of Jesus.

18. Luke's Gospel emphasizes prayer (for example, 1:10; 3:21; 9:29; 23:46).

Quotable Quotes

There is no gospel which more shows the mind and love of God than this of Luke. None is more truly and evidently inspired. Nevertheless there is none so deeply marked by traces of the human hand and heart. —William Kelly

There is something especially attractive about this Gospel. —Donald Guthrie

The message of this Gospel is not a simple message. The more carefully we study this book the more we are impressed with its profundity, with the wonder and spaciousness of the thing it has to say to us concerning Christ. . . . What is the message of this Gospel to the world? Carry it to the ends of the earth, let it speak its own truth to the men who are lost, and it tells them of a Kinsman Who, to borrow the old Hebrew figure, is able to discharge their debt, destroy their enemies, make possible the redemption of their persons, and the redemption of their inheritance, as offspring of God. —G. Campbell Morgan

Notable Notes

A very old tradition dating back to the sixth century asserts that Luke was a painter and that he painted a portrait of Mary, the mother of Jesus. Certainly, Luke painted beautiful pictures with his words. His account is viewed as being by far the best literary work of the four Gospels. This is evidenced by the instance when French rationalistic critic and notorious nonbeliever Ernest Renan once said that Luke's Gospel was "the most beautiful book ever written."

Christ Connections

Christ can be found in Luke as:

Son of Man

Sympathetic High Priest

Savior

JOHN

Important Information

Author: John the Apostle
Theme: The Deity of Christ
Category: Gospel

Fascinating Facts

1. John's Gospel contains the shortest verse in the Bible, "Jesus wept," (11:35).

2. The names Jesus and Christ appear more times here (over 170) than in any other book of the Bible.

3. John's Gospel contains the longest prayer of the New Testament, chapter 17.

4. One-third of John's Gospel is a record of the last eight days of Christ's life before His death, from Palm Sunday to Easter Sunday.

5. John is the most theological of the four Gospels.

6. John's Gospel contains no parables and only eight miracles, five of which are not recorded in the other Gospels.

7. John 3:16 is undoubtedly the most quoted and most familiar verse in all of Scripture.

8. In John's Gospel, the word *believe* appears some one hundred times, emphasizing the gospel message.

9. John's Gospel presents the strongest evidence for the deity of Jesus Christ.

10. Over 90 percent of John's Gospel is unique from the other three synoptic Gospels.

11. Only John's Gospel contains Jesus's "I am" statements that speak of His being the Messiah.

12. John begins his Gospel with the same language of Genesis: "In the beginning."

Quotable Quotes

The Gospel of John is the most influential book that has ever come from the pen of any man. —Philip Schaff

This is the Gospel of the Divine Life of Jesus. The eagle has always been its recognized emblem, as denoting its sublime and heavenly character. And, clearly, in its dictation, its insights into the deepest truths, its repeated testimony to the Glory and Deity of our Lord, it holds a unique place among the records of His life. —F. B. Meyer

No Gospel of the New Testament is more greatly loved than the Gospel of John. Among young and old alike its profound message, beautiful imagery, and simple language have won their way into countless hearts. —Homer A. Kent Jr.

Notable Notes

The oldest surviving New Testament text that we have is a fragment of John 18:31–33, 37–38, which includes Pilate's question to Jesus:

"Are You the King of the Jews?" That fragment dates to about AD 125, roughly one generation after the original was written. It is located in the John Rylands Library in Manchester, England.

Christ Connections

Christ can be found in John as:

Son of God

One Who Brings Eternal Life

ACTS

Important Information

Author: Luke
Theme: History and Life of the Early Church
Category: History

Fascinating Facts

1. Acts is the most historical book of the New Testament.
2. Without the book of Acts, we would have very little background information on many of the other New Testament epistles and churches.
3. The Holy Spirit is mentioned over fifty times in Acts, more than any other New Testament book.
4. Acts records the birth of the church (ch. 2).
5. Acts is the only unfinished book in the Bible, as the history of the church still continues to this day.

6. Acts records many church firsts, such as the first martyrs, the first deacons, the first pastors, the first missionaries, and the first Gentile converts.

7. Almost every chapter in Acts refers to prayer, and every chapter shows the result of prayer.

8. Luke, the author of this book, is the only known Gentile author of Scripture.

9. Acts contains the longest recorded sermon in the New Testament, preached by Stephen in chapter 7.

10. In Acts, believers are called *Christians* for the first time (11:26).

11. In Acts, we have the last two biblical resurrections of identified people, Dorcas (9:40–41) and Eutychus (20:9–12).

12. In Acts, Luke makes references to more than one hundred people and approximately eighty locations.

13. Acts, with its three major missionary journeys, has been called the greatest missionary story ever told.

14. In the New Testament, there are four resurrections recorded by Luke, two in his Gospel and two in the book of Acts.

Quotable Quotes

It is no exaggeration to say that the book of Acts is one of the most graphic pieces of writing in all literature. . . . Acts is a dawn, a glorious sunrise, a bursting forth in a dark world of eternal light; it is a Book precious beyond all price. —W. Graham Scroggie

No book of the New Testament is more appealing as it beckons the church of today to look at the church as it was at the beginning. . . . It is thrilling narrative, striking characterization, and dynamic achievement. —Ralph G. Turnbull

The story of the church which unfolds in the Acts of the Apostles is one of the most fascinating stories of the Bible. It is the story of young churches in action—not in meditation, contemplation, or worship—but action. In fact, action is the theme as well as the name of the book of Acts. It is its atmosphere, story, movement, and inspiration. —Roy Laurin

Notable Notes

On the day of Pentecost, as Peter preached the gospel, some three thousand people were saved. In contrast, after the golden calf tragedy at Mount Sinai, some three thousand people lost their lives. Consequently, when the law was first given at Mount Sinai, three thousand souls died—and when grace was first preached in the church on Pentecost, three thousand souls were saved. The law kills, but grace saves!

Christ Connections

Christ can be found in Acts as:
    One Sitting at the Right Hand of God
    Prince of the Kings of the Earth

ROMANS

Important Information

Author: Paul
Theme: Salvation by Grace through Faith
Category: Pauline Epistle

Fascinating Facts

1. In Romans, Paul quotes more from the Old Testament (especially from Isaiah and Psalms) than in all of his other epistles combined.

2. In Romans, just about every major doctrine of the Christian faith is put forth.

3. Romans is one of only two epistles in which Paul includes several personal and individual greetings (see also Colossians), and, in both cases, he had not visited either church previously.

4. The epistle of Romans is Paul's most formal and systematic writing.

5. In Romans, there are well over two hundred words not found in any of Paul's other writings; nearly one hundred of those words are unique to the New Testament.

6. Although Romans is Paul's second largest epistle (see 1 Corinthians), it is his most important work.

7. Romans is the first of three New Testament books to quote Habakkuk 2:4 (see also Galatians and Hebrews).

8. In Romans, three key words appear numerous times: *law* (seventy-eight times), *righteousness* (sixty-six times), and *faith* (sixty-two times).

9. In Romans, Paul makes reference to many Old Testament figures, including Adam, Abraham, Sarah, Jacob, Esau, Rebekah, David, and others.

10. Romans 16 contains Paul's most eloquent benediction (vv. 25–27).

11. Many scholars believe that the epistle to the Romans was hand-delivered by Phoebe, the faithful sister Paul describes in chapter 16.

12. Romans is so foundational to the faith that it has been called the "Constitution of Christianity."

Quotable Quotes

This epistle is the chief part of the New Testament, and the very purest Gospel. . . . It can never be read or considered too much or too well; and the more it is handled, the more precious it becomes, and the better it tastes. —Martin Luther

It opened the door to all of the treasures in Scripture. —John Calvin

It is the greatest and richest of all the apostolic works. —F. B. Meyer

This epistle has ever been considered as St. Paul's masterpiece, whether judged from an intellectual or theological standpoint, and the greatest of men have ever valued it most highly. —Robert Lee

Notable Notes

John Chrysostom had this epistle read to him once a week for eighteen years. Martyn Lloyd-Jones, the great expositor of Scripture, spent fourteen years teaching through the book of Romans and yet never finished his series before he resigned from his church. Donald Grey Barnhouse broadcast weekly messages through Romans for eleven years on the radio. Several hundred years ago, one church leader copied the entire book of Romans by hand—twice—in order to become more familiar with it. Early church father Augustine was converted by reading Romans. It propelled Martin Luther into the Protestant Reformation. And it inspired John Wesley into the great Wesleyan Revival of England.

Christ Connections

Christ can be found in Romans as:
Lord Our Righteousness
Justifier, Redeemer, and Savior

1 CORINTHIANS

Important Information

Author: Paul
Theme: Correcting a Carnal Church
Category: Pauline Epistle

Fascinating Facts

1. 1 Corinthians is the longest of Paul's epistles.
2. 1 and 2 Corinthians are, by content, Paul's most practical epistles.
3. In 1 Corinthians, Paul uses the title "the Lord Jesus Christ" six times in just the first ten verses, emphasizing Christ's Lordship.
4. 1 Corinthians is an epistle of reproof and correction.
5. 1 Corinthians addresses practically every existing church problem.
6. 1 Corinthians contains the most extensive treatment of spiritual gifts found anywhere in the New Testament.
7. 1 Corinthians provides us one of the most vivid windows into the life of the early church.

8. In 1 Corinthians 15 we find the greatest and earliest New Testament discourse on the Resurrection.

9. The church at Corinth was the least spiritual of all the churches addressed by letter in the New Testament.

10. In 1 Corinthians there are more than 230 words not used in any of Paul's other writings, and one hundred of those words are unique to the New Testament.

11. 1 Corinthians contains one of the earliest references to the Lord's Supper, found in chapter 11.

Quotable Quotes

This Letter is addressed not just to a few people in Corinth, a city that is now in ruins, but to the church of Jesus Christ in any city of the world in any era of history, even the times in which we live. —Alan Redpath

First Corinthians is so vital to us. Conditions have not changed much. Many of the problems that confronted the Corinthians plague present-day believers as well. Living wisely for God is not easy in the midst of a sinful and materialistic age. But 1 Corinthians is filled with valuable and important lessons . . . which [are] so essential for our walk with the Lord. —J. Allen Blair

These epistles [Corinthians] . . . in reference to all practical measures in the establishment of the church among the heathen, and in its conduct in Christian lands, are among the most important portions of the word of God. —Charles Hodge

Notable Notes

According to 1 Corinthians 5:9, 11, Paul had written an earlier letter to the church at Corinth, which has since been lost. Also,

2 Corinthians 2:4 points to still another letter not found today. Therefore, 1 and 2 Corinthians are actually Paul's second and fourth letters to that church. Consequently the church at Corinth is the only known church to which Paul ever sent four letters.

Christ Connections

Christ can be found in 1 Corinthians as:

Foundation of the Church

Unifier

Great Sacrifice

Resurrected One

Coming Lord

2 CORINTHIANS

Important Information

Author: Paul
Theme: The Ministry of the Church
Category: Pauline Epistle

Fascinating Facts

1. 2 Corinthians is the most autobiographical of all of Paul's epistles.
2. In 2 Corinthians different forms of the word *ministry* are used some eighteen times, underscoring the epistle's theme.
3. 1 and 2 Corinthians are perhaps Paul's most practical epistles.

4. 2 Corinthians is one of Paul's least doctrinal letters.

5. The church at Corinth was the least spiritual of all the churches addressed by letter in the New Testament.

6. 2 Corinthians is the least systematic of all of Paul's epistles.

7. In 2 Corinthians there are at least 170 words that Paul does not use anywhere else, and at least ninety of those words are unique to the New Testament.

8. In 2 Corinthians chapters 8 and 9 we find the longest New Testament passage on the subject of giving.

9. In 2 Corinthians Paul's companion and helper Titus is referred to by name no less than nine times, far more than anyone else.

10. In 2 Corinthians the person and the ministry of Satan are emphasized (for example, 4:4; 11:14).

Quotable Quotes

Nowhere does Paul open his heart to his readers so completely as he does in his second letter [to the Corinthians] as he relates some of God's dealings with him in his inner life. —Alan Redpath

The two [epistles of Corinthians] together are valuable beyond all estimate for an understanding of the problems of first-century Christians, and for an appreciation of the greatest missionary of the Christian era. —W. Graham Scroggie

This book reveals the warm, human character of Paul. Many have pictured Paul as the methodical logician of Romans or Galatians. . . . This epistle, however, is emotional, full of tears and grief. It was written more with the heart than with the head. —Robert G. Gromacki

Notable Notes

In chapter 12 of this epistle the apostle Paul briefly describes his experience of being caught up into the third heaven, or paradise. Paul states that he heard things there that are unlawful for a man to speak. Many commentators believe that this unusual experience in Paul's ministry took place when he was stoned and left for dead by a mob in the city of Lystra (see Acts 14:19).

Christ Connections

Christ can be found in 2 Corinthians as:
   Son of God
   One Who Anoints
   Reconciler

GALATIANS

Important Information

Author: Paul
Theme: Justification by Faith
Category: Pauline Epistle

Fascinating Facts

1. Galatians was most likely the first epistle that Paul wrote.
2. Galatians is Paul's only letter that was addressed to a group of churches (1:2).

3. Galatians is the only epistle of Paul's that does not begin with a word of thanksgiving and praise, and it is the apostle's most severe letter.

4. In Galatians Paul makes no request for prayer from these believers, which was very unusual.

5. In Galatians Paul emphasizes the doctrine of justification by faith more than in any of his other epistles, including Romans.

6. Galatians is Paul's only epistle in which he draws attention to his handwriting (6:11).

7. Only in Galatians do we learn of a three-year period shortly after Paul's conversion in which he went into the deserts of Arabia (1:17).

8. Galatians is undoubtedly Paul's most passionate and emotionally charged epistle.

9. In Galatians there are some forty-seven references made to Christ.

10. In Galatians two key words are *law* (appears thirty-two times) and *faith* (appears twenty-one times).

11. Galatians 5 contains the well-known and very important passage on the fruit of the Spirit (5:22–23).

Quotable Quotes

The epistle to the Galatians is my epistle. I have betrothed myself to it. It is my wife. —Martin Luther

It is a stern, severe, and solemn message. . . . It has been called the Magna Carta of the early church, the manifesto of Christian liberty, the impregnable citadel, and a veritable Gibraltar against any attack on the heart of the gospel. —J. Vernon McGee

Paul's letters are probably the most extraordinary letters in the world, but none of them is more remarkable than Galatians. Its vigor, variety, audacity, and self-revealing frankness, together with its deep and direct insight into religious truth, put it in a class by itself among the books of the New Testament. —Edgar J. Goodspeed

Notable Notes

In Galatians 1:15–16 Paul refers to the fact that he was set apart in his mother's womb for the service to which God had called him. In this regard we are reminded of the Old Testament prophet Jeremiah, who also stated that he was set apart for God's special calling prior to his birth (see Jer. 1:5). Jeremiah even states that God knew him before he was conceived within the womb!

Christ Connections

Christ can be found in Galatians as:
    Great Redeemer
    Seed of Abraham
    Liberator

EPHESIANS

Important Information

Author: Paul
Theme: A Walk Worthy of Our Calling
Category: Pauline Epistle

Fascinating Facts

1. The church at Ephesus is the only church to receive a letter from more than one New Testament writer, as John also addressed them (see Rev. 2:1–7).
2. Ephesians is one of Paul's four prison epistles, along with Colossians, Philippians, and Philemon.
3. The church at Ephesus had many well-known preachers, including Paul, Apollos, Timothy, and John.
4. In Ephesians over one-half of all the verses are repeated in Colossians with some slight variations (the "Twin Epistles").
5. In Ephesians 5 we have the most beautiful New Testament picture of the Christian husband-wife marriage relationship.
6. Ephesians 6 gives us a detailed teaching on spiritual warfare, including the armor of God.
7. Ephesians 1:3–14 constitutes the longest continuous sentence found anywhere in Scripture, as translated from the Greek.
8. The phrase "in the heavenly places" is found five times in Ephesians but nowhere else in the New Testament (1:3, 20; 2:6; 3:10; 6:12).
9. In Ephesians the personality of the Holy Spirit is emphasized throughout the epistle (1:13; 2:18; 3:5; 4:30; 5:18; 6:17).
10. In Ephesians there are no personal greetings, despite the fact that Paul had been to Ephesus twice, staying for three years on the second visit.
11. In Ephesians the word *grace*, one of the key words, is used some twelve times.
12. In Ephesians the terms "in Christ" and "in Him" are used fifteen times.

Quotable Quotes

It is the epistle of the Heavenlies, a solemn liturgy, an ode to Christ and His spotless bride, the Song of Songs in the New Testament. —Philip Schaff

The whole letter is a magnificent combination of Christian doctrine and Christian duty, Christian faith and Christian life, what God has done through Christ and what we must be and do in consequence. —John R. W. Stott

Of all God's wonders in His natural creation, which He has given me to see, none seems more wonderful than the Grand Canyon. . . . Ephesians is the Grand Canyon of Scripture. —Ruth Paxson

Ephesians—carefully, reverently, prayerfully considered—will change our lives. It is not so much a question of what we will do with the epistle, but what it will do with us. —R. Kent Hughes

Notable Notes

The church at Ephesus cross-sectioned the lives of many well-known New Testament figures. Paul went there with Priscilla and Aquila on his second missionary journey (see Acts 18). Apollos and Timothy were both involved there (see Acts 18; 1 Tim. 1). Tradition says that after Paul died, John made his headquarters there and then eventually died there. Tradition also states that Mary, the mother of Jesus, died and was buried there.

Christ Connections

Christ can be found in Ephesians as:

Heavenly King

Reconciler

Head of the Body
Giver of Ministry Gifts

PHILIPPIANS

Important Information

Author: Paul
Theme: Joy in the Midst of All Circumstances
Category: Pauline Epistle

Fascinating Facts

1. Philippians is Paul's warmest and most affectionate epistle.

2. In Philippians, the words *joy* and *rejoice* occur sixteen times and are found in every chapter.

3. Philippians contains one of the most magnificent New Testament passages on the deity and ministry of Christ (2:5–11).

4. Philippians contains no quotations from the Old Testament.

5. The church at Philippi was Paul's most faithful and loyal source of financial support (4:10).

6. The church work at Philippi began with Paul going to jail (Acts 16:25), and this epistle was written by Paul while in jail (Phil. 1:14).

7. Philippians is Paul's only epistle in which he makes reference to church officers in his opening greetings (1:1).

8. Philippians, along with Philemon, are Paul's two most personal letters.

9. Philippians 4:6–8 offers one of the most practical explanations and applications for prayer found anywhere in Scripture.

10. In Philippians 4:4–14 Paul shares a very significant autobiographical sketch of himself.

11. Only in Philippians and Thessalonians does Paul not begin with a declaration of his apostleship.

12. Philippians is one of Paul's four "prison epistles," along with Ephesians, Colossians, and Philemon.

Quotable Quotes

Paul's Letter to the Philippians is like an open window into the Apostle's very heart. In it we have the artless outpouring of his unrestrained love for and his unallayed joy in his devoted and loyal Philippian friends. It is the most intimate and spontaneous of his writings. —D. Edmond Hiebert

This is an epistle of the heart, a true love letter, full of friendship, gratitude, and confidence. —George G. Findlay

Joy is the music that runs through this epistle, the sunshine that spreads all over it. The whole epistle radiates joy and happiness. —R. C. H. Lenski

The Epistle to the Philippians has no doctrines to expound. It has no errors to correct; no issues to refute. It has a living Christ to introduce and commend to human need. Not a Christ disassociated from life's living, but a Christ experienced and proved in the utmost stress of life. —Norman B. Harrison

Notable Notes

The church at Philippi was the first church founded in Europe (see Acts 16). This church work began with the conversion of a woman named Lydia who had been meeting regularly outside of the city, beside a river, for prayer along with other women (see Acts 16:13–15). Other women converts also became prominent within the church (Phil. 4:2–3). This corresponds with the fact that women were held in higher regard in this province of Macedonia. Paul's greatest satanic challenge even came in the form of a demon-possessed girl.

Christ Connections

Christ can be found in Philippians as:

Source of the Fruits of Righteousness

One Equal with God Who Humbled Himself

Coming One

COLOSSIANS

Important Information

Author: Paul
Theme: Complete in Christ
Category: Pauline Epistle

Fascinating Facts

1. Colossians is one of only two of Paul's epistles written to a church that he had never previously visited (see also Romans).

2. Colossians, like Philippians, contains some of the greatest passages on the deity and ministry of Christ (1:15–20; 2:9–10).

3. Colossians contains one of Paul's briefest benedictions (4:18).

4. Over four-fifths of the verses here in Colossians are repeated in Ephesians, with some slight variations.

5. In Colossians Paul dealt with many forms of false teaching and harmful doctrines, including legalism, mysticism, asceticism, and Gnosticism.

6. Though Colossians is a smaller epistle, Paul uses some fifty-five words that are not found in any of his other epistles.

7. There are no references made in Colossians to the Old Testament.

8. Colossians is one of the most Christ-centered books in the Bible.

9. Though the epistle to the Colossians is very important, the city of Colosse itself was by far the least important city to which Paul had ever sent a letter and, afterward, the church disappears from Christian history.

10. Colossians contains many unique titles for Christ, such as "image of the invisible God" (1:15), "firstborn from the dead" (1:18), and so on.

11. Colossians is one of Paul's four prison epistles, along with Ephesians, Philippians, and Philemon.

Quotable Quotes

The Epistle to the Colossians contains the heart of the Christian message. One cannot engage in a serious study of its contents without being deeply and profoundly affected. . . . No other New Testament book is more relevant in our generation, for the manifestations of the heresy at Colosse are present today. —Charles N. Pickell

The Epistle to the Colossians is a short one, but tremendous in its depth and height, its scope and grasp. —A. T. Robertson

As therefore this Epistle forms one of the peaks in the New Testament revelation of Christ, all who desire to reach a correct understanding of His Person must resolve to scale its heights. The message of Colossians is that believers are complete in Christ. —Geoffrey B. Wilson

Notable Notes

Epaphras, the pastor and probable founder of the church at Colosse, traveled well over one thousand miles—from Colosse to Rome—just to seek Paul's counsel and help for handling serious doctrinal attacks against the Christian faith in that region. The epistle to the Colossians is Paul's answer to Epaphras's plea for help. Paul's epistle did not come back with Epaphras, either because he himself was imprisoned with Paul (Philem. 23) or Paul had asked Epaphras to stay and help him there.

Christ Connections

Christ can be found in Colossians as:

Preeminent One

Redeemer in the Image of God

1 THESSALONIANS

Important Information

Author: Paul
Theme: Living in Light of Christ's Return
Category: Pauline Epistle

Fascinating Facts

1. Every chapter in 1 Thessalonians ends with a reference to Christ's return (1:10; 2:19; 3:13; 4:16; 5:23).

2. This was probably the second epistle written by the apostle Paul, and one of the earliest of the New Testament books.

3. 1 Thessalonians contains the earliest New Testament reference to the rapture of the church (4:16).

4. 1 Thessalonians does not contain any quotations from the Old Testament.

5. 1 Thessalonians contains the earliest reference to the trichotomy of our human nature: that we are spirit, soul, and body (5:23).

6. This epistle, along with 2 Thessalonians, has more to do with last-days teaching than any of Paul's other writings.

7. The church at Thessalonica was perhaps the youngest church to which Paul ever wrote, being a year or less old in the Lord.

8. Between 1 and 2 Thessalonians almost every major doctrine of the Christian faith is mentioned.

9. One out of every four verses in 1 and 2 Thessalonians concerns the fact of Christ's return.

10. In 1 Thessalonians there are seventeen Greek words not found elsewhere in the New Testament, and another seventeen words that are unique within Paul's epistles.

11. Only in Thessalonians and Philippians does Paul not begin with a declaration of his apostleship.

Quotable Quotes

On the subject of the Second Coming, Paul assures the Thessalonians what will happen, but not when it will happen. His discussion throughout is dominated by an emphasis on practical living, rather than on speculation. The best way to prepare for Christ's return is to live faithfully and obediently now. —*Nelson's Bible Dictionary*

This Letter, more than any other of Paul's, is characterized by simplicity, gentleness, and affection. —W. Graham Scroggie

The Epistles [of 1 and 2 Thessalonians] are like finely cut gems. They reflect the depths of theological thought, especially in the area of future things. . . . They are a joy to read and a delight to study. —Charles C. Ryrie

Notable Notes

Of all of the churches that the apostle Paul established, only six of them ever received letters from him, and only two of them—the church at Corinth and this church at Thessalonica—would ever receive multiple letters. Timothy is the only person to receive two letters from Paul.

Christ Connections

Christ can be found in 1 Thessalonians as:

Risen Lord

Coming King

2 THESSALONIANS

Important Information

Author: Paul
Theme: The Second Coming of Christ
Category: Pauline Epistle

Fascinating Facts

1. 2 Thessalonians contains one of the main New Testament teachings concerning the antichrist (2:3–12).

2. 2 Thessalonians is Paul's shortest letter to a church and his second shortest epistle overall (see also Philemon).

3. Eleven times in this short epistle, Paul refers to "the Lord Jesus Christ" as he exhorts these young believers to focus on Him.

4. 2 Thessalonians 2 contains three different titles for the antichrist: "man of sin" (v. 3), "son of perdition" (v. 3), and "lawless one" (v. 8).

5. In 2 Thessalonians 2 the sinner's condemnation is everlasting (v. 9) and the saint's consolation is everlasting (v. 16).

6. Only in Thessalonians and Philippians does Paul not begin with a declaration of his apostleship.

7. This epistle, along with 1 Thessalonians, has more to do with last-days teaching than any other of Paul's writings.

8. The church at Thessalonica was perhaps the youngest church to which Paul ever wrote, being a year or less old in the Lord.

9. One out of every four verses in 1 and 2 Thessalonians concerns the fact of Christ's return.

10. Between 1 and 2 Thessalonians, almost every major doctrine of the Christian faith is mentioned.

Quotable Quotes

Second Thessalonians is a sequel to Paul's letter to the church at Thessalonica. Sequels, at least with regard to books and movies, rarely have quite the punch of the original. However, one look at Paul's closing remarks in 2 Thessalonians . . . dispels that conclusion with the swiftness of a left jab and the impact of an upper cut. —Charles R. Swindoll

A wonderful epistle which teaches that the knowledge of prophecy, rather than leading to fanaticism or laziness, brings peace to the heart. —J. Vernon McGee

I am greatly encouraged that the apostle Paul had to write a second letter to the Thessalonians to explain his first! I have had to do that on occasion. —Ray C. Stedman

Notable Notes

In the New Testament there are nearly 320 references dealing with the subject of Christ's return, or one in every twenty-five verses. In 1 and 2 Thessalonians that rate jumps dramatically to one in every four verses. More space is dedicated to the subject of Christ's return in the New Testament than to baptism and communion combined.

Christ Connections

Christ can be found in 2 Thessalonians as:

  Coming King
  Great Judge
  Faithful One

1 TIMOTHY

Important Information

Author: Paul
Theme: Proper Church Conduct
Category: Pauline Epistle

Fascinating Facts

1. Timothy is one of only three individuals, rather than congregations, to whom Paul addressed his epistles (see also Titus and Philemon).

2. 1 Timothy is one of only three pastoral epistles that specifically addresses the pastoral care of churches (see also 2 Timothy and Titus).

3. 1 Timothy is the first New Testament book to give detailed instruction for how the church should operate.

4. Timothy is the only person in the New Testament to be called "man of God" (6:11).

5. 1 Timothy contains Paul's shortest benediction (6:21).

6. Only in the pastoral epistles (1 and 2 Timothy, Titus) did Paul add the word "mercy" to his normal greeting of "grace and peace."

7. Only in 1 Timothy and Titus do we have a detailed description of the qualifications for church leadership (3:1–13).

8. Timothy's name appears in the greetings of Paul's epistles more often than any other person's.

9. The unique phrase of Paul, "this is a faithful saying," is found only five times and only in the pastoral epistles, three of those instances being in 1 Timothy (1:15; 3:1; 4:9).

10. In 1 Timothy the words *doctrine* and *godliness* appear eight times each, tying in with the theme of proper church conduct.

Quotable Quotes

The importance of these Pastoral Epistles lies especially in the instruction they give on character, testimony, and care of local churches, God's lamps of witness in a world of darkness.
—Homer A. Kent Jr.

While the epistle is written to a particular person, and to meet peculiar circumstances, it yet has such wide application to ourselves. —Guy H. King

These [pastoral] epistles are the only part of the New Testament which deals with church problems from an administrative rather than a theological viewpoint. —W. E. Vine

Notable Notes

Out of the city of Lystra came perhaps the apostle Paul's most difficult circumstance and his most delightful companion. On Paul's first missionary journey through Lystra he was stoned by an angry mob, dragged out of the city, and left for dead. However, a young man named Timothy came to faith as a result of Paul's preaching. On Paul's second missionary journey through Lystra, Timothy became Paul's missionary companion. Timothy went on to become like a son to Paul, and he was a constant and faithful companion to the great apostle.

Christ Connections

Christ can be found in 1 Timothy as:
    Enabler Who Ministers
    Mediator
    God in the Flesh
    King of Kings

2 TIMOTHY

Important Information

Author: Paul
Theme: Carrying on the Ministry
Category: Pauline Epistle

Fascinating Facts

1. 2 Timothy was Paul's final epistle and his last written words before his death.

2. 2 Timothy contains one of the two main statements on the inspiration of Scripture in 2 Timothy 3:16 (see also 2 Pet. 1:20–21).

3. 2 Timothy is one of only three pastoral epistles that specifically address the pastoral care of churches (see also 1 Timothy and Titus).

4. 2 Timothy is Paul's only pastoral epistle written from prison.

5. Only in the pastoral epistles (1 and 2 Timothy, Titus) did Paul add the word "mercy" to his normal greeting of "grace and peace."

6. 2 Timothy contains some twenty-five essential directives from Paul to Timothy.

7. Timothy was one of only three individuals, rather than congregations, to whom Paul addressed his epistles (see also Titus and Philemon).

8. Though 2 Timothy contains only eighty-three verses in its four brief chapters, it records the names of some twenty-three different people.

9. Only in 2 Timothy do we learn of the names of Timothy's mother and grandmother (1:5), as well as the names of the magicians who opposed Moses in Egypt (3:8).

10. In 2 Timothy 2 Paul uses many metaphors for the faithful Christian: soldier (v. 3), athlete (v. 5), farmer (v. 6), worker (v. 15), and so forth.

Quotable Quotes

I have often found it difficult deliberately to read these short chapters through, without finding something like a mist gathering in the eyes. The Writer's heart beats in the writing. —H. C. G. Moule

It is in a sense the last will and testament of the greatest missionary-theologian of early Christianity. —Robert H. Mounce

Let us read, let us listen, let us believe. We shall find the dying Letter full of living messages, carried to us by a sure messenger's hand, direct from Him. —H. C. G. Moule

Notable Notes

Though his death is not recorded in the pages of Scripture, tradition states that the apostle Paul was martyred under the cruel hand of the Roman emperor Nero and was beheaded on the Ostian Way, west of Rome.

Christ Connections

Christ can be found in 2 Timothy as:

Victor over Death

Resurrected Seed of David

TITUS

Important Information

Author: Paul
Theme: Setting the Church in Order
Category: Pauline Epistle

Fascinating Facts

1. Titus is one of only three individuals to whom Paul wrote; the others were Timothy and Philemon.

2. Titus is one of only three pastoral epistles that specifically address pastoral care of churches; the others are 1 and 2 Timothy.

3. Only in the pastoral epistles (1 and 2 Timothy, Titus) did Paul add the word "mercy" to his normal greeting of "grace and peace."

4. Only in Titus and 1 Timothy do we have a detailed description of the qualifications for church leadership (1:6–9).

5. In Titus a heavy emphasis is placed upon the importance of good works in the lives of believers (1:16; 2:7, 14; 3:1, 8, 14).

6. In Titus 1:12 Paul quotes the Cretan poet Epimenides.

7. Though Titus is a brief epistle, there are several references made to the key doctrines of the Christian faith.

8. Though closely associated with the apostle Paul and his missionary work, Titus is never mentioned in the book of Acts.

9. Titus was one of only two young men whom Paul referred to as being his true sons in the faith, the other being Timothy (Titus 1:4; 1 Tim. 1:2).

10. Titus is the only epistle written to an island location (Crete).

Quotable Quotes

This is a short epistle, but yet such a model of Christian doctrine, and composed in such a masterly manner, that it contains all that is needful for Christian knowledge and life. —Martin Luther

Somehow, as we ponder this short but weighty note to Titus, we have an uneasy feeling that all too many of us modern Christians live far below its simply worded but searching standards. . . . We have much need to linger often among the purifying paragraphs of this little letter. —J. Sidlow Baxter

The Pastoral Epistles are the last words we have from the pen of the apostle Paul. . . . The hard-earned lessons of Paul's years of service are concentrated here so that these epistles, brief though they are, contain a priceless spiritual treasure. —Philip C. Johnson

Notable Notes

Some Bible students believe that Titus may have been the brother of Luke, author of the third Gospel and the book of Acts. Titus left the island of Crete temporarily, as Paul requested (see Titus 3:12), and was sent by the apostle into Dalmatia (see 2 Tim. 4:10). Following that, tradition states that Titus returned to the island of Crete and became the spiritual overseer of the church work, eventually dying there at a good old age.

Christ Connections

Christ can be found in Titus as:

> One Who Appoints the Leaders in the Church
>
> Coming Savior

PHILEMON

Important Information

Author: Paul
Theme: Forgiveness
Category: Pauline Epistle

Fascinating Facts

1. Philemon is perhaps Paul's most personal letter and one of his least doctrinal.

2. Philemon is Paul's shortest epistle.

3. Philemon is one of only three individuals to whom Paul wrote; the others were Timothy and Titus.

4. Philemon is Paul's only letter written both to an individual (v. 1) as well as to a family and a church (v. 2).

5. Though a brief letter of only twenty-five verses, Philemon mentions eleven people by name.

6. Philemon is one of Paul's most tactful and discreet pieces of writing in the midst of a very controversial subject (slavery).

7. Philemon is possibly the only letter that Paul may have written for himself without the help of a secretary (v. 19).

8. Paul's letter to Philemon is one of the most beautiful examples in all of Scripture of our forgiveness, reconciliation, and justification in Christ.

9. Philemon is the only New Testament book to give us an inside peek into the Christian home of that day.

10. Philemon is one of Paul's four prison epistles; the others are Ephesians, Philippians, and Colossians.

Quotable Quotes

A masterly lovely example of love . . . for we are all His Onesimi (forgiven sinners like Onesimus) if we will believe it. —Martin Luther

This letter is absolutely unique, not only in the Pauline literature, but in all literature. —W. Graham Scroggie

It is a masterpiece, and a model of graceful, tactful, and delicate pleading. —Robert Lee

The whole letter is of pure gold. No wonder the church placed it into the canon. —R. C. H. Lenski

Paul's epistle to Philemon far surpasses all the wisdom of the world. —A. H. Francke

Notable Notes

It has been estimated that there were as many as six million slaves in the Roman empire in Paul's day. There were Christian slaveholders like Philemon within the church. The New Testament does not directly address the institution of slavery as such but instead offers guidelines both for Christian masters and Christian slaves.

Christ Connections

Christ can be found in Philemon as:

Controller of the Destiny of His Servants

HEBREWS

Important Information

Author: Unknown
Theme: The Superiority of Christ and Christianity
Category: General Epistle

Fascinating Facts

1. Hebrews is the only New Testament book with an unknown author.

2. Hebrews is the only New Testament book that deals specifically with the present ministry and activities of Jesus Christ as our High Priest.

3. Hebrews has no introductory greeting, as most New Testament letters do.

4. Hebrews is second only to the book of Revelation in its number of quotations from the Old Testament.

5. More than twenty descriptive phrases are used of Christ in this book ("heir of all things," "High Priest," and so forth).

6. The epistle to the Hebrews, along with 2 Peter and Jude, makes more references to Jewish history than other New Testament books.

7. Hebrews is the only New Testament book to give us some typological understanding of the Old Testament feasts and offerings found in Leviticus.

8. Hebrews contains five very serious warnings against turning away from the Lord (2:1–4; 3:7–4:13; 5:11–6:20; 10:26–39; 12:25–29).

9. Hebrews contains more than 150 Greek words that are unique to this book.

10. Hebrews is considered by many scholars and commentators to be the greatest literary work in the New Testament, written in some of the most elegant Greek of the New Testament.

11. All of the Old Testament quotations in Hebrews are from the Septuagint (Greek) version of the Old Testament rather than the more common Hebrew version.

Quotable Quotes

Only God knows who wrote the book of Hebrews. —Origen

The book of Hebrews was written to the Hebrews to tell them to stop acting like Hebrews. —Donald Grey Barnhouse

The Epistle to the Hebrews is one of the great but much neglected treasures of the New Testament. —D. Edmond Hiebert

We may compare [Hebrews] to a painting of perfect beauty, which has been regarded as a work of Raphael. If it should be proved that it was not painted by Raphael, we have thereby not lost a classical piece of art, but gained another master of first rank! —Thiersch

Hebrews begins like an essay, proceeds like a sermon, and ends like a letter. —T. Rees

Notable Notes

John Owen, the noted Puritan theologian and preacher, spent sixteen years of his life writing an eight-volume commentary just on the book of Hebrews! And William Gouge, an eighteenth-century preacher who pastored one of the largest churches in London for forty-five years, spent thirty-three of those years just preaching on the book of Hebrews!

Christ Connections

Christ can be found in Hebrews as:

Son and Image of God

Captain and Author of Our Salvation

Apostle and High Priest

JAMES

Important Information

Author: James the brother of Jesus
Theme: The Practice of the Christian Faith
Category: General Epistle

Fascinating Facts

1. James is probably the earliest of the twenty-seven New Testament books.

2. James was one of the last books to be accepted into the New Testament canon of Scripture.

3. James is one of only two New Testament books written by a brother of Jesus (see also Jude).

4. The epistle of James has more figures of speech, analogies, and illustrations from nature than all of the apostle Paul's epistles combined.

5. While James does not ever quote Jesus directly, he does present more of Christ's personal teachings than any other New Testament writer.

6. The language of the Sermon on the Mount is reflected more in this epistle than in any other New Testament book.

7. In many ways, James is the Proverbs of the New Testament.

8. James begins and ends with the subject of trials.

9. James is the most practical book in the New Testament, containing very little formal theology.

10. The epistle of James is very Jewish in nature (with no mention of Gentile believers), and contains twenty-two allusions to Old Testament books.

Quotable Quotes

If God gives you St. Paul's faith, you will soon have St. James's works. —Augustus M. Toplady

The Epistle of James is not an epistle of straw; rather it is an epistle of strength. It is not destitute of evangelic character but rather characteristic of the evangel. —Lehman Strauss

Perhaps there was never a time when the testimony of James, rightly understood, had a more necessary application than now. —C. I. Scofield

Notable Notes

Martin Luther, the great leader of the Protestant Reformation, was not fond of the epistle of James. Luther objected to it on the basis that he felt it spoke too much about good works and not enough about faith. He also felt it taught too little about Christ and the gospel. Even though Luther called James "an epistle of straw, and destitute of evangelic character," he nevertheless considered it to be the Word of God, though not one of the chief books.

Christ Connections

Christ can be found in James as:
Unchangeable Father
Wisdom of God
Husbandman
Coming Lord

1 PETER

Important Information

Author: Peter
Theme: Grace in Times of Suffering
Category: General Epistle

Fascinating Facts

1. Peter is one of only three original disciples used by God to write New Testament books or epistles (see also Matthew and John).
2. The suffering of Christ is spoken of in every chapter of 1 Peter.
3. In 1 Peter the subject of suffering is mentioned over fifteen times.
4. 1 Peter has been called the Job of the New Testament, as it deals with suffering and God's sovereignty.
5. In 1 Peter there are more Old Testament quotations, proportionately, than in any other New Testament book.

6. Peter is one of only two New Testament authors to refer to Jesus as a "Lamb" (1:19; see also John 1:29, 36; Rev. 5:6).

7. 1 Peter was probably written in the early stages of the great Christian persecution under Caesar Nero in Rome.

8. In chapter 5, Peter includes a special word of exhortation for the elders of the church, of which he was one (vv. 1–4).

9. 1 Peter was one of the earliest New Testament books to be accepted as inspired, while 2 Peter was one of the last.

10. In writing his epistles, Peter was fulfilling the command given to him by Jesus to feed, teach, and shepherd God's people (see John 21:15–17).

Quotable Quotes

The portrait of Peter in the Gospels and his own writings are amazingly and gloriously different. In the former, Peter saw his Lord transfigured; in the latter, we see Peter transfigured by the boundless grace of God. —Robert Lee

Of all the writings of the New Testament, the First Epistle of Peter is perhaps the most anciently and most unanimously attested. —Dean Farrar

First Peter is a favorite book because of its practical approach to the needs of every believer. . . . This little epistle provides a splendid source of peace and comfort for all God's people who are perplexed and troubled. —J. Allen Blair

Notable Notes

Peter seemed to have an appreciation and fondness for the word *precious*. In his two epistles Peter tells us about seven "precious" things that we either possess or are, by God's grace. In 1 Peter these are salvation (1:7), Christ's blood (1:19), God's people (2:4),

Christ Himself (2:7), and inner Christian beauty (3:4). In 2 Peter these are our faith (1:1) and God's promises (1:4).

Christ Connections

Christ can be found in 1 Peter as:

One Who Was Resurrected

Chief Cornerstone

2 PETER

Important Information

Author: Peter
Theme: Full Knowledge of the Truth
Category: General Epistle

Fascinating Facts

1. The epistle of 2 Peter consists of the apostle's last recorded written words (1:14).
2. The authorship and canonicity of 2 Peter have been challenged and attacked perhaps more than any other New Testament book.
3. Only 2 Peter and Jude contain New Testament references to the fall of angels (see 2 Pet. 2:4; Jude 6).
4. 2 Peter contains one of the two main statements on the inspiration of Scripture, 1:20–21 (see also 2 Tim. 3:16).
5. 2 Peter is the only New Testament book that describes how the heavens and earth will pass away (3:10–13).

6. Peter is the only New Testament writer to refer to the inspired writings of another New Testament writer, Paul (3:15–16).

7. There are many similarities and parallels between 2 Peter and Jude, and Jude probably borrowed from Peter's writing.

8. After the first verse Peter always uses the title of "Lord" in every reference to Jesus.

9. In 2 Peter one entire chapter out of three is devoted to the subject of false teachers (ch. 2).

10. In this second epistle Peter makes reference to his experience on the Mount of Transfiguration (1:16–18).

Quotable Quotes

Peter is quick to remind us that the believer can and will conquer through conflict. Times may be harsh and corruption rampant, but those whose faith rests in the Lord will not only survive, they will be victorious. —Charles R. Swindoll

The letter is a strong appeal to Christians to develop a character and conduct consistent with a true faith. As Peter writes, he has his eye on his own approaching death, but even more upon the glorious coming of Christ. —Cary N. Weisiger III

The best defense is a strong offense. Peter illustrated that axiom by calling his readers to a life of maturity as the best safeguard against the inroads of apostasy. —Robert G. Gromacki

Notable Notes

Though his death is not recorded in the pages of Scripture, tradition states that Peter was martyred under the cruel hand of the Roman emperor Nero. Tradition also affirms that Peter was crucified on a cross outside of Rome; however, because Peter did not feel worthy to die in the same manner as his Lord, he requested to be crucified upside-down, and was obliged.

Christ Connections

Christ can be found in 2 Peter as:

Savior

Coming One

Deliverer

1 JOHN

Important Information

Author: John the Apostle
Theme: Living in the Light
Category: General Epistle

Fascinating Facts

1. 1 John contains no greeting or opening address.
2. John uses the affectionate term of "little children," in reference to believers, a total of nine times—more than any other New Testament writer.
3. 1 John contains two of the three great "God is" statements that John gave (1:5; 4:16).
4. 1 John contains many contrasts: light and darkness, love and hatred, truth and falsehood, Christ and antichrists, and so on.
5. 1 John contains no quotations from the Old Testament.

6. In 1 John the word *know* and its equivalent are used more than thirty times (John's refutation of Gnosticism: to know).

7. 1 John makes a dozen references to Jesus in this brief epistle, and His name is found in every chapter.

8. 1 John provides one of the most definitive statements on worldliness (2:15–17).

9. 1 John is one of only two books in the Bible to use the term *antichrist* (see also 2 John).

10. In John's three epistles *truth* is a key word and is found some twenty times.

Quotable Quotes

It is a family letter from the Father to His "little children" who are in the world. With the possible exception of the Song of Solomon, it is the most intimate of the inspired writings. —C. I. Scofield

John, who was with the Lord from the very first, is the very last to write. It seems as if he, who knew and loved the Lord so intimately and deeply, is set to guard His glory and the infinite worth of the Person of our blessed Lord, against the fearful departure from the truth of God. —August Van Ryn

John is saying that Jesus Christ is God's communication to us. Jesus is the noun of God, the verb of God, the adjective of God. Jesus articulates God. When you look at Jesus Christ you see the love of God. —Jerry Vines

Notable Notes

John was an elderly man around ninety years of age when he wrote his final letters. As far as we know, he is the only one of the original disciples to die of natural causes. Tradition states that the Roman emperor Domitian had John condemned to boil in a cauldron of oil, but God supernaturally protected John and he emerged unharmed. After being banished to the island of Patmos for a period of time, John eventually returned to Ephesus, where he is believed to have died at a good old age.

Christ Connections

Christ can be found in 1 John as:

Word of Life

Advocate

Propitiator

Messiah

2 JOHN

Important Information

Author: John the Apostle
Theme: Walking in Truth
Category: General Epistle

Fascinating Facts

1. 2 John is the second shortest book in the Bible (see also 3 John).

2. 2 John is one of only three personal letters in the New Testament (see also 3 John, Philemon).

3. 2 John is the only book in the Bible addressed to a woman—if the "elect lady" is not a reference to a church (v. 1).

4. 2 John is one of only two books in the Bible to use the term *antichrist* (see also 1 John).

5. In 2 John *truth* is a key word and is found five times—and some twenty times in John's three epistles combined.

6. 2 John was one of the last books to be accepted into the New Testament canon of Scripture.

7. In 2 John the author does not identify either himself or his recipients outright (v. 1).

8. Of the thirteen verses in 2 John, at least eight of them are found directly or indirectly in 1 John.

9. 2 and 3 John are the only two New Testament books addressed from "the Elder."

10. In 2 John we have John's stern warning that false teachers are not to be invited into our homes or even to be bid Godspeed (vv. 10–11).

Quotable Quotes

The Second Epistle of John may be the most neglected book in the New Testament. —Jerry Vines

Though he understood and interpreted the person and work of Jesus more intimately than any other writer in the New Testament, and though he was in a life and death struggle with evil, he took time to pen this little personal note to one Christian woman, bringing joy to her heart and strengthening her in her own battle with evil forces which swirled about her. —Herschel H. Hobbs

Here in the Second Epistle, truth is insisted on. We are shown that love must be in the truth, and does not go beyond the bounds which truth imposes. —August Van Ryn

Notable Notes

An old tradition states that the "elect lady" addressed here in 2 John is Martha, the good friend of Jesus. One scholar suggests that the Greek word for "lady" (*kuria*), is "Martha" in Hebrew. If this tradition about Martha is true, then the "elect sister" mentioned in verse 13 would be Martha's sister Mary.

Christ Connections

Christ can be found in 2 John as:
Son of God
God Come in the Flesh

3 JOHN

Important Information

Author: John the Apostle
Theme: Hospitality
Category: General Epistle

Fascinating Facts

1. 3 John is the shortest book in the Bible.
2. 3 John is one of only three personal letters in the New Testament (see also 2 John, Philemon).
3. 3 John contains one of the briefest New Testament greetings.
4. 3 John is the only book in the Bible dedicated entirely to the subject of hospitality.

5. 3 John is the only New Testament book in which the names Jesus and Christ do not appear.

6. 3 John is written with great affection (vv. 1, 2, 5, 11).

7. In 3 John *truth* is a key word and is found six times—and some twenty times in John's three epistles combined.

8. John's first epistle was written to believers, his second epistle to a woman, and this third epistle to a man.

9. 2 and 3 John are the only two New Testament books addressed from "the Elder."

10. Gaius, to whom this letter is addressed, was probably not one of the three well-known associates of Paul, since this Gaius was evidently converted under John's ministry (v. 4).

Quotable Quotes

My old teacher, A. T. Robertson, was fond of telling us that when we were in the pastorate we must love the people, "warts and all." . . . It is against such a background that we can best understand 3 John. —Herschel H. Hobbs

When truth and love come into conflict, truth must always survive. —J. Vernon McGee

This little letter gives us a glimpse into an early assembly, its people and its problems. As you read this brief letter, you find yourself saying, "Times have not changed very much!" We have similar people and problems today! —Warren W. Wiersbe

Notable Notes

In the early days of Christianity many of the evangelists were called to an itinerant ministry. This meant that they were dependent upon kind and generous believers like Gaius (v. 6) to open their homes and to provide their basic necessities, such as a hot meal and a place to sleep. These evangelists would take nothing from the unsaved (v. 7) lest they appeared to be peddling the gospel.

Christ Connections

Christ can be found in 3 John as:
    Truth
    One Who Is Good

JUDE

Important Information

Author: Jude
Theme: Contending for the Faith
Category: General Epistle

Fascinating Facts

1. Jude is one of only two New Testament books written by a brother of Jesus (see also James).
2. Jude is the only book in the Bible solely devoted to the subject of apostasy.
3. Jude has more noncanonical references (three) than any other New Testament book (v. 9, the Assumption of Moses; vv. 6, 14–15, the book of Enoch).
4. The book of Jude, along with Hebrews and 2 Peter, makes more references to Jewish history than other New Testament books.

5. There are approximately a dozen groups of triads in this brief epistle (v. 1: called, sanctified, and preserved; v. 8: defile, reject, and speak evil; and so on).

6. Jude addresses the most general audience of all the New Testament epistles (v. 1).

7. Only Jude and 2 Peter contain Scripture references to fallen angels being chained (v. 6; 2 Pet. 2:4).

8. Only in the epistle of Jude is Michael referred to as an archangel (v. 9). No other archangels are mentioned as such in Scripture.

9. Jude's epistle is very similar in content and theme to 2 Peter 2, and he apparently continued the previous warnings of Peter (vv. 17–18).

10. In many ways Jude is the book of Judges of the New Testament.

11. Jude has often been referred to as "The Acts of the Apostates."

12. Jude is the only book of the Bible to reference Michael and Satan disputing over the body of Moses.

Quotable Quotes

Studying the little book of Jude is like working a gold mine because of all the rich nuggets which are here just for the mining. — J. Vernon McGee

Jude is the only book in all of God's Word entirely devoted to the great apostasy which is to come upon Christendom before the Lord Jesus Christ returns. Without Jude, the prophetic picture which begins with the teachings of Christ in the Gospels and develops throughout the epistles would be incomplete. —S. Maxwell Coder

A clash of cymbals! A boom of tympani! A cannon blast and a cascade of fireworks! That is what the letter of Jude is like. The words of this apostle thunder from the pages. —Ray C. Stedman

Notable Notes

Even though the early church father Jerome considered the epistle of Jude to be a part of the New Testament Scriptures, he still regarded it as a disputed book. His reasoning stemmed from the fact that Jude alludes to non-biblical sources—those being 1 Enoch and the Assumption of Moses.

Christ Connections

Christ can be found in Jude as:

Preserver

Coming Judge

Merciful One

REVELATION

Important Information

Author: John the Apostle
Theme: The Revelation of Jesus Christ for the Last Days
Category: Prophecy

Fascinating Facts

1. Revelation is the only New Testament book that focuses primarily on prophetic and future events.

2. Revelation is the only book of the Bible that pronounces a special blessing for reading, hearing, and obeying the prophecy within (1:3).

3. Revelation pronounces a distinct curse at the end (22:18–19).

4. Revelation contains more symbolism than any other New Testament book.

5. Revelation begins and ends with the Second Coming of Christ.

6. Revelation is the only book in Scripture that refers to the "thousand years" (millennium) specifically by name (20:2, 3, 4, 5, 6, 7).

7. Revelation contains more references to, and more quotations from, the Old Testament than any other book in the New Testament.

8. In the book of Revelation Jesus is referred to as the "Lamb" some twenty-eight times.

9. Revelation contains more references to numbers, especially seven (more than fifty times) and twelve (over twenty times), than any other New Testament book.

10. Revelation ends much of what Genesis began: the curse of mankind, death, sorrow, tears, and so on.

11. Revelation is the only New Testament book that is based upon a vision (1:10).

12. Revelation is the last book written in the Bible, chronologically (approximately AD 95).

13. Revelation contains John's final recorded written words.

14. Revelation gives more titles for the Savior than any other book in the Bible.

15. Revelation records the name of Satan more than any other New Testament book (seven times).
16. Revelation is the only book in the Bible that gives its own natural outline (1:19).
17. Revelation is one of the few books of the Bible to contain its own title (1:1).
18. Revelation is the only one of the five New Testament books written by John in which he identifies himself by name (1:1, 4, 9; 21:2; 22:8).
19. Revelation is one of the few books in the Bible to state the exact location of its writing (1:9).
20. In Revelation the ministry of angels is very prominent, and angels are mentioned some seventy-four times.
21. John is one of only two biblical figures commanded by God to eat a scroll (see also Ezekiel).

Quotable Quotes

I do not understand all the details of the book of Revelation but there is a special blessing promised to all who read, hear, and keep its message and I don't want to miss that blessing. —Vance Havner

The book of Revelation is a source of happiness to anyone who will read it, hear it in the depths of his heart, and obey its instructions. If ever a generation needed to study this book, it is ours. We are probably living at the time when these things will begin to come to pass. —Tim LaHaye

The book of Revelation has suffered an unfortunate fate. On the whole either it has been abandoned by the readers of the Bible as being almost completely unintelligible, or it has become the happy hunting ground of religious eccentrics, who seek to construct from it a kind of celestial timetable of events to come. —William Barclay

Notable Notes

There are four separate earthquakes foretold in Revelation: at the opening of the sixth seal (6:12), at the opening of the seventh seal (8:5), at the raising of the two witnesses (11:13), and at the pouring out of the seventh vial at Armageddon (16:16–21).

Christ Connections

Christ can be found in Revelation as:

    Coming One

    Beginning and End

    Son of Man

    Great Judge

    Lion of Judah

    Conquering One

    Lamb

    Bridegroom

    Faithful and True

    Word of God

Bibliography

Barker, Kenneth, gen. ed. *The NIV Study Bible.*

Baxter, J. Sidlow. *Explore the Book.*

Deal, William S. *Pictorial Introduction to the Bible.*

Gaebelein, Arno C. *The Annotated Bible.*

Gromacki, Robert G. *The New Testament Survey.*

Guthrie, Donald. *New Testament Introduction,* vols. 1–3.

Hayden, Eric W. *Preaching through the Bible.*

Heibert, D. Edmond. *An Introduction to the New Testament,* vols. 1–3.

Lee, Robert. *The Outlined Bible.*

Lockyer, Herbert Sr., gen. ed. *Nelson's Illustrated Bible Dictionary.*

Luck, G. Coleman. *The Bible Book by Book.*

MacArthur, John F. Jr. *The MacArthur Study Bible.*

Mears, D. Henrietta C. *What the Bible Is All About.*

Ryrie, Charles C. *The Ryrie Study Bible.*

Scroggie, W. Graham. *Know Your Bible.*

Tenney, Merrill C. *Zondervan's Pictorial Bible Dictionary.*

Unger, Merrill F. *The New Unger's Bible Dictionary.*

Wiersbe, Warren W. *Be Committed.*

————. *Be Holy.*

————. *Be Skillful.*

————. *Be Strong.*

Wilkinson, Bruce, and Kenneth Boa. *Talk Thru the Bible.*

Willmington, H. L. *Willmington's Bible Handbook.*

————. *Willmington's Guide to the Bible.*

————. *Willmington's Survey of the Old Testament.*

Information in the Christ Connections sections adapted from http://www.free-bible-study-lessons.com/Christ-in-the-Bible.html

Notes

Introduction

1. Matthew Brown, "Poll: Many Own a Bible, but Not Many Read It," *Deseret News*, April 9, 2013, http://www.deseretnews.com/article/865577728/Poll-Many-own-a-Bible-but-not-many-read-it.html?pg=all.

2. Billy Graham, "Foreword," in Henrietta Mears, *What the Bible Is All About* (Ventura, CA: Regal, 1983), 7–8.

3. Ibid.

Chapter 1 How We Got the Bible

1. David Jeremiah, *The Jeremiah Study Bible: NKJV* (Franklin, TN: Worthy Publishing, 2013), xxv.

2. John MacArthur, *NASB MacArthur Study Bible* (Nashville: Thomas Nelson, 1997), xi.

3. Origen, as quoted in R. Kent Hughes, *Hebrews: An Anchor for the Soul*, vol. 1 (Wheaton, IL: Crossway, 1993), 18.

Chapter 2 Why We Can Trust the Bible

1. "Most American Christians Do Not Believe that Satan or the Holy Spirit Exist," *Barna Group*, April 13, 2009, https://www.barna.org/barna-update/faith-spirituality/260-most-american-christians-do-not-believe-that-satan-or-the-holy-spirit-exis#.Vq_-ivkrIgs.

2. Dennis J. Hester, *The Vance Havner Quotebook* (Grand Rapids: Baker, 1991), 17.

3. John Blanchard, *More Gathered Gold* (Welwyn, England: Evangelical Press 1986), 24.

4. John Wesley, "July 24, 1776," *Journal*, vol. IV (London: Wesleyan Conference Office, 1867), 77.

5. Blanchard, *More Gathered Gold*, 27.

6. C. H. Spurgeon, "Psalm 33," *The Treasury of David*, accessed January 11, 2016, http://www.spurgeon.org/treasury/ps033.htm.

7. Mark Hitchcock, *The Amazing Claims of Bible Prophecy: What You Need to Know in These Uncertain Times* (Eugene, OR: Harvest House, 2010), 8.

8. Origin of quote unknown.

9. Nelson Glueck, *Rivers in the Desert: History of Negev* (Philadelphia: Jewish Publication Society of America, 1969), 176.

10. Bernard Ramm, *Protestant Christian Evidences* (Chicago: Moody, 1957), 232–33.

11. C. S. Lewis, *Surprised by Joy* (New York: Walker and Co., 1955), 337.

12. Ibid., 338.

13. Ibid., 349–50.

Chapter 3 Understanding the Old Testament

1. Max Anders, *30 Days to Understanding the Bible* (Nashville: Thomas Nelson, 2004), 12.

2. Augustine, as quoted in Charles R. Swindoll, *The Tale of the Oxcart and 1501 Other Stories* (Nashville: Word, 1998), 53.

3. Mark Batterson, *All In: You Are One Decision Away from a Totally Different Life* (Grand Rapids: Zondervan, 2013), 126.

4. Clarence Macartney, *The Wisest Fool: Sermons on Bible Characters* (Grand Rapids: Kregel, 1996), 9.

5. Alfred Tennyson, as quoted in J. Vernon McGee, *Thru the Bible Commentary: Job*, vol. 16 (Nashville: Thomas Nelson, 1991), 9.

6. C. H. Spurgeon, *The Treasury of David* (Peabody, MA: Hendrickson, 1990), 250.

7. Anders, *30 Days to Understanding the Bible*, 78.

Chapter 4 The Sounds of Silence

1. Colin Duriez, *The A–Z of C. S. Lewis: An Encyclopaedia of His Life, Thought, and Writings* (Oxford, England: Lion Books, 2013),134.

2. John Walvoord, *Daniel: The Key to Prophetic Revelation* (Chicago: Moody, 1989), 184.

Chapter 5 Understanding the New Testament

1. Paul Harvey, *For What It's Worth* (New York: Bantam, 1992), 147.

2. Augustine, as quoted in Warren Wiersbe, *The Wiersbe Bible Commentary: New Testament* (Colorado Springs: David C. Cook, 2007), 324.

3. Vance Havner, "From the Vantage Point of Patmos," *Standing for God in These Evil Times*, February 10, 2013, http://standingforgod.com/tag/revelation.

4. Mark Hitchcock, *101 Answers to the Most Asked Questions about the End Times* (Colorado Springs: Multnomah, 2001), 200.

Chapter 6 How to Study the Bible

1. J. I. Packer, as quoted in John Blanchard, *Gathered Gold* (Welwyn, England: Evangelical Press, 1984), 23.

Chapter 7 How to Teach the Bible

1. Vance Havner, as quoted in John Blanchard, *Sifted Silver* (Durham, England: Evangelical Press, 1995), 236.

2. Warren Wiersbe and David Wiersbe, *The Elements of Preaching* (Wheaton: Tyndale, 1986), 61.

3. C. H. Spurgeon, *Lectures to My Students* (New York: Sheldon & Co., 1875), 68.

4. D. L. Moody, as quoted in Warren Wiersbe, *Bible Exposition Commentary: Old Testament, the Prophets* (Colorado Springs: David C. Cook), 419.

5. Wiersbe and Wiersbe, *Elements of Preaching*, 20.

6. Unknown author, "Quotes," *Board of Wisdom*, accessed January 15, 2016, http://boardofwisdom.com/togo/Quotes/ShowQuote?msgid=547538#.VgWfgMtViko.

7. John MacArthur, *Preaching: How to Preach Biblically* (Nashville: Thomas Nelson, 2005), 18.

8. Wiersbe and Wiersbe, *Elements of Preaching*, 29.

9. Dietrich Bonhoeffer, *Dietrich Bonhoeffer: A Biography* (Minneapolis: Fortress Press, 2000), 443.

10. Thomas Brooks, *The Select Work of the Rev. Thomas Brooks* (London, England: L. B. Seeley & Son, 1824), 222.

11. C. H. Spurgeon, "Chapter 17: Two Great Controversies," *The Spurgeon Archive*, accessed January 15, 2016, http://www.spurgeon.org/misc/bio17.htm.

12. Chuck Swindoll, as heard by the author in a speech given by Swindoll at his installation as president of Dallas Theological Seminary, 1994.

13. D. L. Moody, as quoted in Martin Manser, *The Westminster Collection of Christian Quotations* (Louisville: John Knox, 2001), 323.

14. Haddon Robinson, as quoted in Scott Gibson, *Making a Difference in Preaching: Haddon Robinson on Biblical Preaching* (Grand Rapids: Baker, 1999), 65.

15. Adam Clarke, as quoted in C. H. Spurgeon, *Lectures to My Students*, vol. 2 (London: Passmore and Alabaster, 1877), 158.

16. Martin Luther, as quoted in John Blanchard, *The Complete Gathered Gold* (Welwyn, England: Evangelical Press, 2006), 60.

17. George Burns, as quoted in R. A. Wise, *Wise Quotes of Wisdom: A Lifetime Collection of Quotes, Sayings, Philosophies, Viewpoints, and Thoughts* (Bloomington, IN: AuthorHouse, 2011), 217.

18. Mark Twain, "Letter to George Bainton, 10/15/1888," *Mark Twain Quotations*, accessed January 15, 2016, http://www.twainquotes.com/Lightning.html.

Jeff Lasseigne has been part of Harvest Christian Fellowship since 1980, and joined the pastoral staff in 1989. He teaches the mid-week Bible study and, as one of the administrative pastors, assists with oversight of the church. Jeff has written two books, *Highway 66* and *Unlocking the Last Days*, a verse-by-verse study through the book of Revelation. Jeff enjoys traveling, reading, and loves all things England. He and his wife, Lorraine, live in Riverside, California.

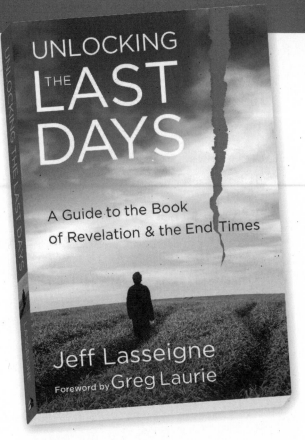